Water Crises and Governance

T0346610

Water Crises and Governance critically examines the relationship between water crises and governance in the face of challenges to provide water for growing human demand and environmental needs. Water crises threaten the assumptions and accepted management practices of water users, managers and policymakers. In developed and developing world contexts from North America and Australasia, to Latin America, Africa and China, existing institutions and governance arrangements have unintentionally provoked water crises while shaping diverse, often innovative responses to management dilemmas. This volume brings together original field-based studies by social scientists investigating water crises and their implications for governance.

Contributors to this collection find that water crises degrade environments, place untenable burdens on stakeholders, and produce or exacerbate social conflict, undermining ecological and social conditions that sustain effective collaboration. At the same time, water crises can promote institutional change that "resets" governance, promoting unusual and creative responses appropriate for local contexts. The studies in this volume provide evidence that, while water crises pose serious threats to environments and societies, they also provide opportunities to learn from experience and recraft water governance with coherent visions of more ecologically and socially sustainable futures.

The introduction and chapters 1–9 of this book were originally published as a special issue of *Society & Natural Resources*.

Peter Leigh Taylor is Professor and Chair of Sociology at Colorado State University, USA, and co-Editor-in-Chief of *Society & Natural Resources*. He has done extensive research and applied work on community-based forest management in Latin America. His current research focuses on environmental flows and agricultural water governance on the Colorado River.

David A. Sonnenfeld is Professor of Sociology and Environmental Policy at the SUNY College of Environmental Science and Forestry, and co-Editor-in-Chief of *Society & Natural Resources*. Recent books include the *Routledge International Handbook of Social and Environmental Change*; *Food, Globalization and Sustainability*; and *The Ecological Modernisation Reader*.

Water Crises and Governance

Reinventing Collaborative Institutions in
an Era of Uncertainty

Edited by
Peter Leigh Taylor and David A. Sonnenfeld

Routledge
Taylor & Francis Group

LONDON AND NEW YORK

First published 2018 by Routledge

2 Park Square, Milton Park, Abingdon, Oxfordshire OX14 4RN
52 Vanderbilt Avenue, New York, NY 10017

Routledge is an imprint of the Taylor & Francis Group, an informa business

First issued in paperback 2019

Introduction, Chapters 1–8 & 10 © 2018 Taylor & Francis
Chapter 9 © 2018 Emma S. Norman. Originally published as Open Access.

British Library Cataloguing in Publication Data
A catalogue record for this book is available from the British Library

ISBN 13: 978-1-138-29976-4 (hbk)
ISBN 13: 978-0-367-23396-9 (pbk)

Typeset in Minion
by RefineCatch Limited, Bungay, Suffolk

Publisher's Note
The publisher accepts responsibility for any inconsistencies that may have
arisen during the conversion of this book from journal articles to book chapters,
namely the possible inclusion of journal terminology.

Disclaimer
Every effort has been made to contact copyright holders for their permission to
reprint material in this book. The publishers would be grateful to hear from any
copyright holder who is not here acknowledged and will undertake to rectify
any errors or omissions in future editions of this book.

Contents

Citation Information

The following chapters were originally published in *Society & Natural Resources*, volume 30, issue 4 (2017). When citing this material, please use the original page numbering for each article, as follows:

Editors' Note
Water Crises and Institutions: Inventing and Reinventing Governance in an Era of Uncertainty
Peter Leigh Taylor and David A. Sonnenfeld
Society & Natural Resources, volume 30, issue 4 (2017), pp. 395–403

Chapter 1
Crises and Institutional Change: Emergence of Cross-Border Water Governance in Lake Eyre Basin, Australia
Jennifer Bellamy, Brian W. Head, and Helen Ross
Society & Natural Resources, volume 30, issue 4 (2017), pp. 404–420

Chapter 2
Scales of Power in Water Governance in China: Examples From the Yangtze River Basin
Qidong Huang and Jiajun Xu
Society & Natural Resources, volume 30, issue 4 (2017), pp. 421–435

Chapter 3
Rescaling Knowledge and Governance and Enrolling the Future in New Zealand: A Co-Production Analysis of Canterbury's Water Management Reforms to Regulate Diffuse Pollution
Ronlyn Duncan
Society & Natural Resources, volume 30, issue 4 (2017), pp. 436–452

Chapter 4
The Practice of Water Policy Governance Networks: An International Comparative Case Study Analysis
Rachel Eberhard, Richard Margerum, Karen Vella, Severine Mayere, and Bruce Taylor
Society & Natural Resources, volume 30, issue 4 (2017), pp. 453–470

Chapter 5
Building Capacities for Sustainable Water Governance at the Grassroots: "Organic Empowerment" and Its Policy Implications in Nicaragua
Sarah T. Romano
Society & Natural Resources, volume 30, issue 4 (2017), pp. 471–487

Chapter 6

Water Crisis and Options for Effective Water Provision in Urban and Peri-Urban Areas in Cameroon
Lotsmart Fonjong and Violet Fokum
Society & Natural Resources, volume 30, issue 4 (2017), pp. 488–505

Chapter 7

Women's Crucial Role in Collective Operation and Maintenance of Drinking Water Infrastructure in Rural Uganda
Resty Naiga, Marianne Penker, and Karl Hogl
Society & Natural Resources, volume 30, issue 4 (2017), pp. 506–520

Chapter 8

When Policy Hits Practice: Structure, Agency, and Power in South African Water Governance
Jan Janosch Förster, Linda Downsborough, and Machaya Jeff Chomba
Society & Natural Resources, volume 30, issue 4 (2017), pp. 521–536

Chapter 9

Standing Up for Inherent Rights: The Role of Indigenous-Led Activism in Protecting Sacred Waters and Ways of Life
Emma S. Norman
Society & Natural Resources, volume 30, issue 4 (2017), pp. 537–554

For any permission-related enquiries please visit:
http://www.tandfonline.com/page/help/permissions

Notes on Contributors

Jennifer Bellamy is an Honorary Senior Fellow at the School of Agriculture and Food Sciences, The University of Queensland, Australia.

Machaya Jeff Chomba is based at the School of Agricultural, Earth and Environmental Sciences, University of KwaZulu-Natal, South Africa.

Linda Downsborough is a Researcher at the Water Research Node, Monash University, South Africa.

Ronlyn Duncan is Senior Lecturer in Water Management at the Department of Environmental Management, Lincoln University, New Zealand.

Rachel Eberhard is a PhD candidate at the Science and Engineering Faculty, Queensland University of Technology, Australia.

Violet Fokum is based at the Department of Political Science, University of Buea, Cameroon.

Lotsmart Fonjong is based at the Faculty of Social and Management Sciences, University of Buea, Cameroon.

Jan Janosch Förster is a Research Assistant at the Water Research Node, Monash University, South Africa.

Brian W. Head is Professor at the School of Political Science and International Studies, The University of Queensland, Australia.

Karl Hogl is Head of the Institute of Forest, Environmental and Natural Resource Policy, University of Natural Resources and Life Sciences, Austria.

Qidong Huang is based at the School of Cultures and Languages, Hohai University, China.

Richard Margerum is Professor and Head of the Department of Planning, Public Policy and Management, University of Oregon, USA.

Severine Mayere is Deputy Student Ombudsman and Senior Lecturer at the Science and Engineering Faculty, Queensland University of Technology, Australia.

Resty Naiga is based at the Department of Development Studies, College of Humanities and Social Sciences, Makerere University, Uganda.

Emma S. Norman is Chair of the Native Environmental Science Department, Northwest Indian College, USA.

Marianne Penker is based at the Institute for Sustainable Economic Development, University of Natural Resources and Life Sciences, Austria.

Sarah T. Romano is Assistant Professor of Political Science and International Affairs at the University of Northern Colorado, USA.

Helen Ross is Professor at the School of Agriculture and Food Sciences, The University of Queensland, Australia.

David A. Sonnenfeld is Professor of Sociology and Environmental Policy at the SUNY College of Environmental Science and Forestry, and co-Editor-in-Chief of *Society & Natural Resources*.

Bruce Taylor is Senior Research Scientist and Team Leader at Sustainable Ecosystems, Commonwealth Scientific & Industrial Research Organisation, Australia.

Peter Leigh Taylor is Professor and Chair of Sociology at Colorado State University, USA, and co-Editor-in-Chief of *Society & Natural Resources*.

Karen Vella is Senior Lecturer in Planning at the Science and Engineering Faculty, Queensland University of Technology, Australia.

Jiajun Xu is based at the School of Public Administrations, Hohai University, China.

Acknowledgements

This edited volume has been made possible through the sustained collaboration and support of many people. Our deep thanks first to the authors and co-authors of the chapters of this collection, for their dedicated research, their conscientious writing and revising over many months, and importantly their commitment to scholarship and practice in support of a more sustainable world. Many thanks also to the many anonymous peer reviewers who provided valuable feedback to the authors through multiple manuscript versions. We acknowledge gratefully the highly competent and professional support throughout of Stacia Ryder, *Society & Natural Resources'* Assistant Editor. Our profound thanks to the International Association for Society and Natural Resources (IASNR) and its leaders, who gave us the opportunity to serve as Editors-in-Chief of *Society & Natural Resources*, and who have steadfastly supported the journal and its activities during our three-year term. We also gratefully acknowledge the organizers of the 2015 International Symposium on Society & Natural Resource Management (ISSRM) in Charleston, South Carolina, USA, for making it possible for us to organize a joint session in support of this project. Finally, we wish to thank the staff of Taylor & Francis for their strong support of *SNR* and this book project, including Meridith Ripa, Paul Cirillo, Ray Bailey, Melody Harris and especially Emily Ross, who worked closely with us on this edited volume.

Water Crises and Institutions: Inventing and Reinventing Governance in an Era of Uncertainty

Ensuring sufficient availability of water for human and environmental needs is one of today's most pressing global challenges. The demand for water—for human consumption, sanitation, power, industry, agriculture and livestock, and other uses—has accelerated more than twice as fast as the rate of population growth over the last century (United Nations [UN] 2013). Efforts to secure and manage water supplies with more than 45,000 major dams and diversions and through unsustainable pumping of groundwater threaten or degrade ecological habitats in the world's rivers, lakes, and wetlands (Postel 2010).

Today's challenge of providing and governing water supplies in sufficient quantity and quality, and across diverse temporal and spatial contexts and scales, involves multiple, interrelated water crises (Linton 2010; Bakker 2014). These crises likely will continue to deepen in complex and unpredictable ways, exacerbated by dramatic shifts in population, demand for water, droughts, severe weather events, and other changes associated with global climate change (Pahl-Wostl 2015).

An extensive and growing literature examines the role that governance plays in unintentionally creating water crises, as well as in shaping responses to the uncertainties of societies' water futures. *Governance* moves beyond government regulation to extend decision-making roles and responsibilities to nonstate actors with a stake in the environment, including formal and informal organizations and practices (Agrawal and Lemos 2007; Eberhard et al. this issue).

Water crises are events in social–ecological systems that are "perceived as significant threats to core social values and structures and to life-sustaining systems (ecological, economic, political or technological) that require urgent responses under conditions of significant uncertainty" (Bellamy et al. this issue, citing Galaz et al. 2011; Homer-Dixon et al. 2015). Resource problems are confronted at specific historical moments and in specific contexts. Multiple, interrelated water crises challenge water users', managers', policymakers', and interest groups' assumptions and accepted practices of managing the resource. Yet crises also provide opportunities for experimentation with new approaches to problems that may generate lessons relevant elsewhere (Ison, Collins, and Wallis 2015; Bellamy et al. this issue).

Aims of this Issue

This special issue of *Society & Natural Resources* brings together original studies exploring water crises around the world, with important implications for environmental governance in the context of uncertainty and change. Contributions examine water crises and governance in the developed world (Australia, France, New Zealand, the United States), the Global South (Cameroon, Nicaragua, and Uganda), and the semiperiphery (China and South Africa), respectively, from a variety of disciplinary perspectives.

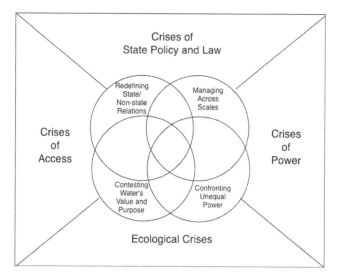

Figure 1. The thematic foci for this special issue: four interrelated sets of global crises in water quality, provision, and governance. *Source*: Authors.

The cases in these studies involve social actors' responses to interrelated water crises triggered by four sets of factors: (1) ecological problems; (2) material and technical infrastructure issues; (3) significant state policy and legal changes; and (4) asymmetrical power exercised by social actors (see Figure 1). In all the cases, governance actors struggle simultaneously with more than one of these crises, though one may dominate. In developing countries, access to safe, secure, and affordable water remains paramount. Problems of coordination of complementary and competing water uses across multiple scales more often take center stage in developed countries.

These studies focus on four sets of cross-cutting governance challenges: (1) struggles to redefine relations between the state and other social actors around water; (2) efforts to manage and coordinate water management across scales; (3) narrowing of access and participation because of actors' inequality; and (4) conflicts over how to ascribe value to water and shape the purpose of governance.

As demonstrated convincingly by the contributions to this special issue, water crises weaken effective governance with respect to both natural resources and the social conditions that sustain effective collaboration. At the same time, such crises also provide opportunities, albeit difficult, even painful ones, for participants to approach water governance with coherent visions of more ecologically and socially sustainable futures.

The Collaborative Turn in Water Governance

Until the 1970s, water resources management was shaped by a "hydraulic paradigm" that approached water management mainly as a technical and scientific problem to be managed by experts. The top-down nature of this approach, according to critics, gave insufficient attention to complex, multiscalar interrelationships among material and technical factors on the one hand, and the political, economic, and social institutions that shape human behavior (Molle 2009; Pahl-Wostl et al. 2012). A paradigm shift emerged (Pahl-Wostl 2015) that aimed to better handle water's complex technical and human interconnections.

Integrated water resources management (IWRM) appeared as a new governance approach in the late 1980s and early 1990s, widely promoted by major global development institutions. IWRM aimed to manage water at the level of ecological units such as river basins and watersheds and to effectively coordinate across diverse scales of water needs. Pahl-Wostl (2015, 4) remarks that IWRM's progress has been slow and has not yet led to major transformations in water governance. Critics have suggested that despite IWRM's emphasis on integration and coordination of diverse water uses, it remains significantly expert driven (Graefe 2011, 24–25). Molle and colleagues remark that IWRM

> implies a degree of centralization of data, water allocation decisions and decision-making power in order to address interactions between users across the basin. This reinforces state control and may militate against the integration of the values and interests of all stakeholders. (Molle, Wester, and Hirsch 2010, 574–575)

Because of IWRM's highlighting of the importance of coordinating diverse water needs across scales, criticisms of its shortcomings, and a broader move in natural resource management toward decentralization, devolution, and greater inclusivity of water users (Ribot, Agrawal, and Larson 2006), a more collaborative turn in water governance has emerged that recognizes the political nature of water and seeks to more effectively include and empower previously excluded non-state actors (Bakker 2012). These collaborative approaches have explicitly acknowledged the varying roles and potential contributions of state and nonstate actors and interests across scales, from more and less centralized water management institutions at national, regional, and basin levels, to nonstate water management and advocacy organizations, to local communities.

Multiple Crises and Cross-Cutting Governance Challenges

The studies in this collection explore recent experiences with interrelated water crises and their impacts on governance arrangements that, consistent with the historical move toward greater inclusivity and cooperation, seek effective collaboration across scales of state and non-state actors. Crises generated by ecological degradation, material or technical problems of basic water access, rapid state policy and legal changes, and the exercise of asymmetrical power have triggered critical reflection on existing assumptions and arrangements by researchers and governance actors alike. In responding to cross-cutting problems (see Figure 1), governance actors redefined relationships between state and other social actors. They strived to manage and coordinate effectively across scales. They struggled with the consequences of unequal power among participants. And they confronted differences over how value is ascribed to water and the purpose of water governance.

Ecological Crises

Ecological crises were the predominant drivers of institutional change in the first three studies in this special issue. In these cases, governance actors responded to environmental degradation even while confronting related shifts in state policy and legal frameworks.

Bellamy and colleagues' historical study of cross-border governance in Australia's Lake Eyre Basin analyzes the relationships at different historical moments between social–ecological and political–administrative crises on the one hand, and institutional change in water governance on the other. Concern within the basin and at the national level with environmental degradation led to a proposal for World Heritage listing of critical wetlands within the basin—a response to a perceived ecological crisis that led to self-organizing advocacy coalitions and strengthened local participation in water governance. Subsequently, plans by powerful external public and private interests to introduce irrigated cotton production in the basin sparked new community-based collaborations among scientists, community members, and other stakeholders in opposition to the development. In parallel, it also led to the creation of a basin-wide, multijurisdictional, cross-border cooperative water governance body, the Lake Eyre Basin Inter-Governmental Agreement (LEBIA). Significantly, later national government natural resource management policy shifts introduced at the regional level eventually undermined self-organized, community-based catchment management arrangements. Nevertheless, the authors argue that in general, these interrelated crises led to the emergence of cross-border water governance, with related shifts in the relative weight and power of local, basin-wide, and government stakeholders and overall, increased basin-wide capacity for self-organized collaboration that could help avoid future major crises.

Huang and Xu's study employs an organizational analysis framework to study multilevel, cross-jurisdictional efforts in China from central government to municipal levels to coordinate responses to water pollution problems in the Yangtze River Basin near Shanghai. In addition to environmental crisis created by pollution, national policy decentralized water quality management to lower administrative levels, including basin and subbasin entities, while simultaneously maintaining key aspects of regulatory control at the central level. Water managers and regulators in the Yangtze River Basin confront wide asymmetries in organizational power as they struggle to manage both endemic pollution sources and extraordinary pollution events. Huang and Xu's analysis responds to two trends in Chinese water governance scholarship that see either a vertical distribution of power that is "strong at two ends (the State Council and local governments) and weak at a middle point (basin commissions)," or alternatively, the obstruction of horizontal flows of power at both the national and local levels. Huang and Xu argue, by contrast, that "scalar configurations of power" among government officials at local, basin, and central administrative levels allow local jurisdictions under certain circumstances to address transjurisdictional pollution by "jumping scale" to exercise regulation across bureaucratic boundaries.

In her article, Duncan focuses on collaborative efforts in the Canterbury region of New Zealand to negotiate and reorganize governance in response to ecological degradation caused by agricultural water pollution. Negotiation and reorganization around water pollution also evolved in contexts of significant changes in national water policy and of problems of scale in involving communities in water governance. Duncan employs an interpretive co-production policy analysis framework that studies the role of science and modeling in "rescaling environmental governance" to involve local communities in design of catchment-level pollution load limits. Scientists and communities worked together to develop water pollution limits. Communities developed their own, value-based water quality objectives, and scientists employed modeling to quantify locally appropriate threshold limits. Duncan argues that a discourse of limits relevant from local to national levels played a key role in rescaling knowledge and governance in New Zealand's national and regional policy realms in ways that are more robust than relying solely on the often legally vulnerable authority of science.

Crises of State Policy and Law

The next two articles in this collection focus on crises generated by changes in state policy, legal, and regulatory frameworks. In these cases, governance actors struggled, as well, with problems posed by environmental degradation and unequal power among participants in water management.

Eberhard and colleagues develop an international comparative study of water policy governance networks, examining "new" networked arrangements encouraged by state water policy changes that involve multiple stakeholders in policy development, negotiation, and implementation. Their governmentality theory approach explores the rationalities and practices of governance, the exercise of power, and outcomes in six large-scale water policy cases in Australia (the Murray–Darling Basin and Great Barrier Reef), the United States (the California CALFED Bay Delta and the Florida Everglades), and France (the Rhone River and Loire River Basin). Case studies examine state and nonstate stakeholders' concerns with interrelated crises triggered by important shifts in state policies and legal frameworks, as well as deteriorating environmental conditions and intense political competition to shape policy outcomes. The authors ask whether the state actually relinquishes control to nonstate actors in governance networks or whether mixed forms develop in which the state remains important. They find that while the purpose of governance is sometimes renegotiated and the scope of responsibilities redistributed, in general, the state has rarely ceded significant power to nonstate governance participants.

Romano's contribution focuses on the impact of a major change in Nicaraguan national policy to "ex post facto" devolve responsibility for drinking-water management to local rural communities, a move that formally recognized a role many rural communities had played for years. Romano writes that the state for many years had not provided adequate financial and technical support to maintain those decentralized systems. In an important sense, this study is also one of cross-scale problems of sustainable water governance in a context of inadequate access to drinking water in rural areas. Romano draws on scholarship at the intersection of common property regime theory and decentralized natural resource management to study cases in which local water committees built local legitimacy by managing small-scale water delivery effectively with little or no state support. She argues that local water committees achieved an "organic empowerment" by organizing together and building on grass-roots legitimacy to act across local and national scales, succeeding in reshaping top-down water policy discourse and developing a more formal role for local water committees in designing new national water legislation.

Crises of Access

Crises shaped by problems involving access to water resources in Africa are the focus of the third set of articles in this collection. In these cases, as governance actors sought to improve access to water, they also had to confront crucial conflicts over who should hold the power and responsibility to manage the resource.

Fonjong and Fokum's study of water crisis and water provision in peri-urban Cameroon analyzes a crisis of basic access to drinking water by low-income populations, a technical crisis nevertheless, closely related to a change in state policy that privatized drinking-water delivery. Fonjong and Fokum report that Cameroon's state-led water system prior to privatization suffered from insufficient delivery capacity, weak bureaucratic institutions, and inadequate capital investment. Privatization, widely promoted by international aid and lending institutions in the 1990s, aimed to solve these problems of efficiency and ensure regular water supplies. The authors argue that in Cameroon's peri-urban areas, because of privatization's valuing of water principally as a commodity, problems of poor coverage, rationing, shortages, and inadequate investment have continued and are now accompanied by higher water rates. Significantly, Fonjong and Fokum observe, study participants report that they place responsibility for their water system's shortcomings on the national government instead of the private firm with formal responsibilities. The authors suggest that in this context, a public–private partnership may provide better results for peri-urban Cameroon by building on the strengths of both state and private institutions.

In their article on drinking-water infrastructure in rural Uganda, Naiga et al. unpack the gendered distribution of local financial and labor resources for operation and maintenance (O&M) of local water systems. The rural communities in their study lack adequate access to safe drinking water, a technical crisis closely linked to the state's decentralization of water management and encouragement of local collaboration. Naiga and colleagues' study develops a gender-sensitive collective action framework to examine how women bear the brunt of water scarcity in rural Uganda. By law women should participate equally in decentralized water governance, yet they are not granted formal recognition of their actual role in maintaining water infrastructure. The study responds to research that emphasizes the difficulty of convincing local community members to contribute financially in support of decentralized water systems. The authors' work highlights that in rural Uganda, women do contribute significant financial and labor resources to O&M. Sociocultural norms and stereotypes combine with technical barriers to adequate water access and weaknesses in state policy implementation to block recognition of women's current contributions and their potential to play a more direct and effective role in drinking water delivery.

Crises of Power

The final two articles in this collection examine crises of asymmetrical power in South Africa and the United States, respectively, both highly racialized settings. In these cases, struggles over control of water management and the distribution of its benefits occurred in the context of state policy and legal frameworks that, formally at least, sought to place greater governance responsibility in local hands.

Förster et al. analyze the implementation of a new post-Apartheid water governance framework in South Africa that aimed to overcome past racial inequalities in basic access to water via international IWRM principles of devolution and collaborative governance. The authors draw on social theories of structure, agency, and power to critically assess how local water user associations are established under the new water governance frame-work. In their case study of the creation of a water user association in the Northwest province, Förster et al. argue that the reality of local elites' power undermined the institutionalization of local stakeholder collaboration and equitable access to water by non-elite farmers and other water users. While national policy and law are crucial for establishing structures supportive of collaborative water governance, agentic factors at the local level largely shape outcomes in practice. Förster and colleagues suggest that prior to establishment of new governance institutions, conditions must be created to enable local actors to meet on a more equal footing.

Norman's study of indigenous peoples' struggles off the northwest coast of the United States focuses on the problem of defending tribes' rights to access and use of waterways that have historically been part of their communities. This problem of basic access to the water resource is simultaneously a problem of unequal power, as outsiders seek to use or control waterways in ways that undermine indigenous peoples' ability to preserve their traditional livelihoods and ways of life. Despite the Point Elliott Treaty of 1855 between the United States and Coast Salish tribes, fragmented governance systems involving federal, state, tribal, county, and municipal actors have left the burden of maintaining their rights on the tribes themselves. Norman employs an ethnographic approach and storytelling, informed by standpoint theory. She looks at the role of indigenous collective action at different scales from individual and tribal to the national and international, to build coalitions to defend their water access rights and communities. Norman develops vignettes of indigenous resistance in defense of individual fishing rights, historical treaty rights in the face of large-scale development proposals in traditional fishing areas, and mobilization against polar oil drilling that threatened their way of life via its contribution to climate change.

Innovations, Reinventions, and Lessons

As poignantly illustrated by all contributions to this special issue, water crises in the contemporary world often produce or exacerbate social conflict, place untenable burdens on water stakeholders, and weaken governance with negative impacts on environments and people. At the same time, they may contribute to conditions conducive to institutional change that "resets" governance systems as participants respond to crises to protect and advance what they value in water. The cases examined here provide strong evidence that such resets have important implications for the technical effectiveness of water management, for how complexity is handled across scales, and for relations between state and nonstate actors and between participants with unequal power.

A number of the responses to water crises analyzed in this special issue were particularly unusual and innovative. Examples include the community-based catchment limits and the extension of water governance beyond spatial spaces to include the temporal (Duncan); the newly recognized identity for a river basin based on a broader understanding of value-based conflicts around water (Bellamy et al.); the possibility of "empowerment across scales" from the grass roots up for a more genuinely collaborative state–nonstate relationship (Romano); and the bureaucratic strategy of "jumping scale" to invent new kinds of coordination within an existing governance system (Huang and Xu). Nevertheless, all of the cases presented here entail important independent and creative responses that are new to their contexts, such as shifts to more centralized state control or, alternatively, toward collaboration involving greater inclusion of local expertise, interests, and values. These "reinventions" tell us that governance actors confront their crises and make changes, a hopeful sign of agency in the face of larger forces of change.

This collection of studies suggests important new lessons about water crises and the governance of natural resources: That crises are moments when existing assumptions and practices are called into question and previously unthinkable alternatives may be considered (Bellamy et al.). That uncertainty is inevitable but not a reason not to make decisions and move forward (Duncan). That rethinking public–private partnerships might serve as a way out of polarized situations (Fonjong and Fokum). That more sophisticated understanding of the power dimension of governance is needed (Eberhard et al.). That legitimacy and empowerment may emerge from diverse sources, calling for more effective negotiation across scales (Romano). That culture matters because it is inextricably linked with power; gender, race and ethnicity, and identity can create and reproduce inequality and provide rich resources for more sustainable governance (Naiga et al., Norman, Förster et al.).

Water is embedded in all aspects of human existence, natural and social. It is nothing less than the "source of life," as Pahl-Wostl (2015, 1) put it recently. Water crises are also crises of sustainability in the larger relationship between humans and the rest of the natural world. We have much to learn about how to create a more sustainable future in the face of unprecedented uncertainty from how states, agencies, communities, and others respond to water crises to pursue healthy environments, technical effectiveness, greater equity, and inclusivity, flexibility, and adaptiveness.

Peter Leigh Taylor
David A. Sonnenfeld

References

Agrawal, A., and M. C. Lemos. 2007. A greener revolution in the making: Environmental governance in the 21st century. *Environment* 49 (5):36–45. doi:10.3200/envt.49.5.36-45

Bakker, K. 2012. Water: Political, biopolitical, material. *Social Studies of Science* 42 (4):616–23. doi:10.1177/0306312712441396

Bakker, K. 2014. The business of water: Market environmentalism in the water sector. *Annual Review of Environment & Resources* 39:469–94. doi:10.1146/annurev-environ-070312-132730

Galaz, V., F. Moberg, E.-K. Olsson, E. Paglia, and C. Parker. 2011. Institutional and political leadership dimensions of cascading ecological crises. *Public Administration* 89 (2):361–80. doi:10.1111/j.1467-9299.2010.01883.x

Graefe, O. 2011. River basins as new environmental regions? The depolitization of water management. *Procedia Social and Behavioral Sciences* 14:24–27. doi:10.1016/j.sbspro.2011.03.014

Homer-Dixon, T., B. Walker, R. Biggs, A.-S. Crépin, C. Folke, E. F. Lambin, G. D. Peterson, J. Rockström, M. Scheffer, W. Steffen, and M. Troell. 2015. Synchronous failure: The emerging causal architecture of global crisis. *Ecology and Society* 20 (3):6–21. doi:10.5751/es-07681-200306

Ison, R. L., K. B. Collins, and P. J. Wallis. 2015. Institutionalising social learning: Towards systemic and adaptive governance. *Environmental Science & Policy* 53:105–17. doi:10.1016/j.envsci.2014.11.002

Linton, J. 2010. *What is water? The history of a modern abstraction*. Vancouver, BC, Canada: University of British Columbia Press.

Molle, F. 2009. Water, politics and river basin governance: Repoliticizing approaches to river basin management. *Water International* 34 (1):62–70. doi:10.1080/02508060802677846

Molle, F., P. Wester, and P. Hirsch. 2010. River basin closure: processes, implications and responses. *Agricultural Water Management* 97:569–77. doi:10.1016/j.agwat.2009.01.004

Pahl-Wostl, C. 2015. *Water governance in the face of global change: From understanding to transformation*. New York: Springer.

Pahl-Wostl, C., L. Lebel, C. Knieper, and E. Nikitina. 2012. From applying panaceas to mastering complexity: Toward adaptive water governance in river basins. *Environmental Science & Policy* 23:24–24. doi:10.1016/j.envsci.2012.07.014

Postel, S. 2010. Water: Adapting to a new normal. In *The post carbon reader: Managing the 21st century's sustainability crises*, ed. R. Heinberg and D. Lerch, pp. 77–94. Healdsburg, CA: Watershed Media.

Ribot, J. C., A. Agrawal, and A. M. Larson. 2006. Recentralizing while decentralizing: How national governments reappropriate forest resources. *World Development* 34 (11):1864–86.

United Nations. 2013. Water scarcity. http://www.unwater.org/statistics/thematic-factsheets/en

Crises and Institutional Change: Emergence of Cross-Border Water Governance in Lake Eyre Basin, Australia

Jennifer Bellamy, Brian W. Head, and Helen Ross

ABSTRACT

Managing large river basins for sustainability is a contentious social–ecological arena challenging traditional scientific and rational planning approaches to water and related natural resources governance. "Crises" are inevitable but double-edged: creating threats and uncertainties, but also new opportunities to shape trajectories of change and avoid adverse consequences. A case study of the large remote cross-border Lake Eyre Basin (LEB), in arid central Australia, shows how over two decades a series of social–ecological and political–administrative "crises" emerged, posing significant environmental and social dilemmas for water governance, while also opening up opportunities for institutional change. This article examines the role of crises in the emergence and evolution of water governance in the LEB, how they were perceived, the challenges and opportunities posed, social and institutional responses, and governance capacity outcomes. Finally, it reflects on emergent crises as opportunities for more systemic and adaptive change in large river basins.

The continuing impact of human activities and climate change on scarce natural resources and vulnerable ecosystems has raised concerns about a global water crisis (Dietz, Ostrom, and Stern 2003; Organization for Economic Cooperation and Development [OECD] 2011; Homer-Dixon et al. 2015). Rather than simply a crisis of water scarcity, however, it is a "crisis of governance" centered on the dynamics of interlinked social and ecological systems (OECD 2011; Pahl-Wostl 2015). Bakker (2012, 616) explains, "As water flows it transgresses geopolitical boundaries, defies jurisdictions, pits upstream against downstream users, and creates competition between economic sectors, both for its use and for its disposal." Considerable uncertainty exists about the long term multiscalar effects of crises (local to global), which raise the challenge that collective societal responses are urgently required across multiple levels of governance to avoid widespread effects that may not become apparent for decades (Wise et al. 2014). This article frames water governance as a complex, contested, and cross-scale problem that encompasses the broad system of governing across a range of political, social, economic, and administrative systems to develop and manage water and related natural resources at different levels of society (Edelenbos and Teisman 2013; Pahl-Wostl 2015). We apply this framing to understand the evolution of governance arrangements for a large river basin in remote arid Australia.

Water governance for sustainability (e.g., waterway health, ecosystem services, and human well-being) is a "wicked" policy problem involving inherently interlinked "social–ecological systems" that challenge traditional scientific and rational planning approaches to their governance (Bellamy 2007; Lubell 2015; Termeer et al. 2015). Social–ecological systems operate as complex wholes embedded within a broader multiscalar institutional landscape (Folke et al. 2005; Levin et al. 2013; Lubell 2015). Feedbacks are important determinants of system behavior, and, in turn, they depend on cross-scale interactions (Folke et al. 2005). Thus, social–ecological systems highlight the interdependence and coevolution of social systems and ecological systems in water governance (Bakker 2012; Levin et al. 2013; Homer-Dixon et al. 2015; Lubell 2015).

As complex systems transcending diverse but interconnected social, institutional, and knowledge boundaries, water governance systems are framed as patterns of interaction that typically evolve incrementally across multiple scales and forms of decision making and action; from local to global, short to long term, and formal and informal (Kallis, Kiparsky, and Norgaard 2009; Edelenbos and Teisman 2013; Homer-Dixon et al. 2015). These interaction patterns include multiple actors (individuals, groups, organizations, governments, etc.); multiple institutions (rules, norms, and beliefs shaping systems of decision making and action); multiple scales and levels (space and time; local to global); and multiple centers of decision making and action (Bellamy 2007; Gerlak and Heikkila 2007; Kallis, Kiparsky, and Norgaard 2009; Wallis and Ison 2011; Osterblom and Folke 2013). Thus, water governance systems refer broadly to the multiscalar mix of formal and informal institutions, actors, and decision-making systems that influence how power is exercised, decisions are made, actors are engaged or disengaged, and conflicts and interests are accommodated in any particular place or instance (Olsson et al. 2006; Edelenbos and Teisman 2013). Self-organization, collaboration, and adaptation are common emergent properties of water governance systems: novel properties of a whole system that arise from the interactions of its component parts (Levin et al. 2013; Homer-Dixon et al. 2015).

At times the dynamics of the pattern of interactions characterizing water governance systems may create water crises (Edelenbos and Teisman 2013): that is, unexpected or sudden shifts in system behavior engendering ecological, social, and institutional change (Seixas and Davy 2008; Pahl-Wostl 2015). We conceptualize water crises as problems of relational dynamics in the governance of coevolving human and ecological systems that can lead to cross-scale changes in social–ecological system behavior, requiring urgent and innovative institutional responses (Ingram 2011; Wallis and Ison 2011; Ison, Collins, and Wallis 2015). Simultaneous crises can interact to cause larger crises, and these can propagate to the global scale (Homer-Dixon et al. 2015).

Crises and Institutional Change

In the complex, evolving, contested, and uncertain domain of water governance systems, crises are inevitable, engendering ecological and sociopolitical change, which can simultaneously pose both challenges and opportunities (Edelenbos and Teisman 2013; Osterblom and Folke 2013). Crises in social–ecological systems are events (or a closely connected series of events) that are perceived as significant threats to core social values and structures and to life-sustaining systems (ecological, economic, political, or technological) that require urgent responses under conditions of significant uncertainty (Galaz et al. 2011; Homer-Dixon et al. 2015).

Crises may emerge abruptly for a number of reasons, including (a) sudden ecological collapse with adverse social–ecological system consequences (Olsson et al. 2006; Galaz et al. 2011), and (b) purposeful implementation of mandated policy reforms and regulation (Lane and McDonald 2002; Osterblom and Folke 2013). Alternatively, they may evolve incrementally, engendered by (a) changes in the social system, including social values, paradigm shifts, and evolving knowledge systems and technical understanding (Lane and McDonald 2002; Seixas and Davy 2008; Rubenstein et al. 2016); (b) the coincidental interaction of coevolving elements of a water governance system (Edelenbos and Teisman 2013; Homer-Dixon et al. 2015); or (c) delayed recognition of connected risks of underlying social and ecological systems behavior (Olsson et al. 2006; Westley et al. 2011).

On the one hand, crises may lead to broad dissatisfaction and tensions over the existing governance system and its likely impacts (Lane and McDonald 2002; Boin et al. 2009; Kallis, Kiparsky, and Norgaard 2009; Westley et al. 2011). On the other hand, a perception of an emergent crisis can have a profound impact on people's understanding of the unfolding problem situation and what needs to be done (Olsson et al. 2006; Boin et al. 2009). Crisis situations may open up unanticipated opportunities for avoiding greater harm and thus enable more systemic and adaptive institutional change (Seixas and Davy 2008; Westley et al. 2011; Osterblom and Folke 2013). Moreover, crises challenge convention and thus may be useful precursors to systemic reform and change (Lane and McDonald 2002; Westley et al. 2011), and may engender collaboration and collective action responses (Prokopy et al. 2014; Pahl-Wostl 2015). At times of crisis, society is more likely to consider novel alternatives that foster innovation and learning (Olsson et al. 2006; Westley et al. 2011), and build governance capacities for catalyzing interaction, self-organization, and collective action that shape trajectories of change (Seixas and Davy 2008; Westley et al. 2011; Wise et al. 2014).

Water Governance: Challenges for Large River Basins

The institutions, organizations, and mechanisms for addressing wicked water governance problems may be weak, or lack the capacity to recognize or deal with emergent water crises or the ensuing challenges of the institutional systems in which they are embedded. Over the last two decades, integrative, collaborative, and adaptive governance frameworks and more flexible and engaged roles for science and society have been the cornerstone of dialogues on water governance in diverse contexts (Dietz, Ostrom, and Stern 2003; Gerlak and Heikkila 2007; Ingram 2011; Pahl-Wostl 2015; Head, Ross, and Bellamy 2016). These dialogues pose high expectations for their contribution toward (a) blurring boundaries and building bridges in contentious social–ecological systems situations; (b) interfacing science–policy–community in more interactive and knowledge-building ways; and (c) enabling evolving governance systems to adapt to ongoing change and uncertainty and avoid crises (Kallis, Kiparsky, and Norgaard 2009; Bellamy, Head, and Ross 2012; Ison, Collins, and Wallis 2015; Termeer et al. 2015). However, the implementation of integrative, collaborative, and adaptive approaches has been largely experimental, with major practical challenges experienced both in Australia (Bellamy 2007; Marshall and Stafford-Smith

2010; Wallis and Ison 2011; Curtis et al. 2014; Head, Ross, and Bellamy 2016; Eberhard et al., this issue) and internationally (Dietz, Ostrom, and Stern 2003; Ingram 2011; Pahl-Wostl 2015). Key challenges that constrain successful implementation include:

- Fragmentation of water governance systems across multiple levels and centers of formal and informal decision making and action (Bellamy 2007; Kallis, Kiparsky, and Norgaard 2009; Wallis and Ison 2011).
- Silo mentalities of planning strategies, compartmentalized and sectoralized decision-making processes, or single-issue policy mandates (Edelenbos and Teisman 2013).
- Poor understanding or framing of the complexity and uncertainty engendered by the inherent multiscalar character of water governance systems (Ingram 2011; Wise et al. 2014; Ison, Collins, and Wallis 2015; Head, Ross, and Bellamy 2016; Rubenstein et al. 2016).
- Diverse sectoral interests creating framing contests and tensions between the various actors seeking to exploit opportunities that emerge (Olsson et al. 2006; Boin, 't Hart, and McConnell 2009; Kallis, Kiparsky, and Norgaard 2009; Wise et al. 2014).
- Disconnection between mandated water-related policy reform processes and local and regional realities in practice, or between local and regional approaches (Bellamy, Head, and Ross 2012; Pahl-Wostl 2015; Rubenstein et al. 2016; Forster et al., this issue).
- Lack of political will and administrative short-termism, leading to systemic policy failure (Kallis, Kiparsky, and Norgaard 2009; Ingram 2011; Rubenstein et al. 2016).

Critical analysts have called for changes in thinking, practices, and institutional arrangements to establish more systemic and adaptive responses in water governance (Rubenstein et al. 2016), particularly in the case of large cross-border river-basin systems (Gerlak and Heikkila 2007; Marshall and Stafford Smith 2010) and at times of crisis (Pahl-Wostl 2015). Empirical research has largely focused on more "formal" or policy-mandated water governance systems and singular policy initiatives, to the neglect of "self-organized" and "informal" social innovations beyond the local scale. The interaction of formal and informal systems has rarely been examined systemically as a multilevel phenomenon over long time frames (Bellamy, Head, and Ross 2012). In particular, a critical gap exists in our understanding of the nature and dynamics of the evolution of large cross-boundary water governance systems over time; the emergence of "water crises" and their nature and role in shaping innovation and institutional change; and the interaction of self-organized and more "formal" or mandated-policy approaches for water governance.

This article addresses these gaps through an empirical study of the emergence and evolution of a cross-border multilevel water governance system for the large remote Lake Eyre Basin (LEB) in arid central Australia. The analytical focus is understanding the dynamics of institutional change and the emergence of governance capacities that shape patterns of interaction in water governance systems and, in turn, trajectories of change. Three core questions are addressed: What were the nature, role, and function of crises in the emergence of cross-border water governance in the LEB over the last two decades? What challenges emerged and what factors shaped responses to crises in dealing with the wicked nature of the water governance problems faced? What are the legacies for the LEB water governance system in responding to future crises?

Water Governance in Australia: A Brief Overview

The nature and evolution of the policy and institutional background for water and related natural resources governance in Australia is complex (Bellamy 2007; Marshall and Stafford-Smith 2010; Curtis et al. 2014). We summarize some aspects of particular relevance to this case study in the following.

Water governance in the Australian federation is multijurisdictional, involving three levels of government: the national government, six state and two territory governments, and numerous local governments. Constitutionally, water and related natural resources policy is the responsibility of the states and territories, which devolve some regulatory roles to local governments. The national government has traditionally been a minor player focusing on matters of national environmental significance and fulfilling international obligations. Since the 1990s, the national government has taken a more prominent strategic role in managing a growing set of international obligations on the environment, in enabling coordination through intergovernmental agreements with the states on standards and strategic goals, and in providing incentive-based funding for achieving performance outcomes in water and related natural resources policy (Curtis et al. 2014; Head 2014).

In this context, the fragmentation of responsibilities and capacities for water and related natural resources governance in Australia, across multiple actors and levels of decision making and action, has created contentious policy dilemmas and crises. Collaboration and cooperation have been relied upon for "harmonization" across Australian federal and state institutions; however, many challenges have emerged in practice (Bellamy 2007; Marshall and Stafford Smith 2010; Wallis and Ison 2011; Eberhard et al. this issue). For example, each level of government typically adopts its own water governance approach, and state and federal governments often continue to develop policy and to design and implement program-specific arrangements that differ in scale, style, resourcing, and accountability standards. This has posed particular challenges for the governance of large cross-border river basins (Kingsford, Boulton, and Puckridge 1998; Gerlak and Heikkila 2007; Marshall and Stafford Smith 2010).

Methods

In the context of large river basins, the research approach recognizes the emergent and contingent character of institutions and the processes changing them. Long-term historical empirical studies are desirable for developing a better understanding of water governance systems as complex adaptive systems (OECD 2011; Edelenbos and Teisman 2013; Ison, Collins, and Wallis 2015), while pluralistic multimethod approaches can enable a systemic focus on the role of institutions and change for enabling and shaping patterns of interaction and the emergence of governance capacities (Poteete, Janssen, and Ostrom 2010; Levin et al. 2013; Rubenstein et al. 2016).

The LEB empirical study is one of four case studies conducted across Australia as part of a larger research project on "Collaboration as a solution to wicked policy problems" (Head, Ross, and Bellamy 2016; Ross, Bellamy, and Head 2016). Key factors in selecting this case were its cross-border multilevel character as a large river basin system in remote rural Australia, and its unique experience over two decades in experimenting with whole-of-basin cross-border catchment management.

The analysis is informed by multiple theoretical perspectives, including complex adaptive systems, social–ecological systems, collaboration, adaptive governance, and institutional change (Bellamy, Head, and Ross 2012; Head, Ross, and Bellamy 2016). It traces the evolution of the LEB water governance system over two decades, and through the lens of collaboration it explores the emergence of episodes of water crisis and institutional change. Three critical elements of water governance capacity are identified by Edelenbos and Teisman (2013): enabling interactions between diverse actors; developing capacity to establish effective interactions between levels, functions, and domains; and the emergence of joint interests and capacities for institutional change. In this context, we examine the role of crises in the emergence of multiscalar governance arrangements (formal and informal) in the LEB and the implications for governance capacity in responding to future crises in a remote rural environment.

The approach involved multiple methods (Poteete, Janssen, and Ostrom 2010), including literature review and archival document analysis; participant observation of a 3-day interactive conference in 2010 engaging 74 stakeholders of the LEB; and 16 in-depth semistructured interviews conducted in 2010 with key informants. The document analysis provided historical and scientific information for triangulation with interview and participant observation data. Participant observation at the conference enabled contextualization through the presentations and opportunities for conversation with the participants, most of whom could not be reached any other way, and allowed introductions toward interviews.

Key informants, selected on the basis of their experience and knowledge of water governance in the LEB, were identified using snowball sampling. They included seven informants from the nongovernment or community-based domain (quotations denoted with C); three research scientists (across the ecology, social, policy science domains) (S); and six informants from the government sector (federal, state, and regional) (G). Interviews lasting 1 to 2 hours were conducted face-to-face or by telephone, recorded, and transcribed. The interviews addressed the issues of: the history of water governance in the LEB since 1990; critical turning points or "hotspots"; collaborative processes and their strengths and weaknesses; factors that supported or hindered collaboration; the cross-scale legacy of the LEB collaborative approach; and the future for multilevel water governance in the LEB. NVivo software was used in the analysis and synthesis of interviews. Codes were derived inductively and deductively from the data and the literature review. Tables, timelines, and matrices were also utilized to: identify trends and linkages; develop timelines and histories of institutional arrangements and processes; and identify relationships and synergies.

Analysis identified four "crises" of importance to the emergence and evolution of the LEB multiscale governance system (Bellamy, Head, and Ross 2012). Further analysis focused on the nature of perceived crises and challenges faced in cross-border water governance; social and institutional responses to crises in practice; whether crises were harnessed as opportunities for change; and the perceived legacy of crises for the LEB water governance system and its long-term future.

The Lake Eyre Basin: A Wicked Problem

The LEB is a large remote cross-border river system in Central Australia spanning four state/territory jurisdictions: Queensland (Qld), South Australia (SA), the Northern

Territory (NT), and a very small area of New South Wales (NSW). It covers one-sixth of Australia (1.14 million km^2) and supports a widely dispersed rural population of about 60,000 people. Its major rivers commence in the NT and Qld, and flow into SA to terminate in Lake Eyre, a large salt pan. Its rivers are free flowing and unregulated except for minor extractions for stock and domestic supplies. Most of the basin lies within the arid zone (annual rainfall less than 125 mm), although the northern headwaters are subject to more regular tropical monsoonal rainfall influences (Reid 1994).

The LEB's river ecology is characterized by prolonged cycles of drought ("bust") punctuated by periods of high flow or flooding after rain that bring intense plant and animal reproductive growth ("boom"), providing food and important wildlife breeding habitats (Reid 1994; Kingsford, Boulton, and Puckridge 1998). Although the basin is in relatively good ecological condition, increasing development pressures (e.g., mining, gas production, irrigated agriculture) are posing significant concerns for sustainable water management (Kingsford, Boulton, and Puckridge 1998; URS 2007; Lake Eyre Basin Ministerial Forum [LEBMF] 2008; Measham and Brake 2009). Benefits from LEB's free-flowing conditions and the ecosystems services they provide include fishery yields, bird breeding grounds, floodplain agriculture, and the cultural significance and recreational enjoyment of native riverine biodiversity (Walker, Puckeridge, and Blanch 1997; Kingsford, Boulton, and Puckridge 1998). Balancing water demands between environmental flows and other economic and social benefits yields invariably controversial issues. This is especially the case in cross-border situations like the LEB.

The LEB water governance system involves five political jurisdictions (four states and the national government), together with scientists and basin communities, in the cross-border management of the dynamics of this highly variable system. The "wicked" challenge relates to the interplay of the complexities and extremes of the ecological functioning of the desert river ecology (Reid 1994; Morton, Doherty, and Barker 1995; Walker, Puckeridge, and Blanch 1997; Kingsford, Boulton, and Puckridge 1998); the social contingencies of a large, remote, sparsely populated, poorly interconnected river basin community characterized by many different perspectives, uncertain and ambiguous understanding, and diverse knowledge systems (Reid 1994; Kingsford, Boulton, and Puckridge 1998; Marshall and Stafford Smith 2010); the fragmentation of institutions, powers, and responsibilities across multiple jurisdictions, levels of decision-making, and centers of action (Bellamy, Head, and Ross 2012); poor capacity for indigenous participation in water and related natural resources management processes; and increasing demands for water extraction to satisfy human needs (Kingsford, Boulton, and Puckridge 1998). Moreover, the system is at risk of impact from climate change.

Water Crises in the LEB

From the late 1980s, national agendas drawing on notions of ecologically sustainable development, biodiversity conservation, and integrated catchment management have dominated the water and related natural resources policy arena in Australia. A collaborative vision emerged at this time in national policy dialogues based on voluntary cooperative efforts of local communities accompanied by complementary actions of governments (Bellamy 2007; Marshall and Stafford-Smith 2010; Head 2014).

Before 1994, there were no jurisdictional or regulatory surface water institutional arrangements within the LEB except for the 1988 listing of wetland areas in South Australia near Lake Eyre under the RAMSAR convention. However, since 1994, an evolving mix of formal and informal arrangements and processes has emerged for managing water and related natural resources in the LEB, spawned by crises of governance. This article identifies four such "crises" that emerged unexpectedly to shape the trajectory of change in water and related natural resource governance in the LEB. Table 1 summarizes how the crises were perceived, the institutional changes involved, and the governance outcomes engendered. The discussion of the crises draws on key informant interviews, literature, and archival sources.

Self-Organized Turn

Crisis 1 (1993–1994): World Heritage Listing Proposal

The first crisis emerged with a proposal by "outsiders" (i.e., national conservation movement, environmental scientists, and the federal government) for World Heritage (WH) listing of wetland areas within the SA portion of the basin. Due to perceived threats to the natural features and future biodiversity of these wetlands, and concerns about water supply due to developmental pressures from growing commercial interests, the proposal created significant community and political conflict (Reid 1994; Kingsford, Boulton, and Puckridge 1998; Parliamentary Library 2000). It was a conservation issue linked with a crisis of governance; federal politicians had different views from state politicians and public officials, while people from the LEB community were outraged by the "outsiders" action, the lack of consultation, and the potential ramifications for future land use options for a much larger upstream area of the basin, particularly in relation to pastoral management and the potential for mining and coal seam gas development (Reid 1994; Parliamentary Library 2000). Thus, the proposal "alarmed commercial interests and state governments, due to the implications of federal intervention and changes in existing management that could follow" (Reid 1994, 273).

The listing proposal galvanized into action two opposing self-organized advocacy coalitions. A pro-listing coalition of nongovernmental organizations (NGOs) from outside the LEB, the Arid Lands Coalition (ALC), was concerned about the future of biodiversity in the Australian arid lands (Gill 1997). An unlikely alliance of Lake Eyre pastoralists, landowners, and mining industry, the Lake Eyre Catchment Protection Group (LECPG), was opposed to WH listing and lobbied federally to stall any progress to the listing (Parliamentary Library 2000). Ultimately, the dispute became highly divisive among LEB interests (Reid 1994). In response, the federal government established a multistakeholder representative technical body, the Lake Eyre Basin Reference Group (LEBRG), to undertake an assessment of the case for WH listing focusing on the natural, indigenous, and nonindigenous values of the SA section of the LEB (Reid 1994; Morton, Doherty, and Barker 1995). Although a majority report of the LEBRG recommended WH listing, a political decision was made by the federal government in 1998 not to pursue WH listing due to the lack of community and state government support and a view that increased community efforts could deliver the best protection for the area's conservation values (Parliamentary Library 2000).

Crisis 2 (1995–1999): Irrigated Cotton Proposal

The second crisis emerged with a submission in 1995 to the Queensland Government by a consortium of NSW cotton growers (seen as "outsiders" to the LEB) for approval to

Table 1. Water crises and institutional change in the LEB, 1993–2012.

Crisis	Type	Perceived challenges	Governance changes	Outcomes	Key sources
1. 1993–1994: World Heritage listing proposal	Social–ecological	Federal intervention; impact on wetland biodiversity; future use options; community conflict and tensions; political tensions	First community-based advocacy group (LEPCG)	Stalled WH listing process; assessment of Lake Eyre values (ecological, social, and cultural); initiated community dialogue	Reid 1994; Morton, Doherty, and Barker 1995; Parliamentary Library 2000
2. 1995–2000: Irrigated cotton development proposal	Social–ecological	Impacts on "boom and bust" character of river ecosystems; cross-border water flows and current water uses; community conflict; political tensions; poor indigenous engagement	Experimentation with self-organized cross-border process (LEBCG, CCCC, GDCC); signing of intergovernmental agreement (LEBIA) 2000; emergent advocacy groups	Emergence of three-tiered LEB governance system and basin identity; information sharing; multi-actor interactions and deliberations; development proposals rejected; investment in scientific knowledge; federal government shelves WH listing nomination.	LEBCG 1997; Walker, Puckeridge, and Blanch 1997; Kingsford, Boulton, and Puckridge 1998; Andrews 1999; Parliamentary Library 2000; LEBCG 1997, 2001; Kingsford 2001; Morton 2007
3. 2003–2007: NHT2 regional initiative implementation	Sociopolitical (administrative)	Resourcing self-organized cross-border process; Shift from community-initiated cross-border priorities to state-based regional group priorities	Demise of LEBCG; catchment committees (CCCC and DGCC) continue but lack resources; 5-year review of LEBIA identifies poor multilevel linkages	Four state-based regional bodies replace cross-border LEBCG; diversified LEBIA processes (indigenous, social scientists); improved indigenous involvement	URS 2007; Curtis et al. 2014;
4. 2008–2012: CfOC policy implementation	Sociopolitical (administrative)	Shift from state-based regionally derived to federally mandated investment priorities; business model and reduced funding for state-based regional NRM groups	Emergence of multisector advocacy groups; strengthening of linkages among LEB stakeholders; basin-level self-organization capacity in response to crises.	Demise of CCCC and GDCC; two-tiered LEB governance system; enhanced interactions between LEBIA, regional NRM groups, and state agencies; enhanced capacity for self-organization	Measham and Brake 2009; Curtis et al. 2014; Head, Ross, and Bellamy 2016

Note. CCCC, Cooper Creek Catchment Committee; CfOC, Caring for Our Country national policy initiative; GDCC, Georgina–Diamantina Catchment Committee; LEBCG, Lake Eyre Basin Coordinating Group; LEBIA, Lake Eyre Basin Inter-Governmental Agreement; LECP, Lake Eyre Catchment Protection group; NRM, natural resource management; NHT2, Natural Heritage Trust Regional initiative; WH, World Heritage. For key sources, additional sources are archival material available at http://www.lakeeyrebasin.gov.au/ and http://archive.is/www.lakeeyrebasin.org.au.

develop large-scale irrigated cotton farming in the Cooper Creek catchment, Queensland (Walker, Puckeridge, and Blanch 1997; Kingsford, Boulton, and Puckridge 1998). The proposal galvanized community, scientist, and conservationist interests to collectively oppose the development due to concerns that it might "open up the door for ongoing extraction of water" that was unsuited to the "boom-and-bust" character of the LEB's arid environment (Kingsford, Boulton, and Puckridge 1998):

> [The crisis] captured the LEB community's attention, but in a very different way [to the WH proposal]—the pastoralists and the conservationists suddenly found they had a lot of common views. That was a really important turning point … [It] really got the cattle industry concerned that there would be a locking up of resources … [and] the floodplain cattle people and also the environment lobby concerned about overdevelopment of resources. (Informant G4)

Importantly, the crisis initiated interactions among LEB conservationists, ecologists and community advocates, and local and state governments (Lake Eyre Basin Coordinating Group [LEBCG] 1997). Wide community discussions on the values of the basin and the legitimacy of various stakeholder interests were generated across the basin (Andrews 1999). Several advocacy coalitions also formed to actively oppose the proposal (Interviews): (1) In 1995, the Australian Floodplain Association (AFA) linked dryland farmer and grazier communities of the Queensland Channel Country with scientists, politicians, and conservation groups; (2) in 1996, the Cooper's Creek Protection Group (CCPG) formed to link a coalition of residents of the catchment (mostly graziers); and (3) a loose alliance emerged linking the Barcoo Shire Council and the LECPG (which previously opposed the WH listing proposal) (Reid 1994). In recognition that "the old divisive ways were not working", a self-organized, community-driven catchment management process linking community, government, and scientists across borders emerged for the LEB based on broad recognition that despite all their differences, the various stakeholders had a fundamental common motivation to look after the basin across borders and to secure their future (LEBCG 2001). For its time, this consensus-based process was experimental and innovative. An informant reflected:

> There was a very strong push from the community to have some arrangement that was effective at managing the catchments of the LEB without drifting to either of those two polar positions: locking it up completely or overexploiting it. (Informant G1)

Public meetings were held around the basin and issues and options papers were prepared, culminating in 1997 with the establishment of a multistakeholder cross-border collaboration, the LEB Coordinating Group (LEBCG), linking interests from the community, science, and government (Andrews 1999; LEBCG 2001). This self-organized process focussed on an integrated partnership approach to managing across borders with a whole LEB vision. By 1998, a two-tiered self-organized process was established with an overarching LEBCG supported by two cross-border Catchment Committees (CC)—one for the Georgina–Diamantina Catchment (GDCC) and the other for the Cooper Creek Catchment (CCCC). Based on a consensus approach and wide public consultation, catchment management strategies for the whole LEB and the two major cross-border catchments were developed (Andrews 1999). A community-based informant explained that:

> [It was] run with funding and involvement from government. … It was very much about a participatory process. What it did do, for the first time, was to get all players sitting around

the table, from the big pastoral companies to the individual owners to conservation, tourism, indigenous people, miners, petroleum … talking about the issues that affected us living out here. (Informant C1)

The second crisis was a major turning point in the LEB with the emergence of: first, an improved understanding of the critical dimensions of the wicked problem faced among diverse stakeholders; second, governance capacity for enabling interactions among diverse interests established through the self-organizing processes; and third, wide recognition of the LEB as an identifiable cross-border entity, which did not exist previously. The cotton proposal was eventually rejected by the Queensland government.

The LEB Inter-Governmental Agreement (LEBIA) in 2000 was a pivotal mandated institutional change, which emerged purposefully to provide an overarching governance arrangement to complement the two-tiered self-organizing community-driven process (Parliamentary Library 2000; URS 2007). It was signed by the federal, South Australian, and Queensland governments (and also the Northern Territory in 2004). The LEBIA formalized a cross-border cooperative multiinstitutional arrangement, in perpetuity. It initially comprised three distinctive forums: the LEB Ministerial Forum or LEBMF (involving relevant Ministers from all governments); a ministerially appointed expert-based Scientific Advisory Panel (SAP); and a representative-based multistakeholder Community Advisory Committee (CAC). LEBIA provided a cooperative framework for jointly addressing water and related natural resources associated with cross-border river systems in the LEB in order to avoid adverse downstream impacts on environmental, economic, and social values. The cross-border management approach was "self-organized" through processes that involved government and community working together:

[LEBIA focused on] bringing people together around the whole idea of managing the LEB as a basin rather than as separate states and territory areas … It did come out of community impetus, but it was also strongly supported by governments at the time. (Informant G1)

Administrative or Mandated Turn

Crisis 3 (2003–2007): Implementation of NHT2 Program

In 2003, a third major crisis emerged but of an administrative character, with the rollout nationally of the federal government's Natural Heritage Trust (NHT2) program (2002–2007). NHT2 created a new regional "architecture" across the whole of Australia involving 56 new multiparty regional bodies for natural resource management (NRM) (Bellamy 2007; Curtis et al. 2014; Head, Ross, and Bellamy 2016), all confined within state boundaries. The regional bodies were linked to a regional delivery funding model based on the development of accredited regional NRM plans reflecting each region's own priorities, but within frameworks defined by respective state/territory governments. Although the NHT2 program transformed natural resource governance arrangements across the whole of Australia, introducing a regional approach for the first time in many instances, it had unintended consequences for the LEB (URS 2007). It created four separate state-based multiparty regional collaborations, each mandated and block funded through different federal–state intergovernmental agreements. Thus, the institutional framework in which the LEBIA and the "self-organized" cross-border catchment processes were developed in the 1990s changed significantly with the NHT2 implementation in the LEB in 2003. The NHT2 reform processes reinstated the very boundaries that the collaborative processes had been established to bridge in response to Crisis 1. The reform strengthened the "top-down" national collaborative arrangements under LEBIA, and undermined the self-organized community-based process. As informants lamented:

> The whole change to the NHT2 arrangements where suddenly everything was regionally funded ... It did sort of lose its basin-wide focus. (Informant G4)

> We went into this new paradigm of regional bodies and because the coordinating group [LEBCG] didn't fit that model—it ran across state borders and sat outside the government ... it ceased to be. (Informant C1)

The consequences were dire for LEB governance capacity for self-organization and addressing change systemically. As each of the new NRM regions was established under different federal–state agreements, they were established as single entities, each on a different basis with responsibilities and action stopping at their respective borders. The two community-based catchment committees (CCCC and GDCC) initially survived this "top-down" mandated reform, albeit fragmented across state borders and very poorly resourced. The overarching whole-of-basin LEBIA arrangements did not find a comfortable fit with the new NHT2 regional arrangements either, as LEBIA had no connections or formal recognition with the new NHT2 regional arrangements.

Crisis 4 (2008–2012): Implementation of the Caring for Our Country Program

A fourth crisis, an "administrative" one, emerged with the rollout of the federal government's Caring for Our Country (CfOC) program, which succeeded the NHT2 program. This replaced agreed regionally derived plans with a competitive project-based funding model for meeting federal government-derived priorities. It changed the funding and administrative relationships between the national and state/territory governments created under NHT2 in an adverse way for the LEB, and it broadened the regional NRM delivery model beyond a focus on the four accredited regional NRM bodies to allow any group within the LEB to compete for funding (Bellamy, Head, and Ross 2012; Curtis et al. 2014). It adversely affected the capacity for managing across jurisdictions and borders and resulted in operational downsizing of the regional NRM bodies, and the final demise of the self-organized cross-border processes (Bellamy, Head, and Ross 2012; Head, Ross, and Bellamy 2016).

Subsequent reforms in 2008 following the 5-year mandated/statutory review of the LEBIA arrangements (URS 2007) enhanced the pattern of institutional interactions across borders through the "perpetual" LEBIA arrangements. These included the establishment of a Senior Officers Group (SOG) for coordination of state-based policies and implementation, and annual meetings of the four regional NRM groups to improve information exchange.

The first two crises were of a mainly "social–ecological" character (Lubell 2015). They catalyzed a significant shift to a more collaborative self-organized cross-border governance approach covering the whole LEB, complemented by a mandated cooperative intergovernmental agreement between the national and state/territory governments. Subsequently, mandated-policy and regulatory changes to national NRM arrangements engendered two further crises but of an "administrative" and "sociopolitical" character that led to the demise of the "self-organized" whole-of-basin process and its replacement by a devolved state-based, regionally fragmented water governance system across the LEB.

Subsequently, the national government's "perpetual" LEBIA arrangements were strengthened but the self-organized cross-border process ceased to exist.

Legacy of Crises

Spawned by crises of governance, an evolving mix of "self-organized" and "mandated" arrangements and processes emerged for managing water and related natural resources in the LEB (Table 1). These mixed arrangements operate across multiple levels of organization (local, regional, state/territory, national), they span borders, and they catalyze interactions among diverse public, private, and community actors through a variety of mechanisms that did not previously exist. The crises also contributed to the emergence of a widely recognized identity for the basin, and a better understanding of the value-based tensions and contests among diverse stakeholder interests, including the ecological values of the river basin system, the indigenous and non-indigenous social and cultural values, and values attached to current commercial production uses.

Concurrently a diverse mix of "self-organized" advocacy coalitions and other alliances (Table 1), variously involving actors from the science, policy, and community domains, has emerged and re-emerged at times of crisis to engage in highly contentious dialogues or debates (Olsson et al. 2006; Head, Ross, and Bellamy 2016). These coalitions enabled the engagement of many diverse people in framing contests (Termeer et al. 2015; Rubenstein et al. 2016), and provided an alternative option for actors to exchange ideas and more vigorously pursue their agendas outside of the more consensual processes of the "self-organized" and "policy-mandated" collaborative cross-border arrangements (see interviews).

Reflecting on the LEB governance capacity for self-organization in response to perceived crises, the LEB water governance system was better prepared to deal with the tensions and community conflict when later controversies rose in different domains. For example, the Queensland Government proposed in 2009 to include the Queensland parts of the LEB for protection under the *Wild Rivers Act 2005*, no longer allowing large-scale irrigation and open cut mines near major creek and rivers. Although receiving a very mixed response (e.g., support from environmentalists and organic graziers but strong skepticism from other agricultural and mining interests), the consultation process in the LEB did not engender bitter conflicts that have typified similar declarations in other regions (e.g., Cape York). Key LEB actors convened a series of forums among regional stakeholders and facilitated open dialogue on the proposed declaration. In 2011, the Queensland Government appointed a group of diverse stakeholders to form the Lake Eyre Basin Wild River Advisory Panel (LEBWRAP) to provide advice on the proposed declarations. Crises thus have been critical in the LEB for enabling governance capacity for self-organization in a more inclusive and knowledgeable way that has avoided other major crises.

Conclusions

In debating sustainable futures, the wide variety of interests and values characterizing stakeholders within large river basins often makes water crises highly complex situations that are prone to controversy, conflict, and divisive framing contests (Boin et al. 2009; Termeer et al. 2015). Solutions to crises are commonly shaped by the way the problem is framed and debated and by how values are mobilized in these debates (Boin et al. 2009; Wise et al. 2014; Ison, Collins, and Wallis 2015). Preferred responses focus on collaborative, multilevel governance approaches, and there is a growing understanding of the impacts, challenges, and limitations they involve (Dutterer and Margerum 2015; Pahl-Wostl 2015; Ross, Bellamy, and Head 2016; Forster et al. this issue). However, a significant gap exists in understanding the role of "crises" in enabling and shaping collaborative multilevel water governance systems to more effectively manage competing ecological and social goals while mitigating conflict in more systemic and adaptive ways.

This article contributes to a better understanding of this gap through a case study of multilevel, cross-border water governance in a large remote rural region of Australia since the 1990s. It shows how emergent crises, both "social–ecological" and "political–administrative," can pose significant environmental and social dilemmas for basin stakeholders, and yet they also can provide opportunities for shaping more systemic approaches to institutional change (Seixas and Davy 2008; Osterblom and Folke 2013).

The historical analysis of water governance in the LEB confirms that adaptation and institutional change in water governance systems for large river basins is an ongoing process rather than a discrete action (Wyborn et al. 2015), and subject to episodic and often externally generated crises (Lane and McDonald 2002). This study confirms that crises create space and opportunities for: new patterns of interactions among actors (Edelenbos and Teisman 2013); more inclusive "self-organized" collaboration and innovation (Folke et al. 2005); critical debate and reflection on established governance systems (Kallis, Kiparsky, and Norgaard 2009); "mandated" cross-border arrangements that can transcend formal organizational structures and boundaries (Gerlak and Heikkila 2007); and for key actors to take collective action and deal with conflict and tensions (Westley et al. 2011). In the LEB example, crises contributed to a more collaborative cross-border approach to water governance that is changing the patterns of interaction among diverse actors (Edelenbos and Teisman 2013) and, in turn, shaping pathways of change in a more systemic and adaptive way (Wise et al. 2014; Wyborn et al. 2015).

Finally, in response to emergent crises, the LEB water governance system has evolved a capacity sufficient to avoid some of the more highly divisive policy failures that often characterize other large river systems, such as the Murray–Darling Basin (Eberhard et al. this issue; Wallis and Ison 2011) and the CALFED Bay-Delta initiative (Kallis, Kiparsky, and Norgaard 2009). There is a need for more research that focuses on a systemic understanding of the role and nature of emergent water crises and how they can be harnessed to improve patterns of interaction in water governance and, in turn, shape trajectories of change in other large river basin systems.

Funding

We thank the Australian Research Council (Discovery Project DP0987727) and The University of Queensland for financial support, and all participants of the study for their contribution.

References

Andrews, K. 1999. Rivers in the Rangelands—What's going on in the Lake Eyre Basin. http://www.lakeeyrebasin.org.au/archive/pages/page25.html (accessed February 7, 2011).

Bakker, K. 2012. Water: Political, biopolitical, material. *Social Studies of Science* 42 (4):616–23. doi:10.1177/0306312712441396

Bellamy, J. 2007. Adaptive governance: The challenge for natural resource management. In *Federalism and Regionalism: New approaches, new institutions?*, ed. A. J. Brown and J. A. Bellamy, 97–120. Canberra, Australia: ANU E-Press.

Bellamy, J., B. W. Head, and H. Ross. 2012. Blurring boundaries and building bridges: Challenges of managing across borders in the Lake Eyre Basin. In Proceedings of 6th Australian stream management conference, Canberra, 6–8 Feb 2012, ed. J. R. Grove and I. Rutherford, 151–58. Canberra, Australia: River Basin Management Authority.

Boin, A., P. 't Hart, and A. McConnell. 2009. Crisis exploitation: Political and policy impacts of framing contests. *Journal of European Public Policy* 16 (1):81–106. doi:10.1080/13501760802453221

Curtis, A., H. Ross, G. R. Marshall, C. Baldwin, J. Cavaye, C. Freeman, A. Carr, and G. J. Syme. 2014. The great experiment with devolved NRM governance: Lessons from community engagement in Australia and New Zealand since the 1980s. *Australasian Journal of Environmental Management* 21 (2):175–99. doi:10.1080/14486563.2014.935747

Dietz, T., E. Ostrom, and P. C. Stern. 2003. The struggle to govern the commons. *Science* 302 (5652):1907–12. doi:10.1126/science.1091015

Dutterer, A. D., and R. D. Margerum. 2015. The limitations of policy-level collaboration: A meta-analysis of CALFED. *Society & Natural Resources* 28 (1):21–37. doi:10.1080/08941920.2014.945054

Edelenbos, J., and G. J. Teisman. 2013. Water governance capacity: The art of dealing with a multiplicity of levels, sectors and domains. *International Journal of Water Governance* 1:89–108. doi:10.7564/12-ijwg5

Folke, C., T. Hahn, P. Olsson, and J. Norberg. 2005. Adaptive governance of social-ecological systems. *Annual Review of Environmental Resources* 30:441–73. doi:10.1146/annurev.energy.30.050504.144511

Galaz, V., F. Moberg, E-K. Olsson, E. Paglia, and C. Parker. 2011. Institutional and political leadership dimensions of cascading ecological crises. *Public Administration* 89 (2):361–80. doi:10.1111/j.1467-9299.2010.01883.x

Gerlak, A. K., and T. Heikkila. 2007. Collaboration and institutional endurance in U.S. water policy. *Political Science & Politics* 40 (1):55–60. doi:10.1017/s1049096507070102

Gill, N. 1997. The contested domain of pastoralism: Landscape, work and outsiders in Central Australia. In *Tracking knowledge—North Australian landscapes: Studies in indigenous and settler knowledge systems*, ed. D. B. Rose and A. Clarke, 50–67. Darwin, Australia: North Australian Research Unit.

Head, B. W. 2014. Managing water crises: Adaptive policy responses to drought and flood in Southeast Queensland, Australia. *Ecology and Society* 19 (2):33. doi:10.5751/es-06414-190233

Head, B. W., H. Ross, and J. Bellamy. 2016. Managing wicked natural resource problems: The collaborative challenge at regional scales in Australia. *Landscape and Urban Planning* 154:81–92. doi:10.1016/j.landurbplan.2016.03.019

Homer-Dixon, T., B. Walker, R. Biggs, A.-S. Crépin, C. Folke, E. F. Lambin, G. D. Peterson, J. Rockström, M. Scheffer, W. Steffen, and M. Troell. 2015. Synchronous failure: The emerging causal architecture of global crisis. *Ecology and Society* 20 (3):6. doi:10.5751/es-07681-200306

Ingram, H. 2011. Beyond universal remedies for good water governance. In *Water for food in a changing world*, ed. A. Garrido and H. Ingram, 241–261. Hoboken, NJ: Taylor and Francis.

Ison, R. L., K. B. Collins, and P. J. Wallis. 2015. Institutionalising social learning: Towards systemic and adaptive governance. *Environmental Science & Policy* 53, Part B:105–17. doi:10.1016/j.envsci.2014.11.002

Kallis, G., M. Kiparsky, and R. Norgaard. 2009. Collaborative governance and adaptive management: Lessons from California's CALFED water program. *Environmental Science and Policy* 12 (6):631–43. doi:10.1016/j.envsci.2009.07.002

Kingsford, R. T., A. J. Boulton, and J. T. Puckridge. 1998. Challenges in managing dryland rivers crossing political boundaries: Lessons from Cooper Creek and the Paroo River, central Australia. *Aquatic Conservation: Marine & Freshwater Ecosystems* 8 (3):361–78. doi:10.1002/(sici)1099-0755 (199805/06)8:3<361::aid-aqc294>3.0.co;2-v

Kingsford, R. T. 2001. Development strains on Australia's greatest desert river system, Cooper Creek. Paper presented at *Beyond Traditional Boundaries*, IPAA National Conference 2001, 28–30 November 2001. Sydney Convention Centre. Sydney, Australia: IPAA.

Lake Eyre Basin Coordinating Group. 1997. Catchment management options paper, October 1997. http://www.lakeeyrebasin.org.au/archive/pages/page26.html(accessed August 11, 2010).

Lake Eyre Basin Coordinating Group. 2001. History of the establishment of Lake Eyre Basin catchment management, 2 March 2001. http://www.lakeeyrebasin.org.au/archive/pages/page11.html (accessed August 11, 2010)

Lake Eyre Basin Ministerial Forum. 2008. *State of the Basin 2008: Rivers assessment*. Report prepared by the Lake Eyre Basin Scientific Advisory Panel. Canberra, Australia: Commonwealth of Australia.

Lane, M. B., and G. McDonald. 2002. Crisis, change, and institutions in forest management: The wet tropics of north-eastern Australia. *Journal of Rural Studies* 18 (3):245–56. doi:10.1016/s0743-0167(02)00008-6

Levin, S., T. Xepapadeas, A.-S. Crépin, J. Norberg, A. de Zeeuw, C. Folke, T. Hughes, K. Arrow, S. Barrett, G. Daily, P. Ehrlich, N. Kautsky, K.-G. Mäler, S. Polasky, M. Troell, J. R. Vincent, and B. Walker. 2013. Social–ecological systems as complex adaptive systems: Modeling and policy implications. *Environment and Development Economics* 18 (2):111–32. doi:10.1017/s1355770x12000460

Lubell, M. 2015. Collaborative partnerships in complex institutional systems. *Current Opinion in Environmental Sustainability* 12:41–47. doi:10.1016/j.cosust.2014.08.011

Marshall, G. R., and D. M. Stafford-Smith. 2010. Natural resources governance for the drylands of the Murray-Darling Basin. *Rangeland Journal* 32 (3):267–82. doi:10.1071/rj10020

Measham, T. G., and L. Brake eds. 2009. People, communities and economies of the Lake Eyre Basin. DKCRC Research Rep. No. 45. Alice Springs, NT, Australia: Desert Knowledge Cooperative Research Centre.

Morton, S. R. 2007. Ecology of Desert Rivers. *Historical Records of Australian Science* 18:281–287.

Morton, S., M. Doherty, and R. Barker. 1995. *Natural heritage values of the Lake Eyre Basin in South Australia: World Heritage assessment*. Canberra, Australia: Division of Wildlife and Ecology, CSIRO.

OECD. 2011. *Water governance in OECD countries: A multi-level approach*. Paris, France: OECD Publishing.

Olsson, P., L. H. Gunderson, S. R. Carpenter, P. Ryan, L. Lebel, C. Folke, and C. S. Holling. 2006. Shooting the rapids: Navigating transitions to adaptive governance of social-ecological systems. *Ecology and Society* 11 (1):18. doi:10.5751/es-01595-110118

Osterblom, H., and C. Folke. 2013. Emergence of global adaptive governance for stewardship of regional marine resources. *Ecology and Society* 18 (2):4. doi:10.5751/es-05373-180204

Pahl-Wostl, C. 2015. *Water governance in the face of global change. From understanding to transformation*. Cham, Switzerland: Springer International Publishing.

Parliament of Australia. 2000. Lake Eyre Basin Intergovernmental Agreement Bill 2001. Bills Digest No. 104 2000–01. Canberra, Australia: Department of Parliamentary Library. 2000.

Poteete, A. R., M. A. Janssen, and E. Ostrom. 2010. *Working together: Collective action, the commons, and multiple methods in practice*. Princeton, NJ: Princeton University Press.

Prokopy, L. S., N. Mullendore, K. Brasier, and K. Floress. 2014. A typology of catalyst events for collaborative watershed management in the United States. *Society & Natural Resources* 27 (11):1177–91. doi:10.1080/08941920.2014.918230

Reid, J. 1994. The Prime Minister's pre-election promise of World Heritage listing for the Lake Eyre Basin: Flight or flight of fancy? *Rangeland Journal* 16 (2):273–97. doi:10.1071/rj9940273

Ross, H., J. Bellamy, and B. Head. 2016. Collaboration challenges in addressing natural resource management problems: Australian regional case studies. In *The challenges of collaboration in environmental governance: Barriers and responses*, ed. R. D. Margerum and C. J. Robinson, 175–96. Cheltenham, UK: Edward Elgar Publishing.

Rubenstein, N., P. J. Wallis, R. L. Ison, and L. Godden. 2016. Critical reflections on building a community of conversation about water governance in Australia. *Water Alternatives* 9 (1):81–98.

Seixas, C. S., and B. Davy. 2008. Self-organization in integrated conservation and development initiatives. *International Journal of the Commons* 2 (1):99–125. doi:10.18352/ijc.24

Termeer, C. J. A. M., A. Dewulf, G. Breeman, and S. J. Stiller. 2015. Governance capabilities for dealing wisely with wicked problems. *Administration & Society* 47 (6):680–710. doi:10.1177/0095399712469195

URS. 2007. Review of the Lake Eyre Basin Intergovernmental Agreement. Report prepared for the Commonwealth Department of Environment and Water Resources, 14 June 2007. Southbank, Victoria, Australia: URS Australia Pty Ltd.

Walker, K. F., J. T. Puckeridge, and S. J. Blanch. 1997. Irrigation development on cooper creek, central Australia: Prospects for a regulated economy in a boom-and-bust ecology. *Aquatic Conservation: Marine and Freshwater Ecosystems* 7:63–73. doi:10.1002/(sici)1099-0755(199703)7:1<63::aid-aqc218>3.3.co;2-x

Wallis, P., and R. L. Ison. 2011. Appreciating institutional complexity in water governance dynamics: A case from the Murray-Darling Basin, Australia. *Water Resources Management* 25 (15):4081–97. doi:10.1007/s11269-011-9885-z

Westley, F., P. Olsson, C. Folke, T. Homer-Dixon, H. Vredenburg, D. Loorbach, J. Thompson, M. Nilsson, E. Lambin, J. Sendzimir, B. Banerjee, V. Galaz, and S. van der Leeuw. 2011. Tipping toward sustainability: Emerging pathways of transformation. *AMBIO* 40 (7):762–80. doi:10.1007/s13280-011-0186-9

Wise, R. M., I. Fazey, M. Stafford Smith, S. E. Park, H. C. Eakin, E. R. M. Archer Van Garderen, and B. Campbell. 2014. Reconceptualising adaptation to climate change as part of pathways of change and response. *Global Environmental Change* 28:325–36. doi:10.1016/j.gloenvcha.2013.12.002

Wyborn, C., L. Yung, D. Murphy, and D. R. Williams. 2015. Situating adaptation: How governance challenges and perceptions of uncertainty influence adaptation in the Rocky Mountains. *Regional Environmental Change* 15 (4):669–82. doi:10.1007/s10113-014-0663-3

Scales of Power in Water Governance in China: Examples From the Yangtze River Basin

Qidong Huang and Jiajun Xu

ABSTRACT

Theories that explain the governance of water, such as integrated river basin management and multilevel water governance, point to scalar configurations of power as critical determinants of success (or failure). This article explains how the scalar configurations of power in water governance mirror those of the Chinese State, and influence water governance in powerful ways. We use the case of the Yangtze River and Shanghai, a megacity in the Yangtze estuary, as examples, showing how a local jurisdiction exercises its regulatory measures against different types of transjurisdictional water pollution and how these regulatory measures mirror the fluidity (or rigidity) of power configurations in hydropolitics in China. China's evolving water resource management institutions are as yet unable to address the scalar configurations of power in water governance.

Scale is a foundational concept in geography. We argue that to date there are two main theoretical principles concerning scale: (1) Scale is geographically and politically constructed, and (2) scale is both fixed and fluid (e.g., Boelens 2014; Dinar et al. 2015; Hoogesteger and Verzijl 2015). For water governance, scales of power have been viewed as critical determinants of success (or failure).

Scalar configurations of power, as an integral part of social strategies and struggles for control and empowerment, involve continuous reshuffling and reorganizations of power at various scales (Thiel and Egerton 2011; Romano 2016). It is clear that the scales at which, for example, social activities and political authority are constituted are not fixed but periodically transformed (Herod 1991). Scalar configurations of power are important factors that complicate water governance, since many regulations that would involve an entire basin might only act on parts of it, while some local policies "jump" scales to affect adjacent areas (Sneddon 2002).

The complexity of scalar configurations of power might be well exemplified by transjurisdictional water pollution, which is characterized by the physical movement of pollutants across jurisdictional boundaries (Bolin, Collins, and Darby 2008). When transjurisdictional water pollution arises, the distribution of the "public bad" is no longer local but more regional or scalar. Thus, transjurisdictional water pollution might be seen as a prism that splits power into different strands at various scales. Through transjurisdictional water pollution we can examine how the scalar configurations of power in water governance mirror those of the Chinese State, and influence water governance in powerful ways.

When conducting their research on scale and power in water governance, scholars typically adopt a national or basin-wide rather than a local perspective, and consider the entire waterscape rather than a specific element, such as flood risk management or trans-jurisdictional water pollution. Our research examines how a local jurisdiction exercises its regulatory measures against different types of transjurisdictional water pollution and how these regulatory measures mirror the fluidity (or rigidity) of power configurations in hydropolitics in China. In the next section we briefly review the literature regarding water governance research (especial trans-jurisdictional water pollution) in China. We then explain the research method used in our analysis, and present our results, followed by a discussion and key conclusions.

Reviews

Management of transjurisdictional water pollution typically entails conflicts of power. The federal government of the United States is responsible for the overall development of water resources and has primary authority for environmental regulation related to issues such as endangered species and water quality management, but relies on states to implement programs and regulation (Eberhard et al. 2016). The federal government also established a number of water resources management committees based on the river basins, which have full authority over the relevant matters (Chaffin et al. 2016). The European Union (EU) Water Framework Directive (WFD) is "one of the most ambitious policy initiatives worldwide to reconfigure power around the hydrological scale of river basins" in the European Union (Hueesker and Moss 2015, 40). In Australia, the power of the basin is located in the federal level. Australia has set up a Commonwealth Environmental Water Holder to protect and restore the Murray-Darling Basin's environmental assets. The Murray–Darling Basin Authority ensures integrated sustainable management of water resources (Alston et al. 2016). These countries face issues similar to those of China: Transjurisdictional water pollution management is challenged by the coordination of power among federal (or central), state (or provincial), county, and municipal governments. However, what make China different from other countries are the power relations within its political hierarchy and the scalar configuration of power in its water governance.

Studies of transjurisdictional water pollution of China are typically divided into two categories according to their research perspectives: "micro-technological" and "macro-institutional." In micro-technological studies, scholars usually focus on econometric measurements of pollution loss within river basins (Liu et al. 2010; Zhang et al. 2010), game-theory analyses of regional pollution disputes (Chau and Jiang 2003; Deng et al. 2010), and regulatory instruments against transjurisdictional water pollution (Ma et al. 2009; Li et al. 2011). In macro-institutional studies, researchers advocate strengthening the central government's power over water resources to ensure balanced and unitary water management across basins (Shen 2004; Zhang et al. 2011) and changing the unilateral policy pattern of central regulation by establishing effective coordination mechanisms across scales (Wang et al. 2008; Huang et al. 2013). We note that both types of studies typically examine the efficacy of environmental regulatory tools under the assumption of a rigid and forceful government.

Some recent studies have shifted somewhat to view water governance in China from a soft and fluid perspective, paying attention to the scope for power shifts at different scales. One strand of the literature views the vertical distribution of power as strong at two ends (the State Council and the local governments) and weak at a middle point (basin commissions), which blocks the vertical flow of the power at basin commissions (Wei, Pang, and Luo 2014). The other strand of the literature holds that the horizontal flow of power is obstructed both at the national level (different ministries) and at the local level (local administrative jurisdictions) (Tang and Yang 2014; Luo, Pang, and Xu 2015). However, these studies do not adequately consider the potential for a local jurisdiction to cope with different types of transjurisdictional water pollution by exercising regulations across scales, and thus fail to achieve a better understanding of fluidity (or rigidity) of power configurations in hydropolitics in China.

Methods

We classified the government entities into four groups according to their levels or geographical scales. At the national level there is the Ministry of Water Resources (MWR) and the Ministry for Environmental Protection (MEP); at the basin scale the Yangtze River Basin Commission (YRBC) and Taihu Lake Basin Commission (TLBC); at the regional scale the Yangtze Estuary Joint Session of Cooperation and Development (YEJS-CD) and the Yangtze Estuary Joint Session of Emergent Disposal of Transjurisdictional Pollution (YEJS-EDTP); and at the local scale the Shanghai Water Bureau of Resources (SBWR), Shanghai Bureau of Environmental Protection (SBEP), and Shanghai Committee of Construction and Transportation (SCCT).

Field research took place between March 2013 and November 2015. As detailed in the following, we designed and conducted a number of surveys, semistructured interviews, and informal discussions. Our approach is qualitative; we have not used random sampling methods (Table 1).

Table 1. Research methods and data collection.

Method	Number	Description
Surveys	6	Four surveys were respectively designed and conducted in the four levels of governmental institutions (270 respondents) and two surveys in the nongovernmental field (285 respondents). In the governmental surveys, we collected data about the process of policymaking, mechanisms of cooperation, responsibilities of institutions, and strategies and discourses used by state actors to obtain political leverage. In the nongovernmental surveys, we collected the data about effects of the regulatory measures on individuals.
Semistructured interviews	42	The respondents were chosen based on their involvement in or knowledge of transjurisdictional water pollution. They come from four categories of institutions: (1) governments at different levels(55 respondents); (2) key hydraulic projects (such as Yangtze-to-Taihu Diversion Project, Dongfengxisha Reservoir Project, etc.) (18 respondents); (3) water quality monitoring centers (such as Taihu Lake Basin Water Environment Monitoring Center) (12 respondents); and (4) source water reservoirs and water plants of Shanghai (such as Qingcaosha reservoir, Pudong Veolia Water Plant, etc.) (12 respondents). Through these interviews, we collected data about institutional duties, transjurisdictional cooperative agreements, environmental policies, structure of the administrative system, and local regulatory measures.
Informal discussions	80	Through 80 informal discussions (approximately 160 respondents), we collected information about regulations and the regulations' effect on individual's livelihood.
Secondary data	/	We collected secondary data both from published literature and government hydrological bulletins. We also visited the archives of Shanghai Municipal Public Affairs Administrative Bureau to get relevant information about the city's change of source water supply.

Results

Finding New Water Sources: A Passive Response

Shanghai is located in the Yangtze estuary near Taihu Lake (Figure 1). The Yangtze River, with a total length of 6,380 km, runs through 15 provinces, two autonomous regions, and two municipalities to finally reach the East China Sea at Shanghai (Wang et al. 2011). Taihu Lake, the third largest freshwater lake in China, is located in the highly developed and densely populated delta region (see Yang, Qin, and Lin 2012). It has a total surface area of 2,338 km^2 and covers parts of the Jiangsu and Zhejiang provinces, as well as Shanghai (Liu et al. 2013). Shanghai's water supply is mainly from the Yangtze River and Taihu Lake (via the Huangpu River).

Transjurisdictional water pollution has been the main driver of the changes in where Shanghai sources its water (Figure 1). Before 1950, Shanghai got its source water mainly from the Huangpu River and Suzhou Creek (a branch of the Huangpu). After 1950, water plant intakes gradually moved to the Huangpu's middle stream due to heavy pollution downstream. In the 1970s, the main intakes were moved to upstream near Taihu Lake. Since the 1980s, the water quality of Taihu Lake has decreased rapidly and currently 80% of Taihu Lake's water does not meet the lowest national drinking standards (Luo, Pang, and Xu 2015). To accelerate water quality improvements in Taihu Lake, Shanghai participated in the construction and operation of the 38-km Yangtze-to-Taihu Diversion Project (Figure 1). Although the water quality of parts of the lake has been improved, the water quality in general has not improved markedly.

Shanghai has now gradually shifted its main intake sources from Taihu Lake to the Yangtze River. Three water reservoirs—Chenhang, Qingcaosha, and Dongfengxisha—were built in the Yangtze estuary to supply water for Shanghai's 125 water plants. To ensure the safety of the urban water supply, a 20-km pipe is being built to link Chenhang and Qingcaosha. The pipe will be used to transfer clean water between the two reservoirs when either of them is under the threat of water pollution. The daily supply volume from Taihu Lake has dropped by 16%, while the daily supply volume from the Yangtze increased by 20% since 2010 (Table 2).

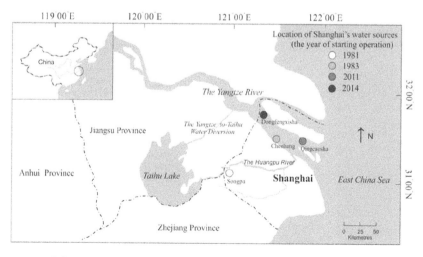

Figure 1. Map of the Yangtze estuary and location of Shanghai's water sources.

Table 2. Source water distribution in Shanghai.

Type	River	Location	Daily supply volume (104 m³) (Proportion)				
			2010	2011	2012	2013	2014
Centralized water	Huangpu	Songpu	350 (55%)	332 (51%)	302 (45%)	283 (43%)	272 (39%)
supply	Yangtze	Chenhang	248 (40%)	236 (36%)	230 (35%)	225 (34%)	198 (28%)
		Qingcaosha	0	53 (9%)	113 (17%)	136 (20%)	135 (19%)
		Dongfengxisha	0	0	0	0	93 (13%)
Dispersed water supply	Suburbs	Surface/ground water	30 (5%)	28 (4%)	25 (3%)	20 (3%)	8 (1%)

Note. Adapted from Shanghai Water Resources Bureau Bulletin (2010, 2011, 2012, 2013, and 2014), http://www.shanghaiwater.gov.cn/indexZh.html.

Institutional Responsibilities

As representatives of the State Council, MWR (the Ministry of Water Resources) and MEP (the Ministry of Environmental Protection) are national environmental authorities and are primarily responsible for the environmental governance of basins. MWR is mainly responsible for water quantity issues such as water resources allocation, hydraulic planning, project construction, and water use supervision, whereas MEP is mainly responsible for water quality issues such as establishment of standards for pollutants discharge and planning of ecological functional areas. However, MWR (including the basin commissions) and MEP (including its designated agencies) each operate their own water quality monitoring system, and the two monitoring systems are parallel and even overlap in many aspects. For example, among the 37 indicators of surface water monitored by MWR, there are 15 indicators monitored by MEP; some important indicators, like river flow measurement (essential for pollution load calculation), are only monitored by MWR and mainly for MWR's internal use. Other ministries like the Ministry of Agriculture and Ministry of Communications and Transports also have a role in water governance. The power of the ministries overlaps, and this always results in blurred responsibility for water pollution.

Basin commissions serve as designated agencies of MWR. YRBC (the Yangtze River Basin Commission) and TLBC (Taihu Lake Basin Commission) determine the basin's overall capacity for carrying pollutants on the basis of environmental capacity, and then break it down to regional capacity for carrying pollutants. The commissions, for much of their existence, have been hydro-technical agencies devoted to water conservancy, and to disaster prevention and mitigation. This restricts the commissions to a professional authority rather than an integrated platform (Tang and Yang 2014) (Figure 2).

At the subbasin level, Shanghai and its neighboring provinces (Jiangsu and Zhejiang) have established the YEJS Framework, encompassing YEJS-CD (the Yangtze Estuary Joint Session of Cooperation and Development) and YEJS-EDTP (the Yangtze Estuary Joint Session of Emergent Disposal of Trans-jurisdictional Pollution). The YEJS Frame is aimed at coordination and cooperation in economic development and environmental protection in the Yangtze estuary.

At the local level, three institutions—SWRB (The Shanghai Water Resources Bureau), SBEP (The Shanghai Bureau of Environmental Protection), and SCCT (The Shanghai Committee of Construction and Transportation)—constitute an internal frame, which is in charge of water affairs within Shanghai's jurisdiction. The internal frame is, of course, not completely free of external constraints and influence, since major planning and construction of water facilities in Shanghai involves a number of national funds and is thus supervised by national water authorities (Table 3).

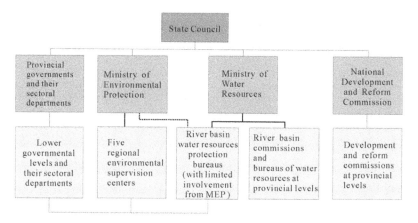

Figure 2. Elements of the hierarchy as relevant to water governance in China.

Local governments are authorized by the central government to manage the water resources that flow through their jurisdictions. Within the scope of the local administrative jurisdictions, local governments are responsible for regulating internal usage patterns of water resources and establishing external coordination mechanisms. When transjurisdictional pollution disputes arise, the local governments concerned will negotiate, sometimes through their authorized government departments. If local governments fail to reach an agreement, the dispute will be mediated by a higher administrative body. Some respondents from local governments even pointed out that the central government in practice gained control over all major resource management decisions although it announced decentralization in water governance. The respondents reported that some "unitary plans" in water resources always "limit" or even "hinder" their coordination. The symbolic decentralization might "represent an abandonment of central government responsibility for resource management without a concomitant establishment of local-level authority" (Sigman 2005, 90).

Regulatory Measures

Regulatory measures, including treaties, agreements, plans, orders, memoranda of understanding, memoranda of cooperation, and memoranda of agreement, act as an essential means of enhancing the interaction and aggregation across scales. We sort regulatory

Table 3. Relevant institutions and mechanisms.

Scale	Institution	Responsibilities
National	MWR MEP	MWR are responsible for water resources allocation, hydraulic planning, project construction, and water use supervision, whereas MEP sets the goal of ecological protection, establishes national standards for pollutants discharge, and operates environmental monitoring system.
Basin-wide	YRBC TLBC	Overall basin planning, risk mitigation, and project construction
Regional	YEJS-CD YEJS-EDTP	Develop an evolving negotiation mechanism against environmental risks within the region
Local (Shanghai)	SWRB SBEP SCCT	Establish a united force to enhance water management within Shanghai jurisdiction

Note. We just list MWR and MEP in the table. Other ministries like the Ministry of Agriculture and Ministry of Communications and Transports also have a role in water governance.

measures into four categories according to their levels: (1) Regulatory measures at the ministerial level refer to ministerial orders, ministerial plans, administrative penalties or interventions from the ministries, and so on. (2) Regulatory measures at the basin level refer to measures that are taken by a basin commission to facilitate water governance like water function areas planning, basin-wide regulations, monitoring water quality at trans-provincial boundaries, and so on. (3) Regulatory measures within the YEJS Frame refer to measures or common consensus made by two joint sessions of the Yangtze estuary like issue linkage, data sharing, information exchange, joint scientific projects, joint risk source screening, integrated planning, coordinated development and regular meeting mechanisms, and so on. (4) Regulatory measures at the local level refer to the measures that are taken by Shanghai to cope with pollution, such as improving technology for purifying raw water, sewage interception, planning for water pollution, source water planning, coordination among municipal bureaus, and so on.

We further classify transjurisdictional water pollution into two types: normal transjurisdictional water pollution (Type I) and emergent transjurisdictional water pollution (Type II). Type I water pollution refers to the pollution caused by daily industrial waste-water, urban domestic sewage, and agricultural non-point-source pollution from the upstream, which are not unexpected. Type II water pollution refers to serious and sudden contamination accidents that seriously threaten the water security of downstream cities or towns.

Figure 3 shows an upward trend in basin and subbasin involvement in regulations against Type I water pollution in terms of number of regulatory measures (the unit of Y axes). The trend displays a high degree of horizontal cooperation between Shanghai and other provinces, and the increasing importance of regional environmental standards set by basin commissions and the YEJS Frame (the Yangtze Estuary Joint Session, at a subbasin scale) in preventing environmental degradation. A sudden increase of the YEJS Frame measures occurred in 2012. In January 2012 the State Council released a policy titled "Implement the Strictest Water Resources Management System," requiring local governments to strengthen unified water resource governance.[1] In this situation, Shanghai, a local actor, adopted a strategy of "jumping scale" and strode over the jurisdictional boundaries to negotiate with upstream provinces within the YEJS Frame.

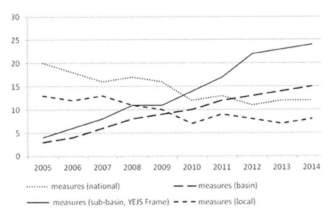

Figure 3. Regulatory measures against normal transjurisdictional water pollution in Shanghai (Type I) at various scales.

Figure 3 also shows that the number of nationwide (ministerial) and local (Shanghai) measures have dropped, from which we can infer a lack of vertical coherence among governments at different levels. At the national scale, ministries are mostly issue oriented and lack the power to settle cross-provincial water disputes, and this, as some respondents explained, has offered Shanghai a range of possibilities of cooperating with upstream provinces. Some respondents (officials from the Ministry of Water Resources and Ministry of Environmental Protection) reported that they were often "asked" by Shanghai to "jointly" hold some "coordination meetings" between Shanghai and upstream provinces. However, the ministries concerned are strengthening their political and financial control over provinces by retaining the power of investment approval. In choosing between the priorities of an efficient coordination mechanism and political control, ministerial actors are likely to choose the latter to maintain their positions in future policymaking.

In the absence of national incentives for interjurisdictional cooperation, Shanghai adopts a strategy of encouraging (or stalling) water project construction (or regulatory measures) in neighboring jurisdictions by "pitting elements of the central bureaucracy against one another" (Moore 2014, 12). The Yangtze-to-Taihu Diversion Project, a project designed against Type I water pollution, is decided and planned by the State Council and implemented by Shanghai, Jiangsu, and Zhejiang (2002–2004). Obviously, Shanghai supports the project because it gets part of its source water from Taihu Lake via the Huangpu River and Suzhou Creek. Some jurisdictions of Jiangsu Province, however, oppose the project because the project has a negative impact on them. For example, some respondents (technicians from the diversion project) reported that Zhihu Port and Wujing Port (northwest part of Taihu Lake in Jiangsu Province) typically suffered from "increased wastewater retention" and "sediment deposition" while the diversion project operates. They admitted that regional differences were "ignored" under the current system of centralized management.

Figure 4 shows that Shanghai adopts a different distribution of regulatory measures when it is confronted with Type II water pollution. The number of YEJS Frame measures (the unit of the y axis) has steadily increased. YEJS-CD (the Yangtze Estuary Joint Session of Cooperation and Development), a generalized coordination mechanism, meets every 12 months to coordinate economic development in the Yangtze Estuary, while YEJS-EDTP

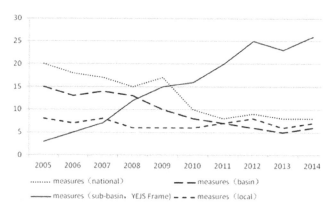

Figure 4. Regulatory measures against emergent transjurisdictional water pollution in Shanghai (Type II) at various scales.

(the Yangtze Estuary Joint Session of Emergent Disposal of Trans-jurisdictional Pollution), a specialized environmental organization, holds a joint meeting every 6 months to perfect the joint session mechanism and solve various environmental problems in a timely manner. YEJS-CD and YEJS-EDTP have been jointly facilitating the cooperation at both provincial and prefectural levels.

The YEJS Frame advocates the establishment of an evolving negotiation mechanism against environmental risks in the region. Specifically, the negotiation mechanism includes (1) regular joint conferences of five mayors to discuss regional development plans including environmental issues; (2) negotiation channels among the water administrative departments facilitating the discussion and design of watershed-scale regulatory measures; and (3) advisory agencies comprised of experts and scholars established in the hope of breaking the pattern of the regional segmentation. Respondents from the YEJS Frame emphasized that the frame is a newly born mechanism and provinces or cities involved in the YEJS Frame always desired more policy support and directives from the ministries or the central government than currently in place.

It is also evident that the number of nationwide (ministerial), basin-wide, and local (Shanghai) measures drops slowly and then remains at a low level. Some respondents (technicians of two basin commissions) explained that Type II water pollution usually causes sudden and serious impacts on the affected areas and the crises might not be controlled by rigid governance mechanisms from higher levels of government. They reported that it was much more effective for the affected areas to "negotiate and coordinate with their neighbors" than to "invite interventions from higher levels of government." Some officials from the ministerial levels also admitted that they always "eventually run into some trouble" when they tried to "authoritatively" guide the local governments to settle Type II water pollution disputes. A case in point is "the Huangpu River dead pigs" disaster in 2013.[2] In addition to collaborating with Zhejiang Province to intercept the pigs and strengthen boundary water quality monitoring, Shanghai engaged in a series of emergent negotiations over a number of issues within the YEJS-EDTP Frame: Shanghai helped Zhejiang standardize construction of pig-breeding zones and establish centers for animal epidemic prevention and control. In return, Zhejiang Province established a long-term mechanism for animal epidemic prevention and control, reinforced information exchange, and strengthened collaborative boundary water quality monitoring. However, some respondents (the pig farmers in Zhejiang Province) reported that their income had dropped sharply due to the decreasing number of pigs.

Table 4 further explores the types of regulatory measures against transjurisdictional water pollution in 2014 across scales. Overall, almost half of the 106 regulatory measures (47%) were at the subbasin scale (within the YEJS Frame, i.e., the Yangtze Estuary Joint Session), which is in agreement with the findings in Figures 3 and 4. By further sorting the measures into binding and nonbinding ones (treaty or nontreaty) we find that the basin measures rely more heavily on nonbinding relationships (76%), whereas subbasin measures rely more on binding relationships (82%). This is not surprising, given the capacity for Shanghai and the provinces that cluster geographically in the Yangtze estuary to create "binding" or 'formal' agreements under the YEJS Frame. The frame has established institutionalized linkages among actors with binding mandates. However, there is no stable environmental coordination mechanism within the whole river basin.

Table 4. Types of Shanghai's regulatory measures against transjurisdictional water pollution by scale (2014).

Type	National Number (proportion)	Basin Number (proportion)	Subbasin (YEJS Frame) Number (proportion)	Local Number (proportion)
Binding	11 (55%)	5 (24%)	41 (82%)	13 (87%)
Nonbinding	9 (45%)	16 (76%)	9 (18%)	2 (13%)
Total	20	21	50	15

Discussion

Power and Geographical Scales

Geographical scales are physically predetermined and relatively fixed. Water users at different geographic locations possess different natural endowments, with upstream water users being in more advantageous positions than their downstream counterparts. This situation forces downstream water users to enhance their own regulatory measures. Even water users at the same geographic location (e.g., the water users around Taihu Lake) face severe conflicts: They compete for limited water resources for drinking, irrigation, industrial and agricultural production, power generation, and shipping.

The Yangtze Estuary, in comparison with the overall basin, is on a smaller geographical scale. Close geopolitical relations, similar levels of development, and a rapid-response negotiation mechanism of newly presented YEJS Frame (the Yangtze Estuary Joint Session) mean that Shanghai and its neighboring provinces can work closely to deal with Type II transjurisdictional water pollution. By adopting the strategy of "issue linkage," Shanghai provides technological and economic support for the upstream jurisdictions in exchange for their regulatory measures and environmental investment. Respondents from these jurisdictions note that they are geographically clustered and thus have a preference for small-scale policymaking units. The respondents also pointed to some reluctance of state actors to facilitate cooperation on subbasin scales. Accordingly, what the YEJS Frame needs is more central directives, instead of greater centralization of policymaking and intervention from the government at higher levels in the name of integrity and continuation of regional interests.

Power and Political Scales

In China's political hierarchy, provinces are agents of the central government and the departments within provincial governments are agents of the central government ministries. As such, there is no constitutional separation of responsibilities between the provinces and the central government. Instead, the sharing of responsibilities between the central and provincial-level governments is negotiated, and periodically changes. And importantly, central ministries and provincial-level governments (provinces and municipalities) have the same rank. This implies that a central government ministry is unable to impose its will on a provincial-level government. This authority structure often makes intervention from a supraministerial organ—or even the State Council itself— essential for basin-wide policymaking because MWR (the Ministry of Water Resources) simply does not have any formal leverage over other ministries and provinces. It should be noted that the water bureaucracy and its branch units, in the formal bureaucratic hierarchy, are a notch below central or provincial bureaucratic units with the same official labels. For example, Shanghai is at the same level as MWR, which means MWR cannot tell provinces or Shanghai what to do; only the State Council can do that.

Type I transboundary water pollution typically arises on a relatively large geographical scale, and usually cannot be managed promptly due to a mismatch between biophysical and institutional levels. Both MEP (the Ministry for Environmental Protection) and MWR (the Ministry of Water Resources) have no formal leverage over Shanghai or other provinces. MEP is "supposed to have a mediating role to resolve the conflict over the transregional environmental problem" (Yang et al. 2013, 730), but "MWR is actually in charge of the dispute since trans-boundary water pollution conflicts usually take place in a river" (Zhou and Zhang 2006, 25). Basin commissions, as designated agencies of MWR, are authorized to resolve it. However, the low position of basin commissions in China's administrative hierarchy has become a significant obstacle to integrated water resource management. For a long time, commissions did not constitute an independent level of authority within the government hierarchy of China. Basin commissions typically do not receive much cooperation from provincial governments. Shanghai's regulations against Type I water pollution might stop working properly when ecological processes and responsibility reside at different scales, and when there are no sufficient cross-scale linkages.

Type II transjurisdictional water pollution typically arises on a subbasin scale. YEJS, a subbasin scale frame, can be a source of great dynamism and initiative in dealing with Type II water pollution. The frame is trilayered: provincial, executive vice-provincial, and cities. At the third layer, cities like Wuxi, Suzhou, and even Kungshan have been empowered as leading cities and growth engines in driving national and regional economic development since the State Council made profound adjustments "such as city administering counties and converting entire counties to county-level cities" in 1990s (Li and Wu 2012, 60). These "startup cities," the primary actors in the environmental games, are inextricably linked together in a relationship characterized by interdependence and reciprocity. The ultimate target of their cooperation is the attainment of joint goals of fairness and equity in utilizing limited water resources.

Reconfiguring Power and Scale

On paper, China has a centralized regulatory system to manage environmental problems at the basin scale. The State Council delegates to basin commissions the duties of water governance within the basin on behalf of the central government. China's centralized regulation appears to be very reasonable if judged from the fact that transjurisdictional pollution involves many subjects. It seems to transcend the boundaries of local governments and realize the internalization of adverse externalities.

In reality, when it comes to critical issues such as development and utilization of water resources, the power for dealing with such affairs undoubtedly lies with local governments at various levels. Driven by local interests, local governments engage in planning, including agricultural regionalization, land-use planning, and water conservancy regionalization, but there are hardly any comprehensive ecological environment plans across jurisdictions. Moreover, the continuous downscaling of power in environmental decision making encourages a view of "the local" in isolation from the larger social, political, and economic entity, which means that the geographical and political context of a certain place is ignored.

Within YRBC (the Yangtze River Basin Commission) and TLBC (Taihu Lake Basin Commission), the coordination is often quite difficult. Downstream governments can only improve the intensity of environmental regulations to ensure the rational use of limited water resources in their own regions. Even if fragmentation is resolved by bilateral or multilateral coordinating arrangements (such as within the YEJS Frame, i.e., the Yangtze Estuary Joint Session), the resolutions are typically beneficial to the welfare of a certain region rather than to that of the whole basin.

The YEJS Frame facilitates scalar configuration of power within the basin commissions. Some local actors in Shanghai, like SWRB (the Shanghai Water Resources Bureau), SBEP (the Shanghai Bureau of Environmental Protection), and SCCT (the Shanghai Committee of Construction and Transportation), turn the balance of power to their advantage through the YEJS Frame by adopting the political strategy of jumping scales to let power flow across the current entrenched structure of scales. The YEJS Frame is conferred with more power independent from the higher authority, as well as with wider responsibilities for local environment. It establishes a cross-border network that reorganizes existing hierarchies of scale by building a new sphere of authority. However, the lack of a good fit between water governance and economic development often gives rise to "coordination traps," which refer to habitual compromises between the conflicting objectives (economic and environmental) rather than decisive choices between them. Local actors tend to remain vague when they are caught between choosing economic development and choosing environmental protection.

Conclusion

On the whole, the central government explicitly attempts to contain local interests and central–local differences through a controlling political system. China's model of water governance is a regionally decentralized authoritarian regime under centralized regulation. The system "effectively limits central–local preference divergence, but does little to solve inter-jurisdictional collective action problems. Such problems are not unique to China" (Moore 2014, 11). This will help us more clearly link the significance of cases of China to larger issues related to water governance beyond China.

Vertically, China adopts a centralized regulation system of water resources—namely, the central government authorizes basin commissions and local governments to carry out unified water resource governance. The system is "characterized by the pursuit of localized preferences within the constraints imposed by a centralized system" (Moore 2014, 15). Under such a premise, subnational administrative jurisdictions adopt political strategies like "jumping scale" or "pitting central bureaucracies against one another" to manage Type I water pollution. Thus, the scalar configurations of power in water governance in China should be regarded as the outcome of conflicts and cooperation within an adaptive regulatory framework, and an evolving system of Type I water pollution regulation may require a clearer division of environmental rights among governments at various levels.

As Moore states, "Although vertical control mechanisms in the Chinese system effectively limit central-local preference divergence, they do little to contain horizontal conflicts between sub-national administrative units" (Moore 2014, 13). Horizontal sharing of responsibilities for water governance in China is constantly negotiated among governments at certain levels. The YEJS Frame (the Yangtze Estuary Joint Session) has effectively strengthened cooperative regulations against Type II water pollution by reshaping the existing power structure at a subbasin scale. This is made possible due to the fact that a loosening of the power structure leaves a lot of scope for cross-scale linkage and power shifts at the subbasin scale. Thus, the subbasin scale, as a "new" spatial scale of power configurations, seems to offer a convincing explanation of current and future environmental policy formation.

Our findings confirm that current hydropolitics of China are characterized by centralized institutional hierarchies (vertically) and polycentric networks of formal organizations at subbasin scales (horizontally). The findings may help to outline some practical considerations in the future. First, policymakers should facilitate power negotiation between different scales and thus encourage interjurisdictional cooperation at subbasin scales. Dialogue and negotiation at subbasin scales can be enabled by interventions from higher scales. Second, the interjurisdictional cooperation at subbasin scales should be under the guidance of the basin or higher levels, although the value of local autonomy should not be underestimated. Given the fact that some local actors take highly competitive measures to "pursue their own localized interests at the expense of neighboring jurisdictions" (Zhou and Zhang 2006, 16), decentralization and delegation of power in water governance may hinder integrated regional water management in China.

Notes

1. The State Council: "Implement the Strictest Water Resources Management System," http://www. gov.cn/zhuanti/2015-06/13/content_2878992.htm (accessed on August 13, 2015).
2. From January to March 2013, nearly 10,000 pig carcasses were found either floating in the Huangpu River or thrown into bushes nearby. The carcasses in the Huangpu are believed to come from pig farms upstream in Jiaxing of neighboring Zhejiang Province. Jiaxing is home to more than 100,000 pig farmers, whose pigs usually live in extremely crowded conditions. When many pigs die, there is not enough land to bury them.

References

Alston, M., K. Whittenbury, D. Western, and A. Gosling. 2016. Water policy, trust and governance in the Murray-Darling Basin. *Australian Geographer* 47:49–64. doi:10.1080/00049182.2015. 1091056

Boelens, R. 2014. Cultural politics and the hydrosocial cycle: Water, power and identity in the Andean highlands. *Geoforum* 57:234–47. doi:10.1016/j.geoforum.2013.02.008

Bolin, B., T. Collins, and K. Darby. 2008. Fate of the verde: Water, environmental conflict, and the politics of scale in Arizona's central highlands. *Geoforum* 39:1494–511. doi:10.1016/j. geoforum.2008.02.003

Chaffin, B. C., A. S. Garmestani, H. Gosnell, and R. K. Craig. 2016. Institutional networks and adaptive water governance in the Klamath River Basin, USA. *Environmental Science & Policy* 57:112–21. doi:10.1016/j.envsci.2015.11.008

Chau, K. W., and Y. W. Jiang. 2003. Simulation of transboundary pollutant transport action in the Pearl River delta. *Chemosphere* 52:1615–21. doi:10.1016/s0045-6535(03)00501-0

Deng, Y., B. Zheng, G. Fu, K. Lei, and Z. Li. 2010. Study on the total water pollutant load allocation in the Changjiang River Estuary and adjacent seawater area. *Estuarine, Coastal and Shelf Science* 86:331–36. doi:10.1016/j.ecss.2009.10.024

Dinar, S., D. Katz, L. D. Stefano, and B. Blankespoor. 2015. Climate change, conflict, and cooperation: Global analysis of the effectiveness of international river treaties in addressing water variability. *Political Geography* 45:55–66. doi:10.1016/j.polgeo.2014.08.003

Eberhard, R., S. Mayere, K. Vella, R. Margerum, N. Sipe, and A. Dale. 2016. The practice of water policy governance networks: an international comparative case study analysis. *Society & Natural Resources* 4:102–115.

Herod, A. 1991. The production of scale in US labour relations. *Area* 23:82–88.

Hoogesteger, J., and A. Verzijl. 2015. Grassroots scalar politics: Insights from peasant water struggles in the Ecuadorian and Peruvian Andes. *Geoforum* 62:13–23.

Huang, T., H. Liu, W. Wu, and X. Chen. 2013. The research on water pollution control in industrial parks under the background of urbanization. *China Water & Wastewater* 22:45–51. (In Chinese)

Hueesker, F., and T. Moss. 2015. The politics of multi-scalar action in river basin management: Implementing the EU water framework directive (WFD). *Land Use Policy* 42:38–47. doi:10.1016/j.landusepol.2014.07.003

Li, J., H. Li, B. Shen, and Y. Li. 2011. Effect of non-point source pollution on water quality of the Weihe River. *International Journal of Sediment Research* 26:50–61.

Li, Y., and F. Wu. 2012. The transformation of regional governance in China: the rescaling of statehood. *Progress in Planning.* 78 (2):55–99. doi:10.1016/j.progress.2012.03.001

Liu, M., G. H. Huang, R. F. Liao, Y. P. Lia, and Y. L. Xie. 2013. Fuzzy two-stage non-point source pollution management model for agricultural systems—A case study for the Lake Tai Basin, China. *Agricultural Water Management* 121:27–41. doi:10.1016/j.agwat.2013.01.006

Liu, X., G. Li, Z. Liu, W. Guo, and N. Gao. 2010. International Society for Environmental Information Sciences 2010 Annual Conference (ISEIS) water pollution characteristics and assessment of lower reaches in Haihe River Basin. *Procedia Environmental Sciences* 2:199–206.

Luo, H., Y. Pang, and X. Xu. 2015. The research on driving factors of changes in water use in Taihu Lake, Jiangsu province. *Chinese Journal of Environmental Engineering* 4:25–32. (In Chinese)

Ma, J., Z. Ding, G. Wei, and H. Zhao. 2009. Sources of water pollution and evolution of water quality in the Wuwei basin of Shiyang river, Northwest China. *Journal of Environmental Management* 90:1168–77. doi:10.1016/j.jenvman.2008.05.007

Moore, S. 2014. Hydropolitics and inter-jurisdictional relationships in China: The pursuit of localized preferences in a centralized system. *China Quarterly* 219:760–80. doi:10.1017/s0305741014000721

Romano, S. T. 2016. Building capacities for sustainable water governance at the grassroots: "Organic empowerment" and its policy implications in Nicaragua. *Society & Natural Resources* 4:133–145.

Shen, D. 2004. The 2002 Water Law: Its impacts on river basin management in China. *Water Policy* 6:345–64.

Sigman, H. 2005. Transboundary spillovers and decentralization of environmental policies. *Journal of Environmental Economics and Management* 50:82–101. doi:10.1016/j.jeem.2004.10.001

Sneddon, C. 2002. Water conflicts and river basins: The contradictions of co-management and scale in Northeast Thailand. *Society & Natural Resources* 15 (8):725–41. doi:10.1080/08941920290069317

Tang, B., and Q. Yang. 2014. Water pollution governance from the perspective of coordinated development: the case of pollution governance in Poyang Lake water. *Theoretical Exploration* 5:24–31. (In Chinese)

Thiel, A., and C. Egerton. 2011. Re-scaling of resource governance as institutional change: The case of water governance in Portugal. *Journal of Environmental Planning and Management* 54 (3):383–402. doi:10.1080/09640568.2010.507936

Wang, M., M. Webber, B. Finlayson, and J. Barnett. 2008. Rural industries and water pollution in China. *Journal of Environmental Management* 86:648–59. doi:10.1016/j.jenvman.2006.12.019

Wang, X., F. Hao, H. Cheng, S. Yang, X. Zhang, and Q. Bu. 2011. Estimating non-point source pollutant loads for the large-scale basin of the Yangtze River in China. *Environmental Earth Sciences* 63 (5):1079–92. doi:10.1007/s12665-010-0783-0

Wei, Y., Y. Pang, and J. Luo. 2014. The research and evaluation on wastewater outlets into Taihu Lake. *Industrial Safety and Environmental Protection* 12:31–39. (In Chinese)

Yang, S. Q., B. Q. Qin, and P. Lin. 2012. Novel SPP water management strategy and its applications. In *Studies on Water Management Issues,* ed. M. Kumarasamy, 240–258. InTech. http://www.intechopen.

com/books/studies-on-water-managementissues/novel-spp-water-management-strategy-and-its-applications (accessed January 10, 2017).

Yang, X., J. Xu, J. Donzier, and C. Noel. 2013. A comparison of the water management system in France and China. *Frontiers of Environmental Science & Engineering* 7 (5):721–34. doi:10.1007/s11783-013-0550-z

Zhang, L. M., W. H. Sun, W. Cheng, W. J. Liu, and C. Wang. 2010. Theory and practice of water pollution prevention and control for inflowing Rivers in Taihu Valley. *Journal of Environmental Science and Engineering* 4 (8):120–32.

Zhang, Y., G. Fu, T. Yu, M. Shen, W. Meng, and E. D. Ongley. 2011. Trans-jurisdictional pollution control options within an integrated water resources management framework in water-scarce north-eastern China. *Water Policy* 13:624–44. doi:10.2166/wp.2011.009

Zhou, H., and Y. Zhang. 2006. Multi-layered consultation strategy for transboundary water pollution control in Yangtze River Delta. *Advances in Science and Technology of Water Resources* 5:20–31.

Rescaling Knowledge and Governance and Enrolling the Future in New Zealand: A Co-Production Analysis of Canterbury's Water Management Reforms to Regulate Diffuse Pollution

Ronlyn Duncan

ABSTRACT

Addressing diffuse agricultural pollution to improve water quality is a socioeconomic, political, and policy challenge worldwide. In New Zealand, catchment load limits are being introduced to regulate nutrient losses from agricultural land. Focused on the South Island region of Canterbury, this article presents an interpretive co-production policy analysis to examine the role of science through modeling in rescaling the knowledge and governance of diffuse pollution. The article assembles a discourse of limits, scientific representations of catchment-scale diffuse pollution, a "fast-track" institutional pathway, and identities of scientists and government as knowledge broker and the community as decision maker. The analysis identifies the paradoxical scripting of "predictable nature" and "uncertain nature" and the enrollment of the future as a governance space essential for resolving water resource conflict. The article illustrates a role for modeling well beyond informing and facilitating environmental decision making to constituting the identities, objects, and spaces of governance.

Introduction

As water resources diminish in both quantity and quality, devising ways to address diffuse pollution while reconciling often-conflicting values, interests, and uses for water is an ongoing and fraught endeavor for governments worldwide (see Bellamy et al., Eberhard et al., and Huang and Xu, this issue). Under state-led hierarchical regimes, expert knowledge and the authority of science have been indispensable warrants for environmental regulation and government-supported developments (Jasanoff 1987). However, on a range of environmental issues not limited to water, the science used by governments to authorize either development or tighter regulations can face debilitating challenge through environmental assessment processes, the media, and the courts. In these arenas, uncertainties of science are routinely exploited to call decisions or project proposals into question or to delay action (Jasanoff 1987, 1990; Bocking 2004). While litigation and controversy continue, for some time governments have been turning to community collaboration to address water resource conflict (Eberhard et al. and Förster et al., this issue). Scaling decision making down and opening it up to a wide range of voices and knowledges are expected to address collective issues and to deliver better outcomes on the basis that dialogue fosters greater legitimacy for the science used in policy and policy implementation (Sabatier et al. 2005; Scholz and Stiftel 2010; Margerum 2011; Wesselink et al. 2011). In line with the international trend, community collaboration is being promoted by New Zealand's central government to implement its National Policy Statement for Freshwater Management (NPSFM) (Ministry for the Environment [MfE] 2014), and collaborative approaches are being adopted by regional councils.

To contribute to calls for further understanding of the role of science in rescaling environmental governance (Cohen 2012; Cohen and McCarthy 2015; van Kerkhoff and Lebel 2015; Wyborn 2015), this article focuses on the use of modeling in regional planning in New Zealand. As the blueprint for central government's NPSFM reforms, collaborative water quality limit-setting has been proceeding across New Zealand's South Island region of Canterbury since 2010. Under its Canterbury Water Management Strategy (CWMS) (Canterbury Mayoral Forum [CMF] 2009), there has been a shift away from trying to manage the environmental effects of agriculture at the property scale with no overarching limits to managing them with catchment scale limits. This article focuses on limit setting in Canterbury, with reference to the subregions known as the Hurunui Waiau and Selwyn Waihora—the first two zones to have completed Canterbury's new hybrid regional planning process of collaboration and statutory force.

A Co-Production Conceptual Framework

Co-production is a conceptual framework well suited to examining the role of science in rescaling environmental governance. As a mode of interpretive critical policy analysis, Jasanoff (2004, 3) describes co-production as a lens through which to trace "how knowledge-making is incorporated into practices of state-making, or of governance more broadly and, in reverse, how practices of governance influence the making and use of knowledge." Drawing insight from constructivist theories of knowledge and the field of science and technology studies (STS), the co-production framework used here stands in contrast to instrumental modes of co-production that aim to produce shared knowledge (van Kerkhoff and Lebel 2015; Wyborn 2015). Co-production as critique identifies discourses, representations, institutions, and identities in-the-making to evaluate their interconnection and reveal "the social arrangements that prop up particular natural orders or in reverse, the epistemologies that help to sustain particular social orders" (Jasanoff 2004, 278).

A foundational STS insight that underpins the Jasanoff (2004) articulation of co-production is that "nature alone" cannot be the sole determinant of the validity or otherwise of scientific knowledge claims (Knorr-Cetina and Mulkay 1983, 4). Hence, although science is often invoked in official statements that account for how regulatory disputes, for example, have been brought to an end, scientific renditions of nature or environmental effects are not sufficient explanations of consensus or closure (Engelhardt and Caplan 1987; Jasanoff 1987; 1990). The full picture also requires understanding the social practices that contribute to the construction, mobilization, and validation of knowledge claims (Shapin and Schaffer 1985; Latour 1987; Jasanoff 2004). In other words, what becomes accepted as "reality" (even if temporary) is not revealed by science as a mere reflection of unmediated nature, nor is it socially determined; "reality" derives from the mutual constitution of both nature and society (Jasanoff 2004). This means that in evaluating the practices of "ordering knowledge," analysis is to look also at practices of "ordering society" (Jasanoff 2004, 13). Jasanoff explains:

> In this view of co-production, human beings seeking to ascertain facts about the natural world are confronted, necessarily and perpetually, by problems of social authority and credibility. … At times of significant change … it may not be possible to address questions of facticity and credibility of knowledge claims without, in effect, redrafting the rules of social order pertaining to the trustworthiness and authority of individuals and institutions. … Only by solving social problems in this way can satisfactory warrants be produced for radically new orderings of nature. Doing science merges, in other words, into doing politics. (Jasanoff 2004, 29)

Jasanoff (2004, 39) states that the instruments of co-production, that is, discourses, representations, institutions, and identities, "operate at the nexus of natural and social order" and "stabilize both what we know and how we know it." From this perspective, knowledge making and state making can be seen as a process of ordering rather than revealing, and modeling as an ordering device that has become indispensable in environmental policy (van Egmond and Zeiss 2010). Hence, tracing the social practices that bring order to our knowledge of nature and vice versa can bring into view "new objects and spaces of environmental governance," for example, understanding how global circulation models constitute global climate change (Cohen and McCarthy 2015, 4).

Methodology

In requiring in-depth research and data triangulation, the qualitative case study (Yin 2013) is useful for grappling with the complexity and fluidity of the "real-life" context of collaborative limit-setting in Canterbury. The empirical resources have been analyzed using discourse analysis, which Hajer and Versteeg (2005, 175) define as follows:

> an ensemble of ideas, concepts and categories through which meaning is given to social and physical phenomena, and which is produced and reproduced through an identifiable set of practices. The "discussion" … is the object of analysis; discourse analysis sets out to trace a particular linguistic regularity that can be found in discussions or debates.

To apply the co-production conceptual framework using discourse analysis, my approach has been deductive and inductive (Merriam and Tisdell 2015). In terms of the former, the instruments of co-production, that is, discourses, representations, institutions, and identities, were used to focus the analysis on how society and nature are being ordered and enacted in the establishment of water quality limits. This was accompanied by an iterative, inductive process, which involved interpreting and conceptualizing statements for their alignment with the instruments, as well as connections between them.

The empirical resources are extensive and include publicly available central government policy documents outlining water management reforms and regional council planning documents, hearings evidence, and scientific reports related to formal water quality limit-setting processes that have been underway across Canterbury since 2010. I have supplemented these official accounts by following limit-setting in practice in the Hurunui Waiau and Selwyn Waihora zones. I have regularly attended monthly zone committee and public meetings in the Hurunui Waiau and participated in limit-setting focus groups in Selwyn Waihora. Through the focus groups and meetings, as well as attendance at regional plan public hearings and briefings for both zones, I have witnessed the different stages of

Canterbury's collaborative limit-setting process, from development through to the beginning of implementation. These attendances have been rich in opportunities to observe and record what has been said and done on the ground to verify the coding of the instruments of co-production from the documents. As such, the attendances and observations have been used in the process of interpreting meaning to draw findings focused on identifying new identities, objects, and spaces of governance.

Background

In brief, under New Zealand's hierarchical Resource Management Act, 1991 (RMA), environmental governance is devolved by central government to two tiers of local government: regional councils and territorial authorities. Through national environmental standards and national policy statements, central government direction on the management of natural and physical resources cascades down to local government. The concept of 'sustainable management' underpins this 'effects-based' legislation, which mandates the control of environmental effects rather than prescribing activities. Regional councils are required to develop regional policy statements to give effect to national standards and statements, as well as identifying resource issues and strategies to address them. While not mandated to do so, regional councils can also develop regional plans to give effect to issues identified in regional policy statements. Regional councils issue consents that authorize resource use (e.g., water takes or discharges to water) under specified conditions. Territorial authorities manage land use and subdivision and develop district plans to give effect to the upper layers of statements and plans (Peart 2007). Managing water resources on a first-in, first-served basis, consent-by-consent, fails to recognize resource bounds and capacity. Hence, many have argued that the consent system under the RMA has (a) been unable to address cumulative effects; (b) foreclosed integrated catchment-based water planning; and (c) fostered too much time-consuming litigation in the Environment Court (CMF 2009; Gunningham 2010; Jenkins 2011; Russell and Frame 2011). In this context, water quality has become a highly charged political issue in New Zealand, in Canterbury especially. The agricultural industry, in particular the dairy sector, is routinely criticized as the cause of degraded water quality (Foote, Joy, and Death 2015).

More than half of New Zealand's land area is dedicated to pastoral and arable farming (Howard-Williams et al. 2010), and one-third is public conservation estate (Department of Conservation [DOC] 2015). Across its varied terrain are 425,000 km of rivers and streams, more than 4,000 lakes, and more than 200 aquifers that are replenished by an estimated 608 billion m^3 of annual precipitation (Ministry for the Environment and Ministry for Primary Industries [MfE and MPI] 2014). In catchments dominated by agriculture, the legacy of past land use and management practices (e.g., excessive fertilizer, deforestation, grazing on erosive slopes) is converging with the more recent effects of water abstraction and nutrient losses from intensified land use (Parliamentary Commissioner for the Environment [PCE] 2012). There is widespread concern that New Zealand's '100% Pure' brand that underpins both tourism and agriculture is under threat (Land and Water Forum [LAWF] 2010; PCE 2012; Foote, Joy, and Death 2015). Clearly, not addressing water quality could have high ecological, social, cultural, economic, and political costs.

Government has responded. Water quality is now on the political, policy, and operational agendas of all levels of New Zealand government. For example, the key purpose of central government's NPSFM is to establish "enforceable quality and quantity limits" for all freshwater water bodies (MfE 2014, 3). Yet diffuse pollution is a challenging socioeconomic, political, and policy issue for governments the world over (Rabotyagov et al. 2014). Measuring nutrient losses and assigning responsibility at the property level for the purpose of enforcing compliance with regulations are very difficult when causes and effects can occur over distant spatial scales and long, often generational, temporal scales. While the highly visible effects of nutrients are ultimately evident through seasonal algal blooms, at their source or at the individual or property scale, nutrient losses of nitrogen and phosphorus from agriculture are easily unnoticed or deemed insignificant. Thus, notwithstanding provisions under the RMA to address cumulative effects, regulation is fraught given the practical impossibility of identifying who is responsible for what, where, and when (Howard-Williams et al. 2010).

The region of Canterbury is where 70% of the country's irrigated agriculture is situated. Its CWMS articulates a vision to "enable present and future generations to gain the greatest social, economic, recreational and cultural benefits from our water resources within an environmentally sustainable framework" (CMF 2009, 6). The vision is to be achieved through long-term targets: ecosystem health/biodiversity, natural character of braided rivers, kaitiakitanga (i.e., Maori stewardship), drinking water, recreational and amenity opportunities, water-use efficiency, irrigated land area, energy security and efficiency, regional and national economies, and environmental limits (CMF 2009, 8). While the targets are to be "advanced in parallel" (CMF 2009, 9), they are to be guided by "environment, customary use, community supplies and stock water" as first-order priorities, with second-order priorities of "irrigation, renewable electricity generation, recreation and amenity" (CMF 2009, 8).

The CWMS is being implemented as a collaborative front end of Canterbury's new hybrid governance framework (Gunningham 2010). The process begins with the establishment of a subregional Zone Committee (ZC) created under New Zealand's Local Government Act, 2002, by the Environment Canterbury Regional Council (ECRC) and the relevant territorial authority. In what would be described by Eberhard et al. (this issue) as a networked governance approach, the ZC works with the regional council and territorial authority in consultation with interest groups, the community, and industry to develop a Zone Implementation Programme (ZIP) to advance CWMS targets. Limit-setting has become a dedicated stage of the CWMS collaborative process after a ZC identifies its community's aspirations for freshwater catchments and priorities to give effect to the CWMS targets in the ZIP. Community-based decisions are then translated by planners into regional plan provisions and rules, which are subsequently plugged into the statutory RMA process, which involves plan notification, public submissions, and public hearings before independent commissioners and, eventually, an operative regional plan (Duncan 2013).

There are 10 CWMS zones in Canterbury in which a number of waterbodies and their catchments are situated (CMF 2009). In December 2013, the Hurunui Waiau zone was the first to complete the new process. Due to limited data, load limits were set only for the Hurunui River. Its catchment loads for nitrogen and phosphorus are a calculation of a 6-year rolling average of monthly observations of in-river nutrient concentrations and river flow measurements from upper and lower catchment sites (ECRC 2013). While these are based on in-river data, interpretation, credibility, lag time, and allocation challenges have arisen (e.g., Duncan 2014a; Hurunui District Council and Environment Canterbury [HDC and EC] 2015a). Selwyn Waihora and all other zones have adopted a modeled catchment load limit approach (ECRC 2015a), which overcomes some of these issues (e.g., the lag time can be modeled in and an allocable load can be calculated) but opens many questions about linking numbers derived from predictive models to compliance and enforcement mechanisms (Duncan 2014b). For example, in all zones, including the Hurunui Waiau, farmers are required to use the government and fertilizer industry-sponsored property-scale nutrient management model, Overseer®(or equivalent approved by ECRC), to demonstrate nutrient loss compliance with regional plan rules. As an empirical model, Overseer® is regularly updated and is being developed to expand its capability for use in policy. While it produces numbers on both nitrogen and phosphorus, its use for compliance within Canterbury beyond the Hurunui Waiau Zone has been confined to nitrogen, given the model's current lack of capability and the less direct pathways of phosphorus getting into water (e.g., via sediment). A shift in the use of Overseer® from decision support for fertilizer application to regulatory tool has been controversial due to, for example, high margins of error and large shifts in output numbers as the science and data systems that operationalize the model are updated (Duncan 2014b). Notwithstanding, Overseer® is central to limit-setting in Canterbury and in many regions across the country (Arbuckle 2015).

A Co-Production Analysis

Making Discourses: A Discourse of Limits

Within the co-production framework, discourse is characterized as a persuasive way of talking about phenomena and constituting identities and representations that are routinely deployed by institutions. The empirical resources show a consensus across government, among scientists and the broad range of stakeholders, that the way to address the issues currently contributing to diminished water quality is by setting enforceable resource limits (CMF 2009; LAWF 2010; 2012a; 2012b; 2015; MfE 2013). For example, central government's national collaborative advisory body, the Land and Water Forum (LAWF), states:

> A central difficulty is that as a nation we have found it hard to set or manage limits. Without limits it is hard to manage diffuse discharges—nutrients, microbes, sediment and other contaminants that wash into water from the land—and impossible to deal with the cumulative effects on water bodies of water takes on the one hand and diffuse and direct discharges to water on the other ... It is in all our interests to maintain and improve the quality of freshwater in New Zealand, including instream values. For that we need limits, standards and targets in line with national needs, values and objectives which are applied taking account of the needs, values and objectives of communities. They must address contaminants and flows. (LAWF 2010, viii–ix)

Concerns about cumulative effects extend to the additional but unknown "load to come" (due to, e.g., the time it takes for nitrogen to move through groundwater to surface water) (Howard-Williams et al. 2010, 134). The modeled load limit approach can incorporate the lag effect. In 2009, in a report commissioned by the ECRC as part of its Land Use and Water Quality Project (LU&WQP), it was argued:

> It would be more certain for environmental outcomes, fairer, less time-consuming and more cost effective, if appropriate water quality objectives and related nutrient load limits were established before the assimilative capacity of a lake (or a river system) is exceeded. This would

make the ground rules for land developers clear before they make investment decisions. Measureable plan objectives and nutrient load caps would clearly quantify the sustainable capacity of the lakes in terms of catchment land use. (Norton et al. 2009, 4–5)

A way to operationalize this proposed limit-setting regime was subsequently offered. It involves a number of steps starting with community decisions on desired water quality objectives informed by community values. Through modeling, these objectives would be quantified by scientists into threshold levels of nutrient enrichment (or nutrient reduction) in water bodies and ultimately translated into catchment nutrient loads. These catchment loads would be translated into property nutrient discharge allowances and used by planners to devise land use rules to be complied with by property owners (Norton, Snelder, and Rouse 2010; Duncan 2013; 2014b). Woven into the LU&WQP's "Preferred Approach for Managing the Cumulative Effects of Land Use on Water Quality in the Canterbury Region" (ECRC 2012), the catchment-based limit-setting framework, with its sequence of community, science, and planning phases, now underpins the Canterbury Land and Water Regional Plan (ECRC 2015a) and has been adopted by central government to operationalize the NPSFM and its accounting regime, which is envisaged to allow resource managers to know when "resource availability is available for current and potential resource users" (MfE 2015, 17).

Making Representations: Catchment-Scale Diffuse Pollution

Scientific representations are ordinarily conceived as reflections, or getting-closer-depictions, of reality revealed by science. From a co-production perspective, they are conceived as outcomes of social, political, and technological practices and imperatives that engage with and constitute the material world (Jasanoff 2004, 39). The CWMS states that a shift from "effects-based management of individual consents [i.e., property scale] to integrated management based on water management zones" is needed to enable the "management of cumulative effects of water abstraction and land use intensification" (CMF 2009, 7; MfE 2015). This planning imperative frames the scale of water quality science and modeling commissioned by the ECRC, thus reconfiguring how environmental monitoring data are interpreted, translated, and communicated into the planning process. Geographic information systems—in conjunction with a range of environmental databases that categorize soil characteristics and land use patterns—render maps, graphs, and charts that depict potential present and possible future diffuse pollution, as well as the extent to which it could be reduced through mitigation alongside modeled regional economic impacts.

In Selwyn Waihora, collaborative and scientific work was undertaken over several years to identify an agreeable catchment load limit. Hydrologic, environmental, and economic models were used to predict and communicate the effects of current and future land use intensification and irrigation expansion under a range of scenarios alongside mitigation options to address environmental effects on the lower catchment's shallow coastal lake, Te Waihora/Lake Ellesmere (Robson 2014). Validated through the collaborative and then the statutory planning process, the regional plan sets a catchment load limit for nitrogen for existing farms of 4,830 tonnes per annum. This load limit is to be achieved by 2037, with an overall 14% reduction in nitrogen by 2022. This will involve farms reducing nitrogen losses beyond what have been estimated to be good management practice loss rates, with different levels of responsibility, for example, dairy 30%, and irrigated sheep, beef, or deer 5% (Robson 2014; ECRC 2015a, 197B).

Making Institutions: A Politically Expedient Institutional Pathway

Within the co-production framework, institutions are characterized as playing a central role in the stabilization of natural and social orders (Jasanoff 2004, 40). In other words, institutional arrangements (e.g., courts or advisory bodies) can bring closure (even if temporary) to scientific disputes. In Canterbury in 2010, a means of closure on resource limits was created when the democratically elected councillors of the ECRC (or ECan) were dismissed by central government under special legislation, the Environment Canterbury (Temporary Commissioners and Improved Water Management) Act, 2010 (the ECan Act) (Rennie 2010; Russell and Frame 2011).[1] This legislation suspends regional council elections and creates a unique institutional pathway that allows the ECRC to temporarily step outside the RMA to establish water quality limits through a nonadversarial process. Specifically, as well as requiring central-government appointed commissioners (ECan commissioners) to take account of the vision and principles of the CWMS, a key provision is that appeal rights on regional plans are restricted to the High Court if a case can be mounted on points of law. This action disallows merit appeals to the Environment Court, which is an adversarial arena. RMA hearings, to which most regional planning in Canterbury is now confined, are inquisitorial. It has been argued by central government (MfE 2013) and the LAWF (2012b) that disallowing merit appeals to the Environment Court is necessary to discourage litigation and to force parties to collaborate and abide by decisions, knowing such agreements cannot be overturned at a later time in court. In practice, this means that catchment-scale water quality limits can be put in place in Canterbury through a truncated process. This pathway is now emulated in a Resource Legislation Amendment Bill that seeks to amend the RMA to allow regional councils across the country to opt into a 'fast track' collaborative regional planning process similar to what has been imposed in Canterbury.

Making Identities: Knowledge Brokers and Community Decision Makers

Within the co-production framework, it is important to consider how identities (human, nonhuman, individual, or collective) are shaped, how they "restore sense out of disorder," and how the roles they play sustain "social roles" and foster "power and meaning" (Jasanoff 2004, 39). The following statement that opens the ECRC CWMS progress report illustrates how the discourse of limits constitutes the ECRC and the community in particular ways:

> The CWMS is underpinned by collaboration; empowering communities to make their own decisions to meet agreed region wide and local targets. Through the CWMS, the process of setting Environmental Limits provides an opportunity for the community to take local ownership of water management and to work together through complex information to reach decisions on their priority outcomes and values. Zone committees and communities are working collaboratively through the Resource Management Act (RMA) plan development timetable. This intensive process supports Environment Canterbury to meet its statutory responsibilities, working with the people of Canterbury to achieve sustainable management of the region's water and land resources and align the planning framework to CWMS targets. (ECRC 2015b, 8)

Setting limits mobilizes a collaborative community that is local, empowered to take ownership, and works together. ZC and community tasks include working through complex information (i.e., the science and modeling) and making decisions. The community, through a ZC, is a collaborator, decision maker (on science, priorities, and values), and supporter of the ECRC, which is scripted as working with and at the behest of the community.

In this collaborative arena, a new identity has been cast for scientists. Invoking Roger Pielke's (2007) repertoire of the roles of scientists in policy, scientists constitute themselves (and the ECRC) as knowledge broker. ECRC's technical report in support of Selwyn Waihora zone's catchment load limit-setting process states:

> Setting outcomes and natural resource limits for catchments and deciding on the available capacity for resource use is not simply a technical question. These decisions are value judgements that involve weighing up, trading off, and balancing between conflicting outcomes and values. The key role for the technical team in these processes is one of informing those decisions, by making consequences transparent, rather than making the decisions themselves.

> This shifts the role of Environment Canterbury from knowledge 'arbiter' to one of knowledge 'broker,' exploring the implications of different management options with the community. It also shifts the role of the science, away from trying to find the 'right' answer and defending that position in scientific terms to a role of supporting and informing. (Robson 2014, 16, emphasis in original)

Hence, the role of science is defined as follows:

> In order to help the Zone Committee and the wider community make informed value judgements recognising the uncertainty that exists in the technical work, the expectations of the technical team were to:
> - Describe the direction of change and likely magnitude of change under future scenarios
> - Predict the likelihood of outcomes being achieved for each of the future scenarios. (Robson 2014, 16)

Rather than claim comprehensiveness, accuracy, or rigor of method to invoke epistemic authority, scientists maintain they have been involved in the supply of information that is "sufficient, relevant and credible" that has been:

> legitimately gathered, analysed and presented to a community in a way for them to understand the connections and make recommendations in the knowledge of the likely consequences—i.e., to make an informed value judgment. This shift also means that an understanding of the inevitable uncertainty of the science or limited information is integral to the nature of the decisions being made, and is not used as a reason for not making them. (Robson 2014, 16)

These statements characterize uncertainty as inevitable rather than something to shy away from:

> There are many sources of uncertainty in a limit setting process such as the Selwyn Waihora. There is uncertainty both in the input sources of information and the numeric models and assessment techniques used to make predictions. Where possible the uncertainty associated with individual technical assessments has been discussed in the technical reports. However, no quantitative assessment of overall uncertainty of the scenario predictions has been attempted. (Robson 2014, 16)

Framing uncertainty as inevitable and everywhere but not a reason not to make a decision avoids miring ZC members in discussions over data, model assumptions, and parameters, and stymies calls for more science.

Importantly, the value judgments of the community derive from a very small group of people. A ZC comprises representatives from the local territorial authority and local Maori (i.e., runanga), and between four and six community members who either live in or have a special interest in the zone. In the context of the ECan Act, an ECan Commissioner contributes to deliberations of each ZC. Each ZC has an ECRC facilitator. The ECRC commissions the science and the modeling used for setting limits and responds with further information, advice, and presentations from experts or stakeholder groups deemed necessary or called for by the ZC. Appointment of community members involves expressions of interest sought by the ECRC from the wider community, with appointees chosen by representatives of the ECRC, the territorial authority, and local runanga on the basis of the "balance of interests required for the Zone" (ECRC 2015c, np). A key criterion for appointment is a member's ability to "work in a collaborative, consensus-seeking manner" (ECRC 2015c, np). Interest or stakeholder groups do not get a dedicated seat at the table. Members could have an affiliation with an environmental or industry organization, for example, or harbor particular interests or values. However, according to the ECRC ZC terms of reference, members are to "work in a collaborative and co-operative manner using best endeavors to reach solutions that take account of the interests of all sectors of the community" and "contribute their knowledge and perspective but not promote the views or positions of any particular interest and stakeholder group" (ECRC 2015c, np).

While ZC meetings occur once a month, meeting preparation for decision making and commitments beyond them, including stakeholder engagement and public consultation, are extensive and time-consuming. Indeed, it has been identified in a report commissioned by the ECRC that these roles have been taking an emotional and physical toll and that "the commitment required to be on a zone committee appears to have been underestimated by just about everyone including ECan" (Henley 2014, 3). Community and local runanga representatives are remunerated with $4,000 per annum for committee members, $5,000 for the deputy chair, and $6,000 for the chairperson (plus travel expenses). Community members cycle through the committees on a 3-year basis (ECRC 2015c). Hence, collaborating, decision making, and supporting the ECRC falls to a small subset of 'the community' who meet particular criteria, and who receive limited remuneration for their high-level workloads and responsibilities.

However, as the wider community has slowly become aware of the implications of the rules and regulations, community ZC members are finding themselves at the center of community division. For example, in the Hurunui Waiau zone in September 2014—9 months after its plan had been finalized—around 350 farmers descended upon the monthly ZC meeting to express their deep concern about how the rules favored high-nitrogen-leaching farms over low-loss farms, and the loss of farm equity. A rule intended to limit further land use intensification that defines land use change as a 10% increase in nitrogen loss (as modeled by Overseer®) has caught the normal operations of dryland farmers in the regulatory net, making their farm businesses technically illegal under the plan's rules (Fulton 2014; HDC and EC 2015b). In Selwyn Waihora, the ZC is defending criticism that nothing is happening (ECRC 2016; see also https://www.youtube.com/watch?v= 3RBi3IlkX30).

Discussion

To address calls for further understanding of the role of science in rescaling environmental governance, I have focused on modeling used in regional planning in New Zealand's South Island region of Canterbury, where catchment nutrient load limits are being instituted to regulate diffuse agricultural pollution. Instigated by the CWMS, water governance in Canterbury has been rescaled from the region to subregional zones, with considerable decision-making power devolved to ZCs. Deliberation and learning are occurring; decisions are being made; plans, limits, and rules are being developed and passed through the statutory RMA process; and on-ground actions are gaining momentum (Henley 2014; ECRC 2015a). It is noted that notwithstanding the considerable decision-making power devolved to communities, the Canterbury case supports the conclusions of Eberhard et al. (this issue), who argue that the so-called shift from 'government to governance' is not appearing to result in a loss of state authority. Instead, networked governance is supplementing rather than replacing traditional hierarchical governance systems.

Pivotal to Canterbury's progress have been the quantitative, aggregative, standardizing, calculative, and predictive capabilities of modeling, which usually escape critical attention. Given the challenges of capturing catchment-scale social–ecological interactions, surface and groundwater dynamics, lag times, the impossibility of knowing what nutrients are actually being leached from what property, and what good management practices have or have not been adopted and when, science's modeled catchment-scale representations bring much order to the intractable indeterminacies, uncertainties, and complexities of the real world.

A co-production analysis focuses on "how knowledge-making is incorporated into practices of state-making, or of governance more broadly and, in reverse, how practices of governance influence the making and use of knowledge" (Jasanoff 2004, 3). This frame-work seeks to bring into view the mutually constitutive epistemological (i.e., how we know) and ontological (i.e., what we know) dimensions of what becomes shared knowledge (Latour 1987; Jasanoff 2004; van Kerkhoff and Lebel 2015; Wyborn 2015). It does so by examining "the social arrangements that prop up particular natural orders or in reverse, the epistemologies that help to sustain particular social orders" (Jasanoff 2004, 278). In other words, as Cohen and McCarthy (2015, 11) argue, "Rescaling of environmental governance plays a significant role in constructing its own objects of governance." To examine closely the identities, objects, and spaces that derive from the 'how' and 'what' of intertwined knowledge and governance practices, I have assembled a discourse of limits, catchment-scale representations of diffuse pollution, a politically expedient institutional pathway under the ECan Act that limits appeal rights, and identities that constitute 'the community' as decision maker and see scientists and the regional council defining themselves as knowledge broker.

The discourse of limits that echoes through New Zealand's national and regional water policy and planning reforms has played a key role in rescaling knowledge and governance. As "an ensemble of ideas, concepts and categories through which meaning is given to social and physical phenomena" (Hajer and Versteeg 2005, 175), this discourse has mobilized a quantitative epistemology through the knowledge practices of science and modeling. Through these practices, diffuse pollution has been made visible and tractable. The scale at which this visibility and tractability has been rendered and given meaning is interwoven with political goals (e.g., strategic resource use), management imperatives (e.g., to overcome a failing consent system), and institutional necessities (e.g., the ECan Act) to create a new object of governance—the catchment. In a Canterbury catchment, the identities of 'the community' as decision maker, with scientists and the ECRC as knowledge broker, are scripted through the goals, imperatives, and necessities that have instigated, facilitated, and validated the process of rescaling and the resultant catchment load limits. Hence, the catchment is as social and political as it is physical.

Further conceptualization through the lens of co-production identifies two further identities scripted through the discourse of limits. The first is 'predictable nature.' The quantitative epistemology renders the nation's water resources measurable, governable, and now allocable at the scale of the catchment. Demonstrating how knowledge making is bound up with state making, 'predictable nature' underpins not only national and regional water policy and planning reforms but also central government's "business growth agenda" with the goal to increase exports from 30 to 40% through, for example, building infrastructure (e.g., large-scale irrigation schemes) and gaining access to natural resources (e.g., water)—while recognizing the need to set limits (Ministry for Business, Innovation and Employment [MBIE] 2015). Constituting a natural resource as predictable is essential for its measuring, accounting, and (re)allocating (Porter 1995; Scott 1998).

Perhaps paradoxically, the second identity is 'uncertain nature.' With the exploitation of uncertainty and model deconstruction substantially averted under the ECan Act, scientists were free to disclose how the models can script only estimates of the current diffuse pollution problem and possible directions of impacts, change, and potential outcomes in the future (Robson 2014). 'Uncertain nature' embodies disclosures essential for scientists working in very close proximity to the ZC and the broader community. Through the knowledge practices of modeling and reconfigured institutional arrangements, the decision-making space was cast by scientists as filled with uncertainty, with resolution deemed to reside with 'the community.'

While they appear diametrically opposed, it is argued that 'predictable nature' and 'uncertain nature' are part of the "ensemble of ideas, concepts and categories" that bring meaning to the discourse of limits (Hajer and Versteeg 2005, 175). Indeed, they constitute a discursive repertoire (Mulkay 1980) that is invoked by actors at different stages of the planning process. For example, 'uncertain nature' influenced the role of scientists, that is, knowledge broker, not arbiter or decision maker. Arguably, it was concern about unleashing 'uncertain nature' into the adversarial arena of the Environment Court that contributed to central government's unprecedented move to limit appeal rights under the ECan Act. In contrast, 'predictable nature' is embedded in the precise numeric renditions of diffuse pollution that are circumscribed by the catchment—a load limit of 4,830 tonnes per annum and a 14% load reduction. Notably, it is 'predictable nature' not 'uncertain nature' that is invoked to construct the regional planning instruments and operationalise the NPSFM accounting regime.

Going further, following the focus of Cohen and McCarthy (2015) on objects and spaces of governance created through rescaling, it is argued that a new space of governance, one that extends spatial concepts of the catchment, has been created in Canterbury. In Selwyn Waihora, the catchment-scale models were used to not only quantify future environmental effects, but also to negotiate and reconcile conflicts between values, interests, and uses for water and to open opportunities to explore a range of mitigation options and potential water quality effects and outcomes. In this respect, the quantitative, aggregative, standardizing, calculating, and predictive capabilities of the modeling are scripting a temporal scale onto what is ordinarily conceived as spatial. Opening up the future to negotiation on possible actions and mitigations, in response to the practical realities of advancing the CWMS targets in parallel, has involved an extension of the governance space beyond the ostensible spatial boundaries of a catchment to enroll the future.

The linchpin of this co-production is central government's orchestration of a means of knowledge closure around the modeling that appears far more resistant (although not completely) to challenge than relying on the authority of science, with its high risk of deconstruction in the Environment Court (Jasanoff 1987). Under the ECan Act, the indeterminacies and uncertainties that pervade the models and predictions are immune from exploitation and the models are relatively safe from those with the means to contest them in court. Arguably, this coproduction is a political, policy, and planning triumph. So enamored is central government with what has been achieved, it has moved to amend the RMA to emulate the Canterbury experiment across the country with a 'fast-track' collaborative pathway available to all regional councils. Hence, the social ordering and politics described by Jasanoff (2004) as necessary to order a new rendition of nature are becoming increasingly explicit in New Zealand.

Conclusion

The co-production analysis brings into view the institutional and political fortifications that have had to be built by central and regional government to create and protect new identities, objects, and spaces of governance to establish limits that can be more swiftly and apparently less contentiously translated into land use rules that are, at least in theory, enforceable. Marked out by a discourse of limits that deploys a quantitative epistemology through science and modeling, water and its assimilative capacity are rendered governable and allocable at the catchment scale with environmental effects apparently knowable far into the future. Their armory is availed by the ECan Act. It has been shown that the use of modeling in regional planning has moved well beyond informing or facilitating. Indeed, the analysis shows that in Canterbury, at least, the modeling is constituting new identities, objects, and spaces of governance.

The implications of the apparent success of this political and institutional stronghold are important to consider. What has occurred in the Hurunui Waiau zone illustrates the risks of the 'fast track' when decisions are made quickly and the implications of innocent-looking numbers are not fully understood by ZC members or are impossible for even planners to think through, given the complexity of the rules and the lack of understanding of the socioeconomic context in which such precise limits and rules seek to intervene (HDC and EC 2015b). Furthermore, ECRC's (and central government's) framing of 'the community' as homogeneous, agreeable, and working together sits in stark contrast to the broader highly diverse groups, communities, and agricultural sectors that are now coming into conflict outside courts of law by virtue of setting resource limits that are creating winners and losers. This unfolding would appear to be the 'collateral damage' governments deem necessary to set limits to address the cumulative effects of diffuse pollution. The big question is: Will the limits be enough? Extending the governance space beyond its spatial bounds far into the future means many of us are unlikely to ever know.

Acknowledgments

I thank the journal editors and the three anonymous reviewers for their helpful feedback.

Note

1. In October 2016, regional council elections were held in Canterbury under central government's mixed model whereby seven councillors were elected to join six central government appointed commissioners on the council. The ECan Act remains in place.

References

Arbuckle, C. 2015. Stocktake of regional council uses of Overseer®. Client Report 001. Dunedin, NZ: Aspiring Environmental.

Bocking, S. 2004. *Nature's experts: Science, politics, and the environment.* New Brunswick, NJ: Rutgers University Press.

Canterbury Mayoral Forum. 2009. Canterbury water management strategy. Strategic framework 2009 targets updated July 2010. http://ecan.govt.nz/get-involved/canterburywater/Pages/Default. aspx (accessed March 11, 2011).

Cohen, A. 2012. Rescaling environmental governance: Watersheds as boundary objects at the intersection of science, neoliberalism, and participation. *Environment and Planning A* 44:2207–24. doi:10.1068/a44265

Cohen, A., and J. McCarthy. 2015. Reviewing rescaling: Strengthening the case for environmental considerations. *Progress in Human Geography* 39 (1):3–25. doi:10.1177/0309132514521483

Department of Conservation. 2015. Annual report 2015. www.doc.govt.nz/annual-report-2015 (accessed December 30, 2015).

Duncan, R. 2013. Converting community knowledge into catchment nutrient limits: A constructivist analysis of a New Zealand collaborative approach to water management. *Nature and Culture* 8 (2):205–225. doi:10.3167/nc.2013.080205

Duncan, R. 2014a. A view from the farm-gate: Farmers' perspectives on water quality. *Lincoln Planning Review* 6 (1–2):18–24.

Duncan, R. 2014b. Regulating agricultural land use to managing water quality: The challenges for science and policy in enforcing limits on non-point source pollution in New Zealand. *Land Use Policy* 41:378–387. doi:10.1016/j.landusepol.2014.06.003

Environment Canterbury Regional Council. 2012. The preferred approach for managing the cumulative effects of land use on water quality in the Canterbury region: A working paper. http://ecan.govt.nz/publications/Reports/luwq-preferred-approach-report-jan2012.pdf (accessed February 9, 2012).

Environment Canterbury Regional Council. 2013. Hurunui and Waiau river regional plan. Operative December, 2013. http://ecan.govt.nz/publications/Plans/hurunui-waiau-regional-plan.pdf (accessed December 24, 2013).

Environment Canterbury Regional Council. 2015a. Canterbury land and water regional plan, Volume 1, December, 2015. http://ecan.govt.nz/our-responsibilities/regional-plans/lwrp/Pages/plan-decisions-version.aspx (accessed February 14, 2016).

Environment Canterbury Regional Council. 2015b. Canterbury water management strategy targets: Progress report June 2015. http://ecan.govt.nz/publications/Reports/targets-report-cwms-2015.pdf (accessed August 1, 2015).

Environment Canterbury Regional Council. 2015c. Information for committee candidates. http://ecan.govt.nz/get-involved/canterburywater/comm-engage/expression-oi/Pages/play-your-part-wm. aspx (accessed May 1, 2015).

Environment Canterbury Regional Council. 2016. Improving water quality—Slowly but surely. Media release, January 19, 2016. http://ecan.govt.nz/get-involved/canterburywater/committees/

selwyn-waihora/our-stories-sw/selwyn-stories/Pages/improving-water-quality.aspx (accessed January 19, 2016).

Engelhardt, H. T., and A. L. Caplan. 1987. *Scientific controversies: Case studies in the resolution and closure of disputes in science and technology.* Cambridge, UK: Cambridge University Press.

Foote, K. J., J. K. Joy, and R. G. Death. 2015. New Zealand dairy farming: Milking our environment for all its worth. *Environmental Management* 56 (3):709–720.

Fulton, T. 2014. Water plan would reward polluters, says farmer. *Stuff.* 6 October. www.stuff.co.nz (accessed October 6, 2014).

Gunningham, N. 2010. Water governance in Canterbury. In *Old problems new solutions: Integrative research supporting natural resource governance*, ed. S. Russell, B. Frame, and J. Lennox, 40–48. Lincoln, NZ: Landcare Research.

Hajer, M., and W. Versteeg. 2005. A decade of discourse analysis of environmental politics: Achievements, challenges, perspectives. *Journal of Environmental Policy & Planning* 7 (3):175–184. doi:10.1080/15239080500339646

Henley, G. 2014. Review report: Review of environmental limit setting process in four zones—Hurunui, Selwyn/Waihora, Hinds and southern coastal and streams. http://ecan.govt.nz/publications/Council/KZC_2014%2010_Agenda%20Paper%207-3_Limit-setting%20Review%20Report_3%209%2014.pdf (accessed December 1, 2014).

Howard-Williams, C., R. Davies-Colley, K. Rutherford, and R. Wilcock. 2010. Diffuse pollution and freshwater degradation: New Zealand perspectives. Selected paper from the 14th International Conference of the IWA Diffuse Pollution Specialist Group, DIPCON 2010, Beaupre, Quebec, Canada, October.

Hurunui District Council, and Environment Canterbury. 2015a. Agenda for meeting of 20 July 2015. http://ecan.govt.nz/publications/Council/hwzc-agenda-20140720.pdf (accessed August 25, 2015).

Hurunui District Council, and Environment Canterbury. 2015b. Agenda for meeting of 20 April 2015. http://ecan.govt.nz/publications/Council/hwzc-agenda-20150420.pdf (accessed May 25, 2015).

Jasanoff, S. 1987. Contested boundaries in policy-relevant science. *Social Studies of Science* 17:195–230. doi:10.1177/030631287017002001

Jasanoff, S. 1990. *The fifth branch: Science advisers as policymakers.* Cambridge, MA: Harvard University Press.

Jasanoff, S. 2004. *States of knowledge: The co-production of science and social order.* London, UK: Routledge.

Jenkins, B. 2011. Sustainability limits and governance options in Canterbury water management. In *Old problems new solutions: Integrative research supporting natural resource governance*, ed. S. Russell, B. Frame, and J. Lennox, 50–58. Lincoln, NZ: Landcare Research.

Knorr-Cetina, K., and M. Mulkay. 1983. Introduction: Emerging principles in social studies of science. In *Science observed: Perspectives on the social study of science*, ed. K. Knorr-Cetina and M. Mulkay 1–17. London, UK: Sage.

Land and Water Forum. 2010. Report of the Land and Water Forum: A fresh start for freshwater. http://www.landandwater.org.nz (accessed March 30, 2011).

Land and Water Forum. 2012a Second report of the Land and Water Forum: Setting limits for water quality and quantity freshwater policy- and plan-making through collaboration. http://www.landandwater.org.nz (accessed February 1, 2013).

Land and Water Forum. 2012b. Third report of the Land and Water Forum: Managing water quality and allocating water. http://www.landandwater.org.nz (accessed February 1, 2013).

Land and Water Forum. 2015. Fourth report of the Land and Water Forum. http://www.landandwater.org.nz (accessed May 1, 2015).

Latour, B. 1987. *Science in action: How to follow scientists and engineers through society.* Cambridge, MA: Harvard University Press.

Margerum, R. 2011. *Beyond consensus: Improving collaborative planning and management.* Cambridge, MA: MIT Press.

Ministry for Business, Innovation, and Employment. 2015. Business growth agenda 2015. http://www.mbie.govt.nz/info-services/business/business-growth-agenda/towards-2025 (accessed February 2, 2016).

Merriam, S. B., and E. J. Tisdell. 2015. *Qualitative research: A guide to design and implementation,* 4th ed. San Francisco, CA: John Wiley.

Ministry for the Environment. 2013. Freshwater reform and beyond. http://www.mfe.govt.nz/publications/fresh-water/freshwater-reform-2013-and-beyond (accessed April 1, 2013).

Ministry for the Environment. 2014. National policy statement for freshwater management. http://www.mfe.govt.nz/sites/default/files/media/Fresh%20water/nps-freshwater-management-jul-14.pdf (accessed August 1, 2014).

Ministry for the Environment. 2015. *A guide to the national policy statement for freshwater management 2014.* Wellington, NZ: New Zealand Government. http://www.mfe.govt.nz/publications/fresh-water/guide-national-policy-statement-freshwater-management-2014 (accessed August 30, 2015).

Ministry for the Environment, and Ministry for Primary Industries. 2014. Delivering freshwater reform: A high level overview. http://www.beehive.govt.nz/sites/all/files/Delivering_Freshwater_Reform.pdf (accessed April 25, 2015).

Mulkay, M. 1980. Interpretation and the use of rules: The case of norms of science. *Transactions of the New York Academy of Sciences.* Series 11, 39:111–125. doi:10.1111/j.2164-0947.1980.tb02772.x

Norton, N., T. Snelder, and H. Rouse. 2010. Technical and scientific considerations when setting measurable objectives and limits for water management. http://www.mfe.govt.nz/publications/fresh-water-rma/technical-and-scientific-considerations-when-setting-measurable (accessed March 30, 2011).

Norton, N., B. Spigel, D. Sutherland, D. Trolle, and D. Plew. 2009. Lake Benmore water quality: A modelling method to assist with assessments of nutrient loadings. http://ecan.govt.nz/publications/Reports/report-lake-benmore-water-quality-000809.pdf (accessed March 30, 2011).

Parliamentary Commissioner for the Environment. 2012. *Water quality in New Zealand: Understanding the science.* Wellington, NZ: PCE.

Peart, R. 2007. *The community guide to the resource management act, 1991,* 2nd ed. Waitakere, NZ: Environmental Defence Society.

Pielke, R. A. 2007. *The honest broker: Making sense of science in policy and politics.* Cambridge, UK: Cambridge University Press.

Porter, T. 1995. *Trust in numbers: The pursuit of objectivity in science and public life.* Princeton, NJ: Princeton University Press.

Rabotyagov, S. S., C. L. Kling, P. W. Gassman, N. N. Rabalais, and R. E. Turner. 2014. The economics of dead zones: Causes, impacts, policy challenges, and a model of the Gulf of Mexico Hypoxic Zone. *Review of Environmental Economics and Policy* 8 (1):58–79. doi:10.1093/reep/ret024

Rennie, H. 2010. The ECan act: Understanding the new provisions for planners. *Lincoln Planning Review* 2 (2):20–21.

Robson, J. 2014. Technical report to support water quality and quantity limit setting in Selwyn Waihora catchment: Predicting consequences of future scenarios: Overview report. http://files.ecan.govt.nz/public/lwrp/variation1/tech-report-sw-overview.pdf (accessed March 1, 2014).

Russell, S., and B. Frame. 2011. From old problems to new solutions. In *Old problems new solutions: Integrative research supporting natural resource governance,* ed. S. Russell, B. Frame, and J. Lennox, 2–11. Lincoln, NZ: Landcare Research.

Sabatier, P. A., W. Focht, M. Lubell, Z. Trachtenberg, A. Vedlitz, and M. Matlock. 2005. *Swimming upstream: Collaborative approaches to watershed management.* Cambridge, MA: MIT Press.

Scholz, J. T., and B. Stiftel, ed. 2010. *Adaptive governance and water conflict: New institutions for collaborative planning.* Washington, DC: Resources for the Future.

Scott, J. 1998. *Seeing life a state: How certain schemes to improve the human condition have failed.* New Haven, CT: Yale University Press.

Shapin, S., and S. Schaffer. 1985. *Leviathan and the air-pump: Hobbes, Boyle, and the experimental life.* Oxfordshire, UK: Princeton University Press.

Van Egmond, S., and R. Zeiss. 2010. Modeling for policy: Science-based models as performative boundary objects for Dutch policy making. *Science Studies* 23 (1):58–78.

van Kerkhoff, L. E., and L. Lebel. 2015. Coproductive capacities: Rethinking science–governance relations in a diverse world. *Ecology and Society* 20 (1):14. doi:10.5751/ES-07188-200114

Wesselink, A., J. Paavola, O. Fritsch, and O. Renn. 2011. Rationales for public participation in environmental policy and governance: Practitioners' perspectives. *Environment and Planning A* 43:2688–2704. doi:10.1068/a44161

Wyborn, C. 2015. Connectivity conservation: Boundary objects, science narratives and the co-production of science and practice. *Environmental Science & Policy* 51:292–303. doi:10.1016/j.envsci.2015.04.019

Yin, R. 2013. *Case study research: Design and methods.* Thousand Oaks, CA: Sage.

The Practice of Water Policy Governance Networks: An International Comparative Case Study Analysis

Rachel Eberhard, Richard Margerum, Karen Vella, Severine Mayere, and Bruce Taylor

ABSTRACT

Governments are increasingly using network governance arrangements to engage stakeholders in tackling complex water policy issues. Claims that this involves a shift from government to governance, with associated loss of state authority, are challenged by empirical literature. We draw on governmentality theory to explore the practices and power dynamics of water policy networks in six significant longitudinal case studies in Australia, the United States, and France. Though contexts differ, the analysis highlights the dynamic nature of these complex policy arenas, where governance arrangements and objectives are periodically revised in response to changing pressures. Governments clearly retain decision-making authority despite adopting more deliberative, networked approaches, and implementation remains challenging. Findings suggest that the hybrid and multiscalar nature of water policy governance warrants a more sophisticated understanding of the power dynamics and political dimensions of networked governance employed within hierarchical systems.

Introduction

Increasing competition for water and the ecological impacts of land and water management are significant policy issues around the world. The governance of water conflicts involves a "system of institutions, including rules, laws, regulations, policies, and social norms, and organizations involved in governing environmental resource use and/or protection" (Chaffin, Gosnell, and Cosens 2014, 56). The effectiveness of governance arrangements to address growing conflicts over water and other resource is a critical question for research and practice.

In embracing more integrated and participatory governance arrangements, governments are adopting "new" networked arrangements that involve stakeholders in policy development, negotiation, and implementation (Rhodes 1996; Klijn and Koppenjan 2000; Kooiman 2003). Though some researchers suggest there has been a shift from traditional, hierarchical forms of governance to more networked arrangements involving the private sector and civil society, others argue that this is more complex in practice

(Jordan, Wurzel, and Zito 2005). Further, governments must manage governance networks alongside other modes of governance. This debate is exacerbated by a lack of comparative research on water governance networks at the policy level (Margerum 2011).

This article seeks to answer two questions:

- Do changes observed in complex water policy conflicts around the world follow similar trajectories toward more networked forms of governance?
- What have been the practical implications for decision-making authority and performance outcomes?

To address this, we undertake a comparative analysis of six large-scale, place-based, longitudinal water policy case studies in Australia, the United States, and France. Drawing on governmentality theory that examines "the art of governing" (Foucault 1991), our analysis explores governance rationalities and practices, the exercise of power, and the outcomes achieved. The evolution of water governance regimes proves to be highly dynamic in all cases, with limited power sharing and significant implementation challenges.

Literature Review

Governance networks describe public policymaking and implementation that involves a set of complex interdependencies between government, business, and civil society actors (Klijn 2008), that is, governments and key stakeholders who can affect and be affected by policy (Freeman 1984). In contrast to more traditional hierarchical forms of governance, network structures are more horizontal and decisions are negotiated through formal and informal rules based on trust and relationships (Agranoff 2007). Governance networks are hypothesized to improve access to information and resources, enhance legitimacy, allow more efficient policy development, and improve policy acceptance (Sørensen and Torfing 2007b). However, networked forms of governance can also be constrained by significant transaction costs, inertia, complex power relationships, and issues of democratic legitimacy (Huxham 2003; Pierre and Peters 2005; Arnouts, van der Zouwen, and Arts 2012; Driessen et al. 2012; Lange et al. 2013). Further, governance networks must manage tensions between inclusivity and efficiency, internal and external legitimacy, and flexibility and stability (Provan and Kenis 2007).

Scholars have asserted a general trend from traditional forms of hierarchical, state-based governance to more pluralistic, networked governance, which Rhodes (2007) termed a shift from "government to governance." The degree to which this change reflects a significant reduction in the role and authority of the state is the subject of ongoing academic debate (Kooiman 2003; Ison and Watson 2007; Pahl-Wostl et al. 2010). Pierre and Peters (2005), for example, argue that more networked forms of governance increase the influence of stakeholders and access to information, but also reduce the authority and capacity of the state and the speed and coherence of policy decisions. Others argue that networks work in and around the apparatus of the state, rather than displacing the state's authority (McGuire and Agranoff 2011; Agranoff 2013).

Longitudinal studies have found that multiple forms or modes of environmental governance occur simultaneously, with shifts occurring both from hierarchical to networked and from networked to hierarchical forms of governance (van Tatenhove, Arts, and Leroy 2000). This suggests that the asserted trend to networked governance is not necessarily consistent and widespread, and that the evolution of governance structures and processes within specific policy domains responds to multiple drivers.

Networked governance approaches exist alongside and interact with regulatory and market-based forms of governance (Holley 2010). Balancing competitive (market), cooperative (network), and authoritative (hierarchical) decision rules to achieve effective policy outcomes can challenge governments (Arentsen 2001). Börzel and Risse (2010) highlight that both networks and markets are often embedded in hierarchical structures, and that negotiation therefore happens in the "shadow of hierarchy" where the state's capacity to impose binding rules on private actors provides an incentive for cooperation (see also Duncan 2017, this issue).

The policy practice of managing networks and their dynamic interplay with hierarchies and markets is known as metagovernance (Sørensen and Torfing 2007a; Meuleman 2008). Through metagovernance, the state facilitates and steers governance networks, seeking to realize the benefits ascribed to networks while addressing their democratic deficit by anchorage them to formal policy processes (Larsson 2015).

Recognizing that governance networks operate within and alongside other modes of governance (hierarchies, markets, and hybrid forms of governance), we turn to the analytical perspective of governmentality theory (Foucault 1991) to focus on the practice of metagovernance. Governing at a distance is considered a key feature of liberal governmentality (Rose and Miller 1992). The relations between government and stakeholder networks and "the political agency and self-association of civil society" are central to the formulation and implementation of policy (Sending and Neumann 2006, 652). Governments seek to both mobilize and control the agency of individuals and groups through the regimes and the rationalities of practice and the "organized ways of doing things" (Dean 1999, 17). In the practice of metagovernance, this is exercised through, for example, problem framing, facilitating network engagement, and judging network performance (Sørensen and Torfing 2007a).

Governmentality theory adds a valuable perspective to the analysis of changing forms of governance by drawing attention to power and its impact on governance outcomes. Power is enacted through established and evolving practices, reflecting historical and cultural contexts (Bevir 2011). Power has been identified as a significant and under-researched area of contemporary water governance (Brisbois and de Loë 2015; Taylor and Sonnenfeld this issue). Our analytical approach therefore examines the evolving practice of governance and specifically the distribution of power and the authority of the state in long-running, evolving water policy conflicts.

Analytical Approach

Our analysis is framed by governmentality theory, examining the rationalities and practices of governance, the exercise of power, and performance of governance networks. We further clarify these themes with relevant elements drawn from the governance network literature already outlined, including the structural and functional characteristics of different modes of governance, tensions within and between these modes, and the kinds of outcomes (at least procedurally) they are likely to generate.

1. What are the rationale and practices of governance?
    a. The scope and objectives of governance arrangements (Mandell and Steelman 2003; Stenson 2008; Edge and Eyles 2015).

b. The evolution of governance network forms over time (Provan and Kenis 2007; Emerson et al. 2011; Arnouts, van der Zouwen, and Arts 2012; Lange et al. 2013).

2. How is power exercised in formal and informal governance arrangements?
   a. The distribution of power through the governance arrangements (centers of decision making) (Rose and Miller 1992; Sending and Neumann 2006; Bulkeley, Watson, and Hudson 2007; McKee 2009).
   b. Stakeholder engagement [participation and roles] (Quirk 2005; Newig and Fritsch 2009; Emerson and Nabatchi 2015b).

3. How have governance arrangements performed?
   a. Outputs and outcomes (Provan and Milward 2001; Voets, Van Dooren, and De Rynck 2008; Emerson et al. 2011; Emerson and Nabatchi 2015a).
   b. Gaps and ongoing challenges (Huxham and Vangen 2005; Newig and Fritsch 2009; Vella et al. 2015).

These elements allow us to consider the impacts of different water governance arrangements through the commonalities (and differences) of experience across multiple case studies.

Research Methods

Empirical governance research is dominated by single case studies (Poteete, Janssen, and Ostrom 2010) that involve intensive examination of bounded processes to test and develop theory (Yin 2014). This study was motivated by the desire to compare governance approaches across countries and across time to better understand how governments are employing network governance approaches and the implications of these institutional trajectories for the management of water resources.

This study adopts a comparative case study analysis to investigate existing water governance research in Australia (Murray–Darling Basin and Reef Partnership), the United States (CALFED and Everglades), and France (Loire and Rhone), allowing their commonalities and differences to be considered. We sought an international comparative study that would allow us to examine collaborative water governance cases that provided variation in political, legal, institutional, and cultural contexts. There are clearly many potential cases to examine; our selection was based upon several criteria: (1) We limited our cases to countries with established liberal democracies and political systems that provide for citizen participation and a role for civil society; (2) we selected cases with a significant history of networked water governance; and (3) we required cases with well-documented analysis by practitioners and academics. We specifically excluded transnational cases to limit between-case variation.

Our research involved a review of plans, evaluations, government reports, and academic research articles relevant to each case. Two members of the team reviewed each case and carried out three data-gathering and analysis steps:

1. We prepared narrative descriptions that summarized the history, political context, institutional changes, and outputs and outcomes. These case narratives also served as a check against the data gathered in our analysis.

2. For each phase of each case study we sought and collated evidence against the analytical themes and elements described in the preceding:
   - Rationale and practices of governance.
     - Scope and definition of the problem.
     - Triggers for governance change.
     - Governance structures (form, hierarchy).
   - Exercise of power.
     - Role and power of elected officials.
     - Role and power of government agencies.
     - Role and power of non-governmental stakeholders.
   - Outcomes.
     - Evidence of outcomes.
     - Documented challenges or failures.
3. After preparing the narratives and data tables, the team conducted a series of workshops where we identified common and divergent trends and compared our results to the themes in the literature.

While the comparative analysis enabled a high-level view of changes over time and a comparison between cases, we were constrained by access to published information and research. Even with careful case selection, the extent to which all analytical criteria were examined varies by case. Our findings are propositional, given the small sample size and low external validity. For this reason, rather than taking our cases as representative, we view them as instrumental cases—that is, their value lies not in their ability to speak for other cases, but in what we might learn from them (Stake and Savolainen 1995). Finally, we are constrained by limited space in this article, in terms of reporting the long and complex history of individual cases. We present highly abbreviated case summaries and a table of the major governance phases, choosing to focus instead on the overarching themes and examples that best demonstrate these themes.

Case Studies

Our six case studies are large, complex water conflicts that have attracted significant, ongoing investment in policymaking, science, and on-the-ground projects over 10–20 years. These six studies were drawn from three countries with complex, multilevel governance arrangements. Australia is a federated constitutional monarchy. The United States is a federal republic. France is a republic and member of the European Union. Pierre and Peters (2005) provide a framework for understanding broad differences in the governance of nation states. The framework describes a spectrum of high to low government authority and capacity, balanced by an inverse spectrum (low to high) of engagement with civil society and associated information flows. Under this classification, France is considered to have a more centralized authority and lower civil engagement than the Australian and U.S. cases. Table 1 briefly describes the responsibilities and the history of water management in each case. Key references are provided in the text that follows for further detail.

Table 1. Phases of the six case studies.

Country	Case	Phase 1			Phase 2			Phase 3		
		Date and name	Triggers	Governance authority	Dates	Triggers	Governance authority	Dates	Triggers	Governance authority
Australia	GBR	2003–2009; Reef Plan I	Environmental concerns (water quality)	Federal and state governments	2009–2013; Reef Plan II	Stakeholder pressure (agriculture, conservation), election	National and state government with stakeholder consultation body	2013 Reef Plan III; Reef 2050 Plan	Risks to World Heritage listing (UNESCO)	National and state government with stakeholder consultation body
	MDB	1915–1992; River Murray Waters Agreement	Water for irrigation and navigation	Federal and three state governments	1992–2007; Murray–Darling Basin Initiative	Water quantity (litigation by the downstream state) water quality, salinity,	National and four state governments with stakeholder consultation body	2007 Murray–Darling Basin Authority	Limits of consensus, drought, climate change	National government, new authority
United States	Bay-Delta	1990s–2000; CALFED I	Environmental concerns (water quality, endangered species)	Federal and state governments, informal leadership	2000–2006; CALFED II	Political changes, litigation (conservation)	Federal and state governments, formalized	2009 Delta Stewardship Council	Litigation, water supply and ecosystem heath	State government, new authority
	Florida	1992–1996 Florida Everglades Review Study I	Litigation (federal government) water quality	Various informal federal government or state government led	1996–1999 Florida; Restoration Taskforce	Litigation; new legislation; water quantity, quality and ecosystem restoration	Federal, state local and tribal governments with stakeholder consultation body	2000- Everglades Restoration Plan	Plan implementation, water quantity and quality, ecosystem health	Federal, state local and tribal governments with stakeholder consultation body
France	Rhone	1990s–2000s Emerging responses	Environmental and flood concerns; Changing legislation	National, regional and local government	2007–2013; Plan Rhone I	Floods Elections New legislation	State and regions with stakeholder consultation body	2014–2020 Plan Rhone II	Flood prevention, economics, climate change, European Union (EU) directives	State and regions with stakeholder consultation body and links to Swiss
	Loire	1994–2006 Plan Loire Grandeur Nature	Environmental and flood concerns; litigation (conservation)	Initially driven nationally, then state–regional	2007–2013 Plan Loire II	Plan review, public engagement; environmental and flood concerns	National and regions with stakeholder consultation body	2014–2020 Plan Loire III	Climate change, economics, EU directives	Multiregion with stakeholder consultation body

Note. GBR = Great Barrier Reef; MDB = Murray Darling Basin.

Australia

Primary responsibility for water management rests with the states, but the federal government has sought greater influence in recent decades through water reform, coordination mechanisms, and community-based natural resource management (Robins and Dovers 2007). The federal government also holds constitutional powers in relation to World Heritage and matters of international and national environmental significance (Ross and Dovers 2008).

The Great Barrier Reef is a World Heritage-listed marine park affected by water quality from 35 catchments, as well as by climate change and coastal development. Bilateral governance arrangements have evolved over 12 years in response to stakeholder and international pressure to manage water quality and coastal development pressures (see Waterhouse et al. 2009; Robinson et al. 2010; Brodie et al. 2012).

The Murray-Darling Basin has had more than a century of collaborative agreements between four states, one territory, and the federal government to manage water allocation conflicts (see Connell and Grafton 2011a; Marshall, Connell, and Taylor 2013; Ross and Connell 2014). New legislation enacted in 2007 provides for greater federal government authority in the basin.

United States

The federal government has primary authority for environmental regulation related to issues such as endangered species and water quality management, but relies on states to implement programs and regulation. States have primary authority over water quantity, but these distinctions tend to be blurred where there are federal water projects and links between water quantity and water quality or endangered species.

The California Bay-Delta (CALFED) history involves bilateral arrangements that have sought to reconcile multiple objectives for California's Sacramento and San Joaquin River Basins and Bay-Delta over 25 years. These have changed from informal to formal collaborative arrangements among state (CAL) and federal (FED) participants, and more recently to a narrower and centralized state-based authority (see Innes, Booher, and Di Vittorio 2010; Dutterer and Margerum 2014).

The Florida Everglades have had a complex series of governance arrangements initiated by both state and federal governments to resolve water quantity and quality issues (see Dengler 2007; Heikkila and Gerlak 2014). Litigation and the threat of litigation have been key drivers of change.

France

Regulatory power is held by the national government; committees and water agencies play important planning and management roles. European Directives and a stronger role for local government have influenced water management arrangements in recent decades (Sangaré and Larrue 2002).

The Rhone River rises in Switzerland, but most of the basin is in France (we focus on the French section). Two rounds of collaborative planning have been completed since 2007, triggered by floods and changing state and European Union regulations (see Bréthaut and Pflieger 2013; Guerrin, Bouleau, and Grelot 2014).

The Loire Valley has had three phases of water planning. Initiated by community action, governance has shifted from a national government-centric response to greater roles for regions and stakeholders over time (see Vreugdenhil et al. 2008; Despointes 2009; Rode 2010).

All six of the cases involve long and complex histories. Our analysis focused on the key governance attributes described earlier under three themes: the rationale and practice of governance; the exercise of power; and governance performance.

Rationale and Practice of Governance

Cycles of Change

Water governance networks in all six case studies undergo periodic cycles of change and renewal. Similar to the triggers for the initial formation of governance structures, triggers for change arise from crises within and beyond the water policy domain. All cases seek to balance competing water uses, and address deteriorating environmental condition. Changes in governance forms and objectives are triggered by a combination of events that collectively make the preexisting arrangements untenable (see Bellamy et al. 2017, this issue). These triggers include elections, legislative changes, litigation, international agreements, stakeholder pressure, implementation failure, changing policy context, and physical events such as floods, droughts, and fish kills.

In the Great Barrier Reef, three phases of bilateral planning have been triggered by stakeholder pressure, elections, and international scrutiny (UNESCO's proposal to list the reef as "World Heritage in danger"). In the Rhone and Loire, floods, new state and European legislation combined with legal challenges, public protests, and growing environmental concerns have driven change. In the Bay-Delta case study, political changes and litigation have been the dominant drivers of change. In each of the three countries, governance change has involved some form of litigation, or threat of litigation by government, conservation, or agricultural industries. This was particularly evident in the U.S. case studies, where litigation was a major trigger for governance reform in both cases.

Renegotiation of Purpose

As these changes occur, the purpose and operation of governance networks are debated across scientific, political, and stakeholder fora. A feature of these negotiations is the need to update and clarify scientific understanding. This allows the issues to be redefined and the objectives of the governance arrangement to be reviewed. Most, but not all, of the cases (the Great Barrier Reef and Bay-Delta are exceptions) showed a widening of planning scope over time. The review of purpose and objectives has significant implications for stakeholders, whose interests may be supported or challenged by the new arrangements. This drives intense debate as the validity of scientific and technical claims are contested.

The Rhone and Loire case studies clearly demonstrate an expanding scope, as the original focus on flood protection and water quality grew to include regional economic development, social innovation, and climate change adaptation. While the Murray–Darling

Basin plan's objective is to restore water to the environment, the social and economic impacts are now receiving greater recognition. In contrast, the Bay-Delta, Florida Everglades, and Great Barrier Reef have maintained their original focus on balancing economic objectives (agricultural production and profitability) with ecosystem restoration.

The debates that accompanied the renegotiation of purpose were seen to follow the classic dichotomy of environmental quality versus economic development (Hanak 2011; Hughes, Day, and Brodie 2015). Particular problem or issue frames may have significant implications for some stakeholder groups, so strong scientific support is required to adjust policy goals (Robinson et al. 2011), and science may be contested by stakeholders to delay policy action (Layzer 2008a). Rather than a consensus-building exercise, these negotiations more closely resemble strategic "policy games" between powerful stakeholders, which result in efforts to restructure the governance approach.

Governance Arrangements

In all six cases, we found that governance models were reviewed when the purpose and objectives of governance were revised and two narratives emerged. In three cases (Reef, Loire, Rhone) the governance structure, membership, and operation largely stayed the same, but governance objectives and strategies were updated. In the other three cases (Murray–Darling, Bay Delta, Florida Everglades), the governance arrangements underwent major revisions, including new structures, members, and operational arrangements.

The network governance models adopted in the case studies range across the idealized forms described by Provan and Kenis (2007). Networks can be governed by the members themselves (participant governed), coordinated through a single participating member (lead organization governed), or led by an entity specifically created to support a collaborative approach (network administrative governed).

In the Great Barrier Reef, governance arrangements resemble a participant-governed network where membership is confined to federal and state governments with links to stakeholder forums. The Rhone case resembles a lead organization network in which Plan Rhone was assigned primary responsibility and its role was to direct implementation efforts. Both of these models have struggled with implementation, discussed further in the following section, but their governance arrangements have been stable over time. In contrast, network structures for Everglades water management in both north and south Florida have changed several times, employing different forms of governance networks.

Both the Murray–Darling and Bay-Delta cases show significant changes to governance arrangements, with a shift from collaborative network arrangements to a more centralized authority with new legislative powers (Connell and Grafton 2011b; Dutterer and Margerum 2014). Whether these more centralized governance models are maintained, and manage to address the perceived limitations of the more networked approaches, remains to be seen. Certainly, the pressure to revise governance objectives and arrangements that is documen-ted in these case studies is consistent with research that shows a wide range of triggers for change, including shock events, adjacent policy arrangements, sociopolitical trends, or the role of policy entrepreneurs (Arts and Leroy 2006). Governance arrangements of any form need to be responsive to changing contexts.

Given the cycles of policy and governance revision that the case studies demonstrate, we must ask whether the potential benefits of a networked approach can be achieved in this context. That is, can collaborative advantage be realized, or do persistent network negotiations become a surrogate for action that overrides implementation? This also raises the question of whether those who want to avoid change or reallocation of resources have utilized deliberation over governance arrangements as a negotiating or delaying strategy.

Exercise of Power

Decision-making Authority

The governance models employed vary, but in all of our cases national and state governments retained primary control and played key leadership roles. Governance structures and processes are used to bring together multiple levels and agencies of government (rather than the full range of stakeholders). Mechanisms to engage nongovernment stakeholders have been incorporated in all cases, but generally have little decision-making authority.

It is clear that government has not ceded power to stakeholder networks or reduced its role in setting the agenda, steering governance arrangements, and commissioning implementation efforts. In fact, in a number of cases, it could be argued that federal or state governments have increased their authority through additional powers, resources, or oversight.

In the California Bay-Delta, collaboration between federal and state governments has significantly increased funding and extended the existing roles of state and federal agencies, and its most recent iteration has resulted in new oversight authority to support the Delta Plan (Hanak 2011; Delta Stewardship Council 2013). Similarly, in the Florida Everglades, the federal government signed a deal with the state to share costs and responsibilities and provide federal stimulus money, though delivery has been delayed (Gerlak and Heikkila 2011). In France, the Plan Rhone and the Plan Loire did not reduce government authority, but added a new layer of collaborative governance arrangements to address a wide range of water resources issues (Guerrin 2013; Guerrin 2014; Guerrin, Bouleau, and Grelot 2014). Similarly, in Australia, efforts to manage impacts to the Great Barrier Reef have attracted substantial state and national investment, and ongoing policy development (Day and Dobbs 2013). Pressure from UNESCO has galvanized renewed government commitment in Queensland, Australia, where a new ministerial portfolio for the Great Barrier Reef has been created.

Deliberation and Politicking

What has changed in all of our cases is a more deliberative approach to defining the policy issues and responses. Deliberations have emerged because of competition for limited resources, major crises and events, and external and internal pressures questioning the effectiveness of existing approaches. They reflect a broader recognition that existing government policies and agencies cannot respond effectively because they don't encompass crosscutting relationships (e.g., flooding and floodplain management) or because they involve decisions with significant costs for some interests (e.g., water allocation) and therefore need to be carefully negotiated.

All of the cases we examined attracted ongoing, high-level political attention through hearings, lawsuits, public protests and campaigns, special commissions, scientific studies, and public policy pronouncements. Furthermore, many observers allude to ongoing political pressures taking place behind the scenes (Connell 2007; Layzer 2008b; Robinson et al. 2011). Far from being apolitical forums for deliberation, these cases demonstrated that deliberations were intimately intertwined with national and state or regional politics. For example, policy stakeholders in the CALFED case cited the early leadership and pressure from the California governor and U.S. Secretary of the Interior as playing a critical role (Lurie 2011). Governance approaches in the Bay Delta have also been the focus of two separate California government commission reviews (Little Hoover Commission 2005; 2010). In the Florida Everglades, the judiciary has played a significant role in mobilizing action either through direct decision making by the courts, or by collaborative processes designed to avoid legal action (Dengler 2007). Several state governors and presidential administrations were involved in negotiations and collaborative governance structures to produce the Restoration Plan in Florida (Harwell 1998), as were state and federal lobbyists and political stakeholders (Dengler 2007). In Australia, significant shifts in reef policies have been associated with elections at both state and federal levels and the political advocacy of key stakeholders (Robinson et al. 2010). In France, there has been continued involvement from national-level agencies (e.g., Rhone-Mediterranean water agency) and leaders from regional councils. High-level attention has also been focused through events such as the 2005 Rhone Summit that engaged a range of policy stakeholders to deliberate on its future.

There is little evidence from these cases to support the claim that there is a shift from "government to governance" that is associated with a transfer of power to other parties within policy-level arenas. Governments are developing networks to engage other governments and other agencies, not to bring nongovernment stakeholders into the decision-making arena. While greater engagement of nongovernment stakeholders has occurred over time, this is generally facilitated through consultative structures and processes. Governance networks are being used to supplement, rather than replace, traditional hierarchical government decision-making processes (Jordan, Wurzel, and Zito 2005).

Accountability

Governance networks involve multiple accountabilities, including individual organizational accountabilities to constituencies and decision-makers, as well as mutual and collective accountability to each other and external sponsors or authorities (Hertting and Vedung 2012). The governance networks described here represent a hybrid arrangement that adopts some of the features of networks, but retains leadership and accountability with the state, not with the network per se (Keast, Mandell, and Brown 2006). Governments occupy a unique position; their legitimate role and public scrutiny limit their capacity to directly negotiate with sectoral interests (Klijn and Koppenjan 2000) and devolve accountability to governance networks. The practice of governance networks is therefore constrained by the traditional accountability of governments to elected representatives as agents of the public through democratic process (Kettl 2006; Agranoff 2007). Political leadership can drive commitment and performance, or can shut down collaboration or constrain debate. While there is a body of research that explores the democratic accountability of networks (see Klijn and Skelcher 2007), the interaction between political process and governance networks is a topic needing further research.

In the Bay-Delta case, the California governor's Little Hoover Commission suggested that both leadership and accountability were significant issues that required major reform (Little Hoover Commission 2005). In Florida, political lobbying by nongovernment stakeholders nearly derailed the Comprehensive Everglades Restoration Plan that had been developed (by the same stakeholders) through networked governance arrangements. Lack of accountability to local stakeholders undermined the implementation of Plan Rhone. Conservation and tribal organizations have effectively used the courts to hold governments accountable for poor performance in the U.S. cases.

Outcomes: Implementation Achievements and Challenges

Despite new and revised governance arrangements, implementation of actions to resolve water policy conflicts remains challenged by insufficient resources, lack of collective authority, and the capacity of vested interests to block or delay actions. While each case has attracted significant investment (e.g., more than US$3 billion in the Bay-Delta, $8 billion for Florida restoration works, more than US$8 billion for water buyback in Australia's Murray–Darling Basin), resources remain insufficient to drive the scale and pace of change to deliver restoration outcomes. This is well documented in the Great Barrier Reef (Brodie and Waterhouse 2012) and the Florida Everglades (Gerlak and Heikkila 2011). In the Murray–Darling Basin, water license buybacks are triggering local community concern and political pressure to slow the pace of change.

Network governance entities lack authority to direct implementation efforts. Typically, networked governance arrangements rely on a range of organizations to implement actions with varying levels of oversight or sanctions to enforce them. These may be government agencies, statutory authorities, or third parties such as industry or community groups, which have had varying levels of input to the decision-making process. This has led to tensions between the steering function of the collaborative governance entity and the array of government and nongovernment parties with a role in the "rowing" function of implementation.

Third parties may effectively block policy implementation by nonconformance or litigation. Litigation has been a significant feature in both American cases—where collaborative governance has been pursued to avoid costly and time-consuming litigious processes, and the resumption in litigation is seen as a failure of governance (Dengler 2007; Layzer 2008a; Lubell et al. 2013). In these cases, litigation has been used to either enforce or prevent implementation of policies. In the Florida Everglades, the slow pace of restoration triggered a federal court ruling in 2010 "that clean water standards were still not being met ordering federal and state governments to amend existing permits for discharges in the Everglades and construct new marsh treatment areas" (Gerlak and Heikkila 2011, 9). In Australia, the threat of litigation from the downstream state has driven governance initiatives in the Murray–Darling Basin (Connell and Grafton 2011a). In the Loire, public campaigns blocked plan implementation.

Two cases, the California Bay-Delta and the Australian Murray–Darling Basin, have created new legislative authorities to drive implementation. In the Bay-Delta, the Delta Reform Act 2009 created an agency to develop a collaborative Delta Plan but also has authority to review the compliance of local and state plans with the Delta Plan (Delta Stewardship Council 2013). In Australia, the Water Act 2007 grants the federal government powers to develop a basin-wide plan, but implementation still relies on state governments to develop and implement compliant water-sharing plans in their jurisdictions (Marshall, Connell, and Taylor 2013).

It is clear in all of the cases that a networked approach to governance has not resolved the ongoing implementation challenges. Networks don't replace government structures, but usually add another layer of complexity (O'Toole 2014). Resource constraints, implementation authority, and veto powers are likely to be issues whether or not governance networks are used (or, indeed, are part of the wicked complexity that is a trigger for adopting a networked approach). These challenges suggest limitations to what a collaborative approach can provide in policy-level collaboration (Margerum 2011). Reaching agreement on objectives is insufficient to deliver outcomes without appropriate resourcing or instruments to underpin implementation. If governance objectives are not aligned with important stakeholder interests, they may be co-opted or challenged in court or through broader public debate.

Conclusion

This study compared six longitudinal case studies of significant water policy conflicts in Australia, the United States, and France. Drawing on governmentality theory, we examined the rationalities and practices of governance, the exercise of power, and evidence of outcomes to test the proposition that there is a trend from "government to governance" that reflects a loss of state authority.

Despite the different political and legal traditions of our case studies, surprisingly consistent themes were evident. Our results challenge the narrative of governments ceding power to governance networks (Kooiman 2003; Rhodes 2007). While governments are adopting more deliberative, networked approaches, these are led by government and employed to supplement, rather than replace, traditional hierarchical governance systems. These attempts to harness collaborative advantage are disrupted by ongoing or cyclical adjustments to policy objectives and governance arrangements. Networked governance is not a panacea for wicked problems. There remain underlying issues of centralization of power, material resource constraints, political legitimacy, and accountability for implementation.

From a research perspective, these findings require further testing in other cases and contexts, including developing economies and transnational cases (e.g., the Rhine, the Danube). Further, are the patterns observed in water governance across our cases consistent with the experiences of other networked governance cases in different policy contexts? Finally, what are the implications of the power dynamics and political dimensions of networked governance employed within hierarchical systems? Are the benefits of networked governance fully realized in this context?

Our results suggest that efforts to employ networked governance approaches to address water policy conflicts struggle to effectively bridge the hierarchical functions and authority of governments with the potential for productive and creative networked relationships. For practitioners, this research emphasizes the need to effectively manage ongoing cycles of change and disruption, and close attention to power and politics. As the scale of water and other resource conflicts continues to increase, the need to better understand and enhance institutional capacity only grows.

Funding

This work was supported by the Australian Research Council (LP130100933), "The Impact of Governance on Regional Natural Resource Planning" project.

References

Agranoff, R. 2007. *Managing within networks: Adding value to public organizations.* Washington, DC: Georgetown University Press.

Agranoff, R. 2013. Bridging the theoretical gap and uncovering the missing holes. In *Network theory in the public sector: Building new theoretical frameworks*, ed. R. Keast, M. Mandell, and R. Agranoff, 193. New York, NY: Routledge.

Arentsen, M. J. 2001. Negotiated environmental governance in the Netherlands: Logic and illustration. *Policy Studies Journal* 29 (3):499–513. doi:10.1111/j.1541-0072.2001.tb02106.x.

Arnouts, R., M. van der Zouwen, and B. Arts. 2012. Analysing governance modes and shifts—Governance arrangements in Dutch nature policy. *Forest Policy and Economics* 16:43–50. doi:10.1016/j.forpol.2011.04.001.

Arts, B., and P. Leroy. 2006. Institutional dynamics in environmental governance. In *Institutional dynamics in environmental governance*, ed. B. Arts and P. Leroy, 1–20. Dordrecht, The Netherlands: Springer.

Bellamy, J., Head, B., and Ross, H. 2017. Crises and Institutional Change: Emergence of Cross-Border Water Governance in Lake Eyre Basin, Australia. *Society & Natural Resources.* doi:10.1080/08941920.2016.1272729.

Bevir, M. 2011. Governance and governmentality after neoliberalism. *Policy & Politics* 39 (4):457–71. doi:10.1332/030557310x550141.

Börzel, T. A., and T. Risse. 2010. Governance without a state: Can it work? *Regulation & Governance* 4 (2):113–34. doi:10.1111/j.1748-5991.2010.01076.x.

Bréthaut, C., and G. Pflieger. 2013. The shifting territorialities of the Rhone River's trans-boundary governance: A historical analysis of the evolution of the functions, uses and spatiality of river basin governance. *Regional Environmental Change* 15:1–10. doi:10.1007/s10113-013-0541-4.

Brisbois, M. C., and R. C. de Loë. 2015. Power in collaborative approaches to governance for water: A systematic review. *Society & Natural Resources* 29:775–90. doi:10.1080/08941920.2015.1080339.

Brodie, J. E., F. J. Kroon, B. Schaffelke, E. C. Wolanski, S. E. Lewis, M. J. Devlin, I. C. Bohnet, Z. T. Bainbridge, J. Waterhouse, and A. M. Davis. 2012. Terrestrial pollutant runoff to the Great Barrier Reef: An update of issues, priorities and management responses. *Marine Pollution Bulletin* 65 (4–9):81–100. doi:10.1016/j.marpolbul.2011.12.012.

Brodie, J., and J. Waterhouse. 2012. A critical review of environmental management of the 'not so Great' Barrier Reef. *Estuarine, Coastal and Shelf Science* 104–5:1–22. doi:10.1016/j.ecss.2012.03.012.

Bulkeley, H., M. Watson, and R. Hudson. 2007. Modes of governing municipal waste. *Environment and Planning A* 39 (11):2733–53. doi:10.1068/a38269.

Chaffin, B. C., H. Gosnell, and B. A. Cosens. 2014. A decade of adaptive governance scholarship: Synthesis and future directions. *Ecology and Society* 19 (3):56. doi:10.5751/ES-06824-190356.

Connell, D. 2007. *Water politics in the Murray-Darling basin.* Canberra, Australia: Federation Press.

Connell, D., and R. Q. Grafton. 2011a. *Basin futures: Water reform in the Murray-Darling Basin.* Canberra, Australia: ANU E Press.

Connell, D., and R. Q. Grafton. 2011b. Water reform in the Murray–Darling Basin. *Water Resources Research* 47 (12):W00G003. doi:10.1029/2010wr009820

Day, J. C., and K. Dobbs. 2013. Effective governance of a large and complex cross-jurisdictional marine protected area: Australia's Great Barrier Reef. *Marine Policy* 41:14–24. doi:10.1016/j.marpol.2012.12.020.

Dean, M. 1999. *Governmentality: Power and rule in modern society.* London, UK: Sage.

Delta Stewardship Council. 2013. *The delta plan.* Sacramento, CA: Delta Stewardship Council.

Dengler, M. 2007. Spaces of power for action: Governance of the Everglades restudy process (1992–2000). *Political Geography* 26 (4):423–54. doi:10.1016/j.polgeo.2006.12.004.

Despointes, F. H. 2009. La Loire, espace d'une gouvernance environnementale? *VertigO—la revue électronique en sciences de l'environnement* (Hors série 6).

Driessen, P. P. J., C. Dieperink, F. Laerhoven, H. C. Runhaar, and W. J. V. Vermeulen. 2012. Towards a conceptual framework for the study of shifts in modes of environmental governance —Experiences from The Netherlands. *Environmental Policy and Governance* 22 (3):143–60. doi:10.1002/eet.1580.

Duncan, R. 2017. Rescaling Knowledge and Governance and Enrolling the Future in New Zealand: A Co-Production Analysis of Canterbury's Water Management Reforms to Regulate Diffuse Pollution. *Society & Natural Resources.* doi:10.1080/08941920.2016.1265187.

Dutterer, A. D., and R. D. Margerum. 2014. The limitations of policy-level collaboration: A meta-analysis of CALFED. *Society & Natural Resources* 28 (1):21–37. doi:10.1080/08941920. 2014.945054.

Edge, S., and J. Eyles. 2015. Contested governmentalities: NGO enrollment and influence over chemical risk governance rationales and practices. *Environmental Policy and Governance* 25:188–200. doi:10.1002/eet.1671.

Emerson, K., A. Gerlak, O. Barreteau, M. B. ten Brink, N. Farahbakhshazad, G. Morrison, and P. Promburon. 2011. A framework to assess collaborative governance: A new look at four water resource management cases. *Journal of Policy Analysis and Management* 22:1–29. doi:10.1093/jopart/mur011.

Emerson, K., and T. Nabatchi. 2015a. Assessing the performance of collaborative governance regimes. In *Collaborative governance regimes,* ed. K. Emerson and T. Nabatchi, 180–206. Washington, DC: Georgetown University Press.

Emerson, K., and T. Nabatchi. 2015b. Collaboration dynamics: Principled engagement, shared motivation, and the capacity for joint action. In *Collaborative governance regimes,* ed. K. Emerson and T. Nabatchi, 57–80. Washington, DC: Georgetown University Press.

Foucault, M. 1991. Governmentality. In *The Foucault effect: Studies in governmentality,* ed. G. Burchell, C. Gordon, and P. Miller, 87–104. Hemel Hempstead, UK: Harvester Wheatsheaf.

Freeman, R. E. 1984. *Strategic management: A stakeholder approach.* Cambridge, UK: Cambridge University Press.

Gerlak, A. K., and T. Heikkila. 2011. Building a theory of learning in collaboratives: Evidence from the everglades restoration program. *Journal of Public Administration Research and Theory* 21: 619–44. doi:10.1093/jopart/muq089.

Guerrin, J. 2013. Le développement durable comme légitimation de l'action publique. Le cas des inondations du Rhône. In Les Cahiers du CRGRNT: Université du Quebec en Outaouais.

Guerrin, J. 2014. A floodplain restoration project on the River Rhône(France): Analyzing challenges to its implementation. *Regional Environmental Change* 15: 559–68. doi:10.1007/s10113-014-0650-8.

Guerrin, J., G. Bouleau, and F. Grelot. 2014. "Functional fit" versus "politics of scale" in the governance of floodplain retention capacity. *Journal of Hydrology* 519:2405–14. doi:10.1016/j.jhydrol.2014.08.024.

Hanak, E. 2011. *Managing California's water: From conflict to reconciliation.* San Francisco, CA: Public Policy Institute of California.

Harwell, M. A. 1998. Science and environmental decision-making in South Florida. *Ecological Applications* 8 (3):580–90. doi:10.1890/1051-0761(1998)008[0580:SAEDMI]2.0.CO;2.

Heikkila, T., and A. K. Gerlak. 2014. Investigating collaborative processes over time a 10-year study of the South Florida ecosystem restoration task force. *American Review of Public Administration* 46:180–200. doi:10.1177/0275074014544196.

Hertting, N., and E. Vedung. 2012. Purposes and criteria in network governance evaluation: How far does standard evaluation vocabulary takes us? *Evaluation* 18 (1):27–46. doi:10.1177/1356389011431021.

Holley, C. 2010. Facilitating monitoring, subverting self-interest and limiting discretion: Learning from new forms of accountability in practice. *Columbia Journal of Environmental Law* 35:127.

Hughes, T. P., J. C. Day, and J. Brodie. 2015. Securing the future of the Great Barrier Reef. *Nature Climate Change* 5:508–11. doi:10.1038/nclimate2604.

Huxham, C. 2003. Theorizing collaboration practice. *Public Management Review* 5 (3):401–23. doi:10.1080/1471903032000146964.

Huxham, C., and S. E. Vangen. 2005. *Managing to collaborate: The theory and practice of collaborative advantage.* Abingdon, UK: Routledge.

Innes, J. E., D. E. Booher, and S. Di Vittorio. 2010. Strategies for megaregion governance. *Journal of the American Planning Association* 77 (1):55–67. doi:10.1080/01944363.2011.533640.

Ison, R., and D. Watson. 2007. Illuminating the possibilities for social learning in the management of Scotland's water. *Ecology and Society* 12 (1):21.

Jordan, A., R. K. W. Wurzel, and A. Zito. 2005. The rise of 'new' policy instruments in comparative perspective: Has governance eclipsed government? *Political Studies* 53 (3):477–96.

Keast, R. L., M. Mandell, and K. A. Brown. 2006. Mixing state, market and network governance modes: The role of government in "crowded" policy domains. *International Journal of Organization Theory and Behavior* 9 (1):27.

Kettl, D. F. 2006. Managing boundaries in American administration: The collaboration imperative. *Public Administration Review* 66 (s1):10–19. doi:10.1111/j.1540-6210.2006.00662.x.

Klijn, E.-H. 2008. Governance and governance networks in Europe: An assessment of ten years of research on the theme. *Public Management Review* 10 (4):505–25. doi:10.1080/14719030802263954.

Klijn, E.-H., and J. F. M. Koppenjan. 2000. Public management and policy networks: Foundations of a network approach to governance. *Public Management an International Journal of Research and Theory* 2 (2):135–58. doi:10.1080/14719030000000007.

Klijn, E.-H., and C. Skelcher. 2007. Democracy and governance networks: Compatible or not? *Public Administration* 85 (3):587–608.

Kooiman, J. 2003. *Governing as governance.* London, UK: Sage.

Lange, P., P. P. J. Driessen, A. Sauer, B. Bornemann, and P. Burger. 2013. Governing towards sustainability– Conceptualizing modes of governance. *Journal of Environmental Policy & Planning* 15 (3):403–25. doi:10.1080/1523908X.2013.769414.

Larsson, O. 2015. The governmentality of meta-governance. Identifying theoretical and empirical challenges of network governance in the political field of security and beyond. Doctor of Philosophy, Acta Universitatis Upsaliensis.

Layzer, J. A. 2008a. Recreating central Florida's meandering Kissimmee River. In *Natural experiments: Ecosystem-based management and the environment*, ed. J. A. Layzer, 205–32. Cambridge, MA: MIT Press.

Layzer, J. A. 2008b. Restoring South Florida's river of grass. In *Natural experiments: Ecosystem-based management and the environment*, ed. J. A. Layzer, 103–36. Cambridge, MA: MIT Press.

Little Hoover Commission. 2005. *Still imperiled, still important. The Little Hoover Commission's review of the CALFED Bay-Delta Program.* Sacramento, CA: Little Hoover Commission.

Little Hoover Commission. 2010. *Managing for change: Modernizing California's water governance.* Sacramento, CA: Little Hoover Commission.

Lubell, M., A. Gerlak, T. Heikkila, J. F. Warner, A. Van Buuren, and J. Edelenbos. 2013. CalFed and collaborative watershed management: Success despite failure. In *Making space for the river: Governance experiences with multifunctional river flood management in the US and Europe*, ed. J. F. Warner, A. Van Buuren, and J. Edelenbos, 63–78. London, UK: IWA Publishing House.

Lurie, S. D. 2011. The CALFED Bay-Delta Program: Lessons from the rise and fall of a large-scale ecosystem management network. *Journal of Natural Resources Policy Research* 3 (3):251–62. doi:10.1080/19390459.2011.591764.

Mandell, M. P., and T. Steelman. 2003. Understanding what can be accomplished through interorganizational innovations the importance of typologies, context and management strategies. *Public Management Review* 5 (2):197–224. doi:10.1080/1461667032000066417.

Margerum, R. D. 2011. *Beyond consensus: Improving collaborative planning and management.* Cambridge, MA: MIT Press.

Marshall, G. R., D. Connell, and B. M. Taylor. 2013. Australia's Murray–Darling Basin: A century of polycentric experiments in cross-border integration of water resources management. *International Journal of Water Governance* 1 (3):197–218. doi:10.7564/13-IJWG14.

McGuire, M., and R. Agranoff. 2011. The limitations of public management networks. *Public Administration* 89 (2):265–84. doi:10.1111/j.1467-9299.2011.01917.x.

McKee, K. 2009. Post-Foucauldian governmentality: What does it offer critical social policy analysis? *Critical Social Policy* 29 (3):465–86. doi:105180 10.1177/0261018309105180.

Meuleman, L. 2008. Metagovernance as the governance of governance. In *Public management and the metagovernance of hierarchies, networks and markets: The feasibility of designing and managing governance style combinations*, ed. L. Meuleman, 66–86. Heidelberg, Germany: Springer Science & Business Media.

Newig, J., and O. Fritsch. 2009. Environmental governance: Participatory, multi-level - and effective? *Environmental Policy and Governance* 19 (3):197–214. doi:10.1002/eet.509.

O'Toole, L. J. 2014. Networks and networking: The public administrative agendas. *Public Administration Review* 75:361–71. doi:10.1111/puar.12281.

Pahl-Wostl, C., G. Holtz, B. Kastens, and C. Knieper. 2010. Analyzing complex water governance regimes: The management and transition framework. *Environmental Science & Policy* 13 (7): 571–81. doi:10.1016/j.envsci.2010.08.006.

Pierre, J., and B. G. Peters. 2005. *Governing complex societies. Trajectories and scenarios.* Basingstoke, UK: Palgrave Macmillan.

Poteete, A. R., M. Janssen, and E. Ostrom. 2010. Small-N case studies: Putting the commons under a magnifying glass. In *Working together. Collective action, the commons, and multiple methods in practice*, ed. A. R. Poteete, M. Janssen, and E. Ostrom, 31–63. Princeton, NJ: Princeton University Press.

Provan, K. G., and P. Kenis. 2007. Modes of network governance: Structure, management, and effectiveness. *Journal of Public Administration Research and Theory* 18 (2):229–52. doi:10.1093/jopart/mum015.

Provan, K. G., and H. B. Milward. 2001. Do networks really work? A framework for evaluating public-sector organizational networks. *Public Administration Review* 61 (4):414–23. doi:10.1111/0033-3352.00045.

Quirk, P. J. 2005. Restructuring state institutions: The limits of adaptive leadership. In *Adaptive governance and water conflict*, ed. J. Scholz and B. Stiftel, 204–12. Washington, DC: Taylor & Francis.

Rhodes, R. A. W. 1996. The new governance: Governing without government. *Political Studies* 44 (4):652–67.

Rhodes, R. A. W. 2007. Understanding governance: Ten years on. *Organization Studies* 28 (8): 1243–64. doi:10.1177/0170840607076586

Robins, L., and S. Dovers. 2007. NRM regions in Australia: The "haves" and the "have nots." *Geographical Research* 45 (3):273–90. doi:10.1111/j.1745-5871.2007.00460.x.

Robinson, C. J., R. Eberhard, T. Wallington, and M. Lane. 2010. Using knowledge to make collaborative policy-level decisions in Australia's Great Barrier Reef. Brisbane: CSIRO water for a healthy country technical report, Australia. http://www/.clw.csiro.au/publications/waterforahealthycountry/2010/wfhc-GBR-collaborative-decisions.pdf (accessed 4 August 2010).

Robinson, C. J., R. D. Margerum, T. M. Koontz, C. Moseley, and S. Lurie. 2011. Policy-level collaboratives for environmental management at the regional scale: Lessons and challenges from Australia and the United States. *Society & Natural Resources* 24 (8):849–59. doi:10.1080/08941920.2010.487848.

Rode, S. 2010. De l'aménagement au ménagement des cours d'eau: Le bassin de la Loire, miroir de l'évolution des rapports entre aménagement fluvial et environnement. *Cybergeo: European Journal of Geography.* 506. http://cybergeo.revues.org/23253 (accessed 24 January 2017).

Rose, N., and P. Miller. 1992. Political power beyond the state: Problematics of government. *British Journal of Sociology* 43:173–205. doi:10.2307/591464.

Ross, A., and D. Connell. 2014. The evolution of river basin management in the Murray-Darling Basin. In *The politics of river basin organisations: Coalitions, institutional design choices and consequences*, ed. D. Huitema and S. Meijerink, 326–55. Cheltenham, UK: Edward Elgar.

Ross, A., and S. Dovers. 2008. Making the harder yards: Environmental policy integration in Australia. *Australian Journal of Public Administration* 67 (3):245–60. doi:10.1111/j.1467-8500.2008.00585.x.

Sangaré, I., and C. Larrue. 2002. *The evolution of the national water regime in France.* Tours, France: Université Francois Rabelais de Tours, Centre de Recherche, Ville Société Territoire (VST).

Sending, O. J., and I. B. Neumann. 2006. Governance to governmentality: Analyzing NGOs, states, and power. *International Studies Quarterly* 50 (3):651–72. doi:10.1111/j.1468-2478.2006.00418.x.

Sørensen, E., and J. Torfing. 2007a. Metagovernance. In *Theories of democratic network governance*, ed. E. Sorensen and J. Torfing, 167–231. Basingstoke, UK: Palgrave-Macmillan.

Sørensen, E., and J. Torfing. 2007b. Introduction. Governance network research: Towards a second generation. In *Theories of democratic network governance*, ed. E. Sørensen and J. Torfing, 1–25. Basingstoke, UK: Palgrave Macmillan.

Stake, R. E., and R. Savolainen. 1995. *The art of case study research.* Thousand Oaks, CA: Sage.

Stenson, K. 2008. Governing the local: Sovereignty, social governance and community safety. *Social Work & Society* 6 (1):2–14.

van Tatenhove, J., B. Arts, and P. Leroy. 2000. *Political modernisation and the environment: The renewal of environmental policy arrangements.* Dordrecht, The Netherlands: Springer.

Vella, K., N. Sipe, A. Dale, and B. Taylor. 2015. Not learning from the past: Adaptive governance challenges for Australian Natural Resource Management. *Geographical Research* 53 (4):379–92. doi:10.1111/1745-5871.12115.

Voets, J., W. Van Dooren, and F. De Rynck. 2008. A framework for assessing the performance of policy networks. *Public Management Review* 10 (6):773–90. doi:10.1080/14719030802423129.

Vreugdenhil, H., J. Slinger, A. Smits, and E. Kater. 2008. Impacts of governance styles on river restoration in NW Europe. Conference of the International Association of Impact Assessments, Perth, Australia, May 2008.

Waterhouse, J., M. Grundy, I. Gordon, J. Brodie, R. Eberhard, and H. Yorkston. 2009. Managing the catchments of the Great Barrier Reef. In *Handbook of catchment management*, ed. R. Ferrier and J. Jenkins, 351–75. Oxford, UK: Blackwell Publishing.

Yin, R. K. 2014. *Case study research: Design and methods*, vol. 5. Thousand Oaks, CA: Sage.

Building Capacities for Sustainable Water Governance at the Grassroots: "Organic Empowerment" and Its Policy Implications in Nicaragua

Sarah T. Romano

ABSTRACT

Many of the most acute water crises globally are "everyday" crises experienced in impoverished rural areas and urban slums across the global South. Confronting these crises are thousands of community-based water management regimes—many operating "below the radar" of formal state policies. Arguably, a foremost challenge to constructing sustainable water governance concerns reconciling long-standing—yet politically and legally unrecognized—locally based governance structures with state policies designed and promoted from above. Bridging the scholarships on common property regimes and decentralized natural resource management, this article examines how policymakers and rural water committees confront the challenge of securing water access for domestic use. Specifically, this article documents the development of what is termed an "organic empowerment" of water committees in Nicaragua, arguing that this grassroots form of empowerment has contributed to the democratization of top-down policymaking. Ultimately, it reveals the complex, multiscalar tensions inherent in efforts to create new and recognize preexisting institutions for water governance.

Introduction

Many of the most acute water crises globally are the "everyday" crises experienced in impoverished rural areas and urban slums across the Global South. Confronting deteriorating infrastructure, political marginalization, and ongoing environmental degradation are thousands of community-based water management (CBWM) regimes—many operating "below the radar" of formal state policies. Despite their unofficial status, CBWM regimes have the potential to intersect and conflict with "higher up" state policymaking and institutions. For example, opposition to state policies that alter water ownership and/or management may be particularly vibrant and assertive among communities intimately involved in water extraction, use, and conservation at the grassroots. This opposition owes to the necessity of water for life and livelihoods, the intimate connection between water and processes of identity formation, as well as the de facto control of water resources on the part of communities and user groups who contest losing certain prerogatives (Perreault 2006, 2008; Boelens 2008; Boelens, Getches, and Guevara-Gil 2010; Romano 2012a; 2012b).

Color versions of one or more of the figures in the article can be found online at www.tandfonline.com/usnr.

Arguably, a foremost global challenge to constructing sustainable water governance concerns reconciling long-standing—yet politically and legally unrecognized—community-based governance structures with state policies designed and promoted from above. Recent policy shifts in Nicaragua, a country with abundant freshwater resources, yet serious problems of distribution and contamination (Baltodano and Olmedo 2001; ENACAL 2008; Kreimann 2010), demonstrate some of the issues and dynamics inherent in trying to reconcile the discrepancies between state policy and water governance in practice. When the government passed the Special Law of Potable Water and Sanitation Committees (Law 722) in 2010 it carried significant weight: The law constituted formal recognition of more than 5,000 water committees, or CAPS, who for more than three decades had been operating without full integration into state policy frameworks. Despite initial state and nongovernmental organization (NGO) investments in rural water systems, financial and technical assistance to CAPS in the wake of system construction has been limited, as well as geographically uneven over time. Limited outside assistance and a long-standing lack of legal recognition make CAPS' water management and provision impressive: CAPS manage thousands of small-scale rural water systems nationally, resulting in more than an estimated 1 million rural residents—a little more than half of the country's rural population—having improved water access (Medrano et al. 2007: 18) (see Table 1).

In practical terms, Law 722 mirrors other decentralization initiatives seeking to devolve resource management authority and responsibilities to communities. Yet the recognition of CAPS, or the Potable Water and Sanitation Committees, via Law 722 reflects more than merely an embracing of the global trend of decentralization (Ackerman 2004; Ribot, Agrawal, and Larson 2006; Dobbin and Sarathy 2015). For one thing, the law constitutes an ex post facto decentralization: Community-based management of rural water systems was an empirical reality in Nicaragua at the time of the law's passing. Second, Law 722 reflects a kind of "decentralization from below" (Larson 2005), given water committees' direct and energetic role in helping to design the law and promote its passage. In fact, 5 years before the law's passing, water committees were mobilizing to contest their exclusion from a different law (Law 620, developed in the context of primarily urban-based anti-water

Table 1. Rural water projects and beneficiaries by region in Nicaragua.

Region	Water projects	Households	Beneficiary households	Population	Population served
I	1,344	123,158	30,343	658827	169,780
II	1,218	89,187	31,769	553772	193,390
III	80	12,990	11,002	84,140	69,003
IV[a]	334	44,702	25,173	262,855	155,680
V	704	37,269	14,035	228,630	95,325
VI	1,175	92,580	40,972	597,848	269,415
VII	58	NA[b]	NA	28676	12,064
VIII	42	NA	NA	23,841	14,796
IX	63	NA	NA	38988	16784
Total	5,017	399,886	153,294	2,477,577	996,237

Note. These figures come from data collected in the National Information System of Rural Water and Sanitation (SINAS), a database created by the Nicaraguan government and international donors in the mid-1990s to document water projects. Data reflect documented water systems and estimated population served through part of 2004 only. Each region corresponds to the following departments: I: Estelí, Madriz, Nueva Segovia; II: León, Chinandega; III: Managua; IV: Carazo, Granada, Masaya, Rivas; V: Boaco, Chontales; VI: Jinotega, Matagalpa, VII: Región Autónoma del Atlántico Norte (RAAN), VIII: Región Autónoma del Atlántico Sur (RAAS), IX: Río San Juan.
[a]Figures include 20 water projects in the Río San Juan and 163 in the RAAS.
[b]Data not available.

privatization protests in the early 2000s), which aimed to provide a comprehensive management framework for the country's freshwater resources (Avendaño 2004; Novo and Garrido 2010; Romano 2012a).

Drawing on extensive field research in Nicaragua, this article examines rural water management over time to assess how a long-standing, de facto empowerment of water committees has helped to democratize top-down efforts to restructure the water sector, largely evident in grassroots mobilization for the passing of a new water law. In so doing, the article explores how policymakers and rural communities of water users and managers confront the governance challenge of securing water access for domestic use across state and nonstate, formal and informal, and urban and rural divides. Specifically, it asks: How have rural water committees become empowered to manage water resources? How does this empowerment affect grassroots actors' legitimacy vis-à-vis residents for whom water access is facilitated? Lastly, how do locally generated empowerment and legitimacy come to bear on top-down, state-led efforts to devise and implement new water policies?

To answer these questions, this article bridges the scholarships on common property regimes (CPRs) and decentralized natural resource management (DNRM) in order to grant attention to formal policies in the first and the role of unofficial actors in natural resource governance in the second. Specifically, the article documents the development of what is termed an "organic empowerment" of rural water committees: that is, an empowerment emerging from the day-to-day labors of water management at the grassroots, rather than from state-conferred responsibilities via decentralization. Examining CAPS as CPRs reveals that an evolving empowerment at the grassroots generates capacities that not only facilitate sustained water access—infusing water committees with legitimacy vis-à-vis system beneficiaries—but also tend to exceed those of urban-based state actors in the sector. Moreover, this bottom-up form of empowerment has influenced top-down efforts to restructure the water sector: CAPS have leveraged their de facto water management roles and responsibilities to contest their political exclusion and promote the passage of a new law "decentralizing" responsibilities to their rural institutions. Ultimately, examining the intersecting realms of unofficial and formal water governance reveals the complex, multiscalar tensions inherent in efforts to create new, as well as to recognize preexisting, institutions for water governance.

Research Design

Research for this article was conducted across 12 months in Nicaragua (during 2007–2010). To document how CAPS have become empowered to manage water resources, semistructured interviews were conducted with 16 water committees, each with their own water system, in addition to two interviews with CAPS representing multiple communities. Those interviewed were selected via convenience sampling based upon their organizations' participation in newly formed "CAPS networks" at the municipal and national levels. CAPS selected for interviews also constitute an intentional sample in terms of how they represent operational common property regimes (see later discussion) in terms of water provision facilitated; in other words, only CAPS reflecting high operational effectiveness were selected.

Fifteen of the interviews were conducted in the municipalities, and in some cases communities, where the CAPS worked; these municipalities include El Tuma-La Dalia,

Esquipulas, Jinotega, Las Sabanas, Masaya, Matagalpa, Muy Muy, San Dionisio, San Ramón, and Sébaco. Other interviews, including numerous informal interviews, were conducted at network meetings in Managua and Matagalpa (for all interview locations see Figure 1). CAPS network meetings also served as sites of extensive participation observation. The geographic scope and age diversity (ranging several years to several decades) of CAPS allowed for assessing origins and operations across time, prior to the passing of Law 722.

This article's analysis is also informed by interviews with staff at multilateral organizations, international and domestic NGOs, and government agencies working in the water and sanitation sector in Nicaragua, some of which had substantial experience in the sector (20–30 years). These interviews help to reveal extralocal perspectives on grassroots water management, and also provide a window of insight into how state actors and NGOs have worked with CAPS over time.

All interviews were recorded and transcribed. Interviews with CAPS members were coded thematically. Five different, albeit overlapping, dimensions of water management emerged across these: technical, financial, organizational, environmental, and legal/political (see Table 2). In the article's analysis, the work performed by CAPS in each of these five areas serves as inductively derived indicators of their empowerment as water managers.

The article also draws upon government, NGO, and foreign donor reports and documents to further contextualize CAPS' water management and provide evidence of the remarkable consistency in water committees' origins and operations over time. The article's conclusion and questions for future research were informed by 2 weeks of exploratory research regarding implementation of the new CAPS law in June 2014.

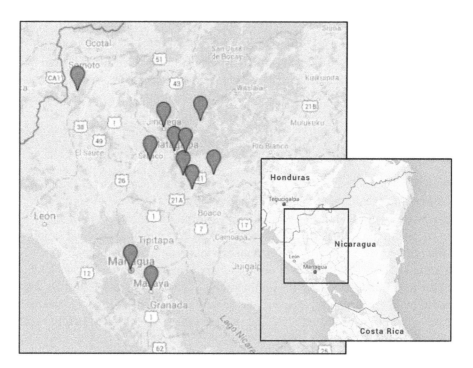

Figure 1. CAPS interview locations.

Table 2. Dimensions of water management demonstrating empowerment.

Technical

Water system construction
Repairing/replacing broken tubes
Installation, maintenance, and reading of water meters
Cleaning water storage tanks and aqueducts
Water chlorination/filtration
Water shutoffs/reconnections

Financial

Collecting user tariffs
Financial record keeping
Fundraising
Appealing to NGOs, international agencies, and local governments for financial support of water projects

Organizational

Maintaining users' registry
Convening/facilitating users' assemblies
Organizing users for participation in water management activities
Enacting formal rule changes
Training incoming leaders
Implementing relevant educational activities
Coordinating with other community groups and state agencies
Design principles 1–6

Environmental

Reforesting around water storage tanks and recharge zones
Day-to-day educational work and periodic campaigns to prevent/regulate deforestation, water contamination, and
   inappropriate and/or excessive water use

Legal/political

Negotiating intracommunity access to water sources and land for water distribution systems
Pressuring state agencies/officials to implement environmental regulations
Advocating for legal recognition of local organizations and ownership over water sources/systems
Design principles 7–8

Note. Each of these areas of water management is meant to be illustrative, rather than comprehensive, nor are these meant
   to imply that each CAPS interviewed and observed during research carry out all of these functions—despite having
   activity in each category.

Empowerment and Legitimacy in Community-Based Natural Resource Management

This article draws together two distinct scholarship areas to account for the increasingly complex and multi-scalar character of CBWM. Independently, the common property regime (CPR) and decentralized natural resource management (DNRM) scholarships have made outstanding contributions toward understanding the conditions under which state and nonstate actors manage resources viably over time. Since their original challenges to Hardin's (1968) "tragedy of the commons" argument, CPR scholars have examined a number of elements associate with "successful" resource management, including small group size, locally devised systems of rules, clearly delineated resource boundaries, and effective local monitoring arrangements (Feeny et al. 1990; Ostrom 1990; 2002; Becker and Ostrom 1995; Gibson, Williams, and Ostrom 2005; Sandier 2010). The CPR scholarship recognizes that local institutions are embedded in and interact with larger scale governance systems (Berkes 2002; Ostrom 2009, 422; see also the scholarship on polycentricity, e.g., Pahl-Wostl 2009; Ostrom 2010). Nevertheless, because of its inherent interest in the microlevel dynamics of resource management, the scholarship has paid relatively less attention to state policies and institutions and the myriad ways these matter for grassroots resource management.

In contrast, scholars of DNRM have emphasized "higher" political and broader geographic scales, shedding light on state devolutions of decision-making authority to lower administrative levels (Narayan 1994; Crook and Manor 1998; Ribot 1999, 2007, 2011; Agrawal and Gupta 2005; Ribot and Larson 2005; Ribot, Agrawal, and Larson 2006). Relevant subnational actors include local governments, as well as community-based groups; however, the DNRM scholarship's emphasis on state policy has often left local-level, unofficial actors involved in resource governance outside the frame of analysis. Murphree, for instance, describes a "properly empowered" regime as one that "operates with the freedom of any public, non-state organization with a legal persona" Murphree (2009, 2559). Kull, citing Ribot (1999), asserts that for "legitimate community institutions" to be "enfranchised … [decision]-making power comes through *empowerment*, which occurs when the decentralization of resource management gives not just responsibilities, but also rights, to local communities" (2002, 58, emphasis in original). Arguably, this emphasis on formal actors results in a missed opportunity to examine alternative, nonstate sources of empowerment and legitimacy in resource governance.

This article refers to an "organic empowerment" as one that evolves at the grassroots, emerging out of the day-to-day labors and relationships associated with managing resources. Not dependent upon formal decentralization initiatives, empowerment may be either a formally conferred or de facto access to, and control over, local resources, entailing significant capacity building, decision making, and leadership (Narayan 1994; see also Fuys and Dohrn 2010). Organic empowerment serves as a conceptual bridge between CPR and decentralization frameworks because it draws attention to the empowerment of grassroots, including "unofficial," actors in resource governance, and facilitates examination of how locally grounded capacities and the legitimacy they generate may influence state policies.

A notable pattern observed in cases of CBWM globally since the 1970s is that the initial moment of empowerment often is indebted to outside financial, technical, and organizational investment in water infrastructure on the part of state and nonstate actors (Trevett and Nuñez 1998; Schouten and Moriarty 2008).[1] Much of this investment reflects short-lived financing and technical support and has not produced organizations embedded within state legal or policy frameworks. As a result, "[Customary] law and practice continues to be the most common source of legitimacy for [resource] access rights" (Fuys and Dohrn 2010, 198). Furthermore, CBWM regimes for both drinking and irrigation water have in many cases emerged without outside investments in attempts to meet water access needs (Murtinho et al. 2013).[2] Nevertheless, we must look beyond the initial moment of "empowerment" to understand this process, given evidence that empowerment can evolve as community-based actors build their capacities and exercise leadership and authority over time.

For example, water rights, or "authorized" use of water within a local system of rules and norms, often develop at the grassroots in the absence of state authorization (Boelens and Doornbos 2002; Boelens and Hoogendam 2002; Hoogesteger 2013). Empowerment to access and control water can emerge out of users "taking part in the organisation, design and construction of the irrigation system, and [when users] *consolidate and re-create their rights by maintaining and rehabilitating the system*" (Boelens 2002, 145, emphasis added). This parallels the Nicaraguan case where problem solving, decision making, and capacity building over time reinforce drinking-water committees' "initial" empowerment and infuse them with legitimacy vis-à-vis system beneficiaries.

Accounting for diverse sources of empowerment to manage resources can help to explain how legitimacy may "scale up" with unofficial CBWM regimes as they act collectively. Legitimacy, identified as buy-in and acceptance of authorities, rules, and norms (Kull 2002), can be understood as both contributing to and resulting from resource management. That is, locally empowered resource managers are likely to generate legitimacy vis-à-vis residents when they effectively facilitate resource access. Simultaneously, beneficiaries' payment of tariffs and participation in community assemblies reflect buy-in and acceptance of resource managers, which may, in turn, serve to strengthen the latter and their access regimes. Importantly, in the case of community-based drinking-water management, resource managers may derive additional legitimacy from the fact that they not only manage natural resources, but are also "service providers," hence fulfilling a function associated with the state (see Romano 2012b).

Understanding how legitimacy transcends the local matters in part because community responses to state water policies and politics are themselves multiscalar. Much scholarship has sought to capture the cross-scalar organizational processes of water users and managers, drawing attention to factors prompting mobilization and bolstering collective action at broader geographic and higher political scales (Perreault 2003; 2006; 2008; Boelens 2008; Thayer 2010; Hoogesteger 2012; 2013; Hoogesteger and Verzijl 2015; Llano-Arias 2015; Romano 2016; see also Fox 1996). This article pays particular attention to how legitimacy "scales up" with community-based actors, potentially influencing interactions with state officials.

The water committees interviewed and observed in Nicaragua for this article are by no means a representative sample. Indeed, the absence of comprehensive documentation of CAPS and water systems nationally challenges efforts to conduct representative research. However, empirical illustrations drawn from these cases generate insight into diverse dimensions of resource management reflected in the CPR scholarship, as well as into how this complex and in ways sophisticated work cannot easily be taken over by state actors, who often lack the necessary capacities and local legitimacy. The following section documents CAPS' organic empowerment as resource managers through examining the technical, financial, organizational, environmental, and legal/political dimensions of their water management (see Table 2, which references overlap with the CPR "design principles" delineating characteristics of enduring CPRs [Ostrom 1990]). The subsequent and final empirical section explores how locally generated empowerment, and resulting legitimacy, have scaled up with CAPS to influence negotiations with public officials, including advocacy for a new law recognizing CBWM regimes in Nicaragua.

"Organic Empowerment": Water Management and Service Provision at the Grassroots

In the absence of an official state policy conferring legal rights and prerogatives, water committees in Nicaragua have become empowered to manage water resources at the grassroots. Historically, most CAPS' "initial" moment of empowerment in regard to gaining access to and control over drinking water supplies (via new infrastructure like wells and gravity-fed systems) has depended upon the resources of NGOs, multilateral organizations, and state agencies. Indeed, since the mid-1970s, the synergistic efforts of domestic and international, as well as state and nonstate, actors have funded water projects—reflecting a pattern of contributions to the sector across Central America

(Donahue 1983; Trevett and Nuñez 1998; Fresh Water Action Network Central America [FANCA] 2006). Over time, these contributions have provided the necessary funding and initial training for the emergence of grassroots committees devoted to management of drinking water in rural areas (INAA 1989; Medrano et al. 2007; Romano 2012b), even though they have not taken place within a formal DNRM framework devolving resource management responsibilities to communities.

Undoubtedly, lack of *personería jurídica*—or legal personality—challenges aspects of CAPS' water management, like legal control over water systems. As one water-sector report explained, "Once the [water] systems are constructed, they are handed over the CAPS, who, lacking legal status, legally cannot receive them" (Government of Nicaragua and PAHO 2004, 100). However, a tenuous relationship to formal policies and state actors has granted, even if unwittingly, the space for water committees to work autonomously and develop solutions to water access and environmental problems. Indeed, the roles of NGO and state actors have been limited and uneven across communities in regard to helping generate and maintain water provision capacities over time. This owes to limited public resources; a bias toward investing public resources in urban, as opposed to rural, infrastructure; and high levels of government turnover that limit development of human capacities in the sector (INAA 1989; Baltodano and Olmedo 2001; Government of Nicaragua and PAHO 2004; Gómez, Ravnborg, and Rivas 2007; Medrano et al. 2007; Romano 2012b; Smit et al. 2012).

In an important, survival-related, sense, the sustained work of many CAPS is not surprising; water as a resource "*requires* a permanent spatially, socially, and functionally bound organization" (Hoogesteger 2013, 71, emphasis added). What is noteworthy for understanding the evolution of empowerment, though, is how the "the practical work of the organization" (Beccar, Boelens, and Hoogendam 2002, 17) promotes reinforcing and strengthening of CAPS' capacities. In other words, empowerment evolves organically at the grassroots via the significant capacity building, decision making, and problem solving that water management entails.

CAPS' everyday practices to manage infrastructure and facilitate water provision have fostered know-how and capacities in the technical, financial, organizational, environmental, and legal realms of local water management. Communities typically receive some minimal technical training from donor organizations or government staff at the time of water system construction. Yet because they are unable to depend on continued assistance, CAPS seek ways to sustain water provision as problems arise. One particular, increasingly prevalent, issue is that of water systems ceasing to function or verging on obsolescence. As confirmed by NGO staff members working in system construction, most systems are intended to last for 15–20 years. As of 2002, an estimated 18% of the 4,886 documented water systems were "out of use" (Government of Nicaragua and PAHO 2004). Some have become defunct from old age, and others are broken because residents lack the technical skills and/or resources to maintain them. As a 2003 report found, "Very few new CAPS members receive a (formal or informal) training from a [Municipal Operation and Maintenance Unit] (Regional or Municipal) promoter" (ENACAL 2003).

Yet even when they have not been trained for certain tasks, CAPS demonstrate having developed certain capacities, as well as innovations to problem solve. An estimated 70% of communities have a resident sufficiently qualified to do basic plumbing work on systems (Government of Nicaragua and PAHO 2004). One CAPS coordinator in Muy Muy explained that because of this internal capacity, communities can be largely self-sufficient in managing their water systems: "We have people who know how to plumb, who know how to build, and who have other skills we can use" (interview, August 22, 2008). An engineer who began working in rural water and sanitation in Nicaragua as part of UNICEF in 1988 expressed surprise that many CAPS function as well as they do without much external support (interview, January 26, 2010). He observed CAPS' technical ingenuity in the municipality of San Isidrio: Residents in one community utilized old hand pumps imported from India that UNICEF had installed 20–25 years ago; they were still functional because CAPS members began to build spare parts for the system as repair needs arose. This technical innovation ensured not only ongoing water access, but also organizational sustainability as the CAPS could "work" again as water managers.

Notably, the more rural, geographically isolated CAPS tend to be those with greater capacities, compared to peri-urban, or semirural, communities (Kreimann 2010). A lack of access to capable state actors in the sector means that communities often have no choice but to problem solve independently—a behavior that may also be reinforced through experience with local government in particular. A water *técnico* in Pueblo Nuevo, Estelí, recounted his response to a resident's request to have him dismantle the community's well pump. He responded, "I had never dismantled that. It would be irresponsible of me to take it apart [and] people in the community were trained to do that" (interview, February 4, 2010). Interestingly, although the *técnico* believed the CAPS "should" have the capacity to dismantle the pump on their own, this seeking of support does not necessarily mean the capacity was absent, but rather that rural residents held certain expectations of local government officials (Narayan 1994). However, a perhaps more significant observation is that the government water and sanitation "expert" in this case had inadequate working knowledge of the infrastructure used by residents in the municipality.[3]

CAPS' capacities to modify and implement local rules not only strengthen their water management, but also generate legitimacy vis-à-vis system beneficiaries. Arguably, the capacity to collect user fees (between $0.23 and $2.85 per month per household for water service) reflects legitimacy of these local authorities. Rules regarding fees also may be "broken," reflecting local norms and CAPS' appropriate accommodations for residents. As the Compasagüe 2, Muy Muy, coordinator explained:

> We don't enforce them because we have few resources. The majority of the women, we leave to harvest coffee each year. When we get back ... the majority of us only pay 120 *córdobas* a year [for our water]. It's a difficulty of the project, not complying with the rules, but it's not that we don't want to, but rather that we have scarce resources, [and that] we understand each other [in the community]. (interview, August 21, 2008)

Across CAPS, similar accommodations are made for families engaged in seasonal labor and without a constant flow of monetary resources during the year. In La Labranza, Matagalpa, the CAPS remains "flexible," according to its treasurer, "because we're the same family" (interview, December 11, 2009). The tendency not to cut off residents' water supply negates many CAPS' by-laws stipulate cutting off water for nonpayment of user fees or for lateness. While rules such as this could reflect the influence of NGOs and state actors at the time of system construction, they point to a more important issue CAPS confront: Their water systems are inherently expensive, and sustaining them proves challenging in local contexts with high levels of poverty. While the capacity to collect fees varies across CAPS, their "breaking" the rules reflects a local social embeddedness—one generating legitimacy not easily taken over by extralocal actors.

Legitimacy also emerges out of and is reflected in CAPS' ability to organize and engage residents in water management. Rules vary by community, though they typically include provisions for elected leadership turnover, system maintenance, payment for water service, environmental stewardship, and financial management. Rules can be hard to enforce; for example, even though collective choice arrangements, such as users' assemblies, may exist (Ostrom 1990), they may not be embraced. In El Zapote, San Dionisio, the CAPS once struggled to get residents to attend community-wide assemblies (interview, May 19, 2010). The CAPS implemented a risky, albeit ingenious, strategy to increase participation: They cut off the water. The secretary proclaimed that they no longer had problems with attendance after sending this "message." Notably, breaking one of their own rules (i.e., related to water shutoffs) contributed to improving the effectiveness of another one (i.e., participation in community-wide assemblies). Residents' compliance with the rules—in this case via coercion—speaks to the CAPS' legitimacy as local authorities.[4]

Addressing environmental issues also reinforces CAPS' empowerment and engenders legitimacy. Observed CAPS embraced various measures to slow or counter environmentally degrading processes like contamination of water sources and deforestation (at the same time that many recognized that such problems transcend their communities in physical terms). CAPS undertake health and sanitation education and promote cleanups around water sources. Many reforest around water storage tanks to produce shade and to promote better holding of underground water. These kinds of environmental "solutions" may intersect with financial problem solving as well: One community in Sébaco reforested their water source with fruit, and sells this fruit locally to raise money for the CAPS (interview, February 3, 2010). Notably, one local government water *técnico* emphasized the importance of CAPS' environmental stewardship, given his office's own limited capacity to contribute to problem solving (interview, February 26, 2010). Overall, the proactive behavior of CAPS to fulfill the function of environmental stewardship—one legally assigned to the state—lends legitimacy to these local institutions and bestows on them "public" authority (Lund 2006).

The legal–political dimensions of local water management, while complicated by most CAPS' lack of legal status, also provide evidence of how an empowerment process evolves "organically" at the grassroots. The navigation of legal gray areas can develop CAPS' political capacities and sense of agency. A San Ramón CAPS depends upon its relationship to the local cooperative to uphold its non-legally binding agreement with a previous landowner to concede the water source to the community. Contrastingly, in San Dionisio, a CAPS used community donations to ensure that water piping was laid on public, versus private, property, thus avoiding sometimes tricky negotiations with landowners. In San Esteban 2, Jinotega, community members amassed 10,000 *córdobas* to purchase access to the water source upon which they currently depend. Despite the disadvantages of operating in a legal gray area—including tenuous land and water rights—CAPS must negotiate use of local resources in order to facilitate water access for residents, which in turn has a legitimacy-enhancing effect.

Empowerment and Legitimacy Across Scales: Water Committees' Policy Interventions

How does an "organic empowerment" come to bear on political negotiations and policy interventions at extralocal scales? Arguably, insight into the instrumentality of CAPS' empowerment beyond the local can be gained through examining extralocal perceptions of and responses to water committees as they mobilized, starting in the mid-2000s. Similar to dynamics observed in the Andes (see Boelens 2002; Hoogesteger 2013), extralocal allies in Nicaragua, including NGOs and bilateral/multilateral organizations, played crucial roles facilitating the mobilization of water committees. To assist in the formation of transcommunity "CAPS networks," allies provided funding for transportation, food, and lodging for meetings; led capacity-building trainings on national legislation; and supported the process of coordinating a "National CAPS Network," including its (successful) application for legal status as a nonprofit association.[5] These relationships and alliances reflect an understanding and promotion of CAPS as legitimately empowered actors in water governance. From another angle, these forms of bridging social capital (Woolcock and Narayan 2000) demonstrate the transcendence of CAPS' legitimacy as resource managers beyond "local" water governance realms.

When the government passed the General Water Law (Law 620) in 2007, CAPS had already started to mobilize, protesting their exclusion from the first "legal institutional framework for the administration, conservation, development, [and] use ... of all existing water resources in the country" (Art. 1) that "hid the CAPS," as one key informant expressed (interview, August 18, 2008). Yet, as it was in regard to allies, a "popular acceptance" (Kull 2002) of CAPS was observed on the part of media and government officials. National media depictions of CAPS prior to the passing of Law 722 reflected CAPS as legitimately empowered, albeit underrecognized, authorities in water management. As one national newspaper article articulated, CAPS "were not contemplated nor included in the General Water Law ... *despite the fact that the CAPS provide [water] service to 53 percent of the rural population*" (García 2008). Government officials echoed buy-in to CAPS' legitimacy as water managers: As the director of the regional office for watershed management in Estelí asserted, "The CAPS are the cornerstones of the [rural] water systems. [State] institutions don't help them ... but in one way or another they are maintaining their systems" (interview, February 3, 2010).

Most consequentially for public policy processes, state lawmakers' public discourses in early 2010 reflected an understanding of CAPS as empowered and legitimate actors in water governance. An Environment and Natural Resources Commission report sent to the President described CAPS as

> groups of voluntarily organized people at the community level, in charge of the maintenance and sustainability of potable water and sanitation projects. In few words, *taking actions and making efforts [gestiones] that correspond to the state* to assure the population's access to the vital liquid in the urban-rural zones in the country. (Rodríguez et al. 2008; emphasis added)

This kind of recognition of water committees encourages enlarging DNRM frames of analysis: CAPS are not yet "legitimate community institutions" via state policy (Kull 2002), but they are, undeniably, "empowered." Moreover, the state-like nature of CAPS' work clearly contributed to the acceptance of CAPS as legitimate actors in water governance. Strikingly, the bipartisan commission worked with the National CAPS Network to draft a new law. This collaboration constituted novel political recognition and inclusion in water policy formation and stood in stark contrast to CAPS' recent exclusion from the development of the General Water Law.

Negotiations regarding content of the law were not without tensions, however. One of the main struggles ensued between CAPS and the state water company (ENACAL) over whether or not CAPS would keep their "S." At a November 2009 meeting at the National Assembly, CAPS defended the S on the basis of their basic sanitation work, despite ENACAL staffs' claims that water committees do not construct *pilas de recepción*, or waste storage tanks. As one CAPS member recounted:

> We said to the deputies that maybe we didn't do that, but we were chlorinating water in the communities and examining sanitation [practices], seeing that people don't burn trash, that they don't allow water to pool. That yes, it wasn't the sanitization that [ENACAL] provides, but it was a basic sanitation. How are we going to make [waste] storage tanks? (interview, June 14, 2010)

CAPS' strategy to defend the "S" was successful.[6] What this negotiation shows, in part, is the practical importance of cross-sectoral dialogue in policymaking spheres. Crafting a legitimate, inclusive, and, in ways, accurate "decentralization" policy was only possible through bringing CAPS to the table as stakeholders in water governance.

The Special CAPS Law (Law 722) passed in 2010 delineates CAPS' responsibilities in water system rehabilitation, maintenance, and expansion; prevention and control of water contamination at the subnational level; and water distribution in accordance with systems' technical capacities. Day-to-day organizational tasks, such as convening meetings, collecting fees, and authorizing and suspending service in accordance with local by-laws, are also detailed. Importantly, the law outlines a process for CAPS' registration with local governments and the national regulatory agency for water and sanitation, INAA; this legal pathway must be followed for a CAPS to benefit from certain provisions of the law like differentiated energy tariffs and tax exemptions, provisions for which water committees themselves advocated.

Conclusion: Toward a Broader Theory of "Community-Based" Water Management

Resolving tensions inherent in a process of ex post facto decentralization necessitates dialogue across state and nonstate, urban and rural, and formal and unofficial "divides." Navigating these interfaces may be particularly important, albeit challenging, in national contexts in which urban-based state actors have played a limited role in rural water management and thus have little experiential or substantive basis for designing a law delineating the work of rural water governance institutions. In contrast to irrigation systems that may have been state managed and then transferred to local residents, small-scale drinking-water regimes in rural areas in Latin America tend not to replace the state because, in most cases, the state was never there. The Nicaraguan case may offer a useful public policy experience to other countries and regions where de facto CBWM regimes have historically been, and remain, the most prevalent means of drinking water access in rural areas.

In conceptual and theoretical terms, the concept of an "organic empowerment" to manage resources proves useful for articulating the intersection of CPR and DNRM frameworks. Unofficial, yet operational, resource management regimes engender legitimacy that may transcend grassroots realms of water management to influence formal decentralization policy. While the Nicaraguan case confirms the significance of the micro-level resource management CPR scholars have documented, not least in terms of the local empowerment and legitimacy this work reflects, it also encourages enlarging the frame of analysis to examine CPR institutions' interactions beyond the community level.

Similarly, better understanding of organically empowered resource management regimes requires expanding the DNRM's conceptual and analytical frames to encompass alternative, nonstate sources of empowerment embodied by many CPRs. The Nicaraguan case confirms the importance of the scholarship's emphasis on empowerment and legitimacy in community-based resource governance. Yet it challenges the idea that these qualities must be transferred from above to local actors. Resource management regimes have diverse sources of empowerment from which legitimacy is ultimately derived. Recognizing this in studies of DNRM has the potential to produce more comprehensive understandings and characterizations of water governance, as well as to inform more comprehensive and appropriate water policies, like the CAPS Law in Nicaragua (see also Bellamy et al. and Duncan, this issue, on the participation of community-based actors in water governance in Australia and New Zealand, respectively).

Not surprisingly, CAPS' official empowerment in Nicaragua raises new practical and policy questions. Future research must assess the short- and long-term effects of attempting to integrate water committees into state legal-institutional frameworks, especially as countries across Latin America continue to move in this direction (e.g., Ministerio del Medio Ambiente y Recursos Naturales [MARN] 2011; Urbano Rural 2015). Formalization, like unofficial legal status, will likely be a double-edged sword for CAPS. How will the trend of greater formalization influence capacities and the availability of resources for water management at the grassroots? For CAPS choosing to register with the state, how will oversight and reporting mechanisms affect the diversity of current community norms and practices, especially those that reflect heterogeneous local circumstances and needs—and thus do not conform to the liberal state's tendency to treat local water rights systems as homogeneous (Boelens 2009)? The implications of Law 722 beyond certain practical aspects merit examination as well. How has novel inclusion in policy processes affected CAPS' sense of political efficacy and legitimacy beyond the communities in which they work? What is the potential for sustained attempts at political engagement at broadened geographic and political scales, especially as CAPS start to confront the implications of greater formalization? Pursuit of these kinds of questions would be fruitful toward assessing the dynamism of water governance in practice, including its state and nonstate, formal and informal, and urban and rural complexity. Across diverse contexts, the challenge for scholars and policymakers will continue to be recognizing what lies "below the radar," yet remains fundamentally connected to, multidimensional and multiscalar landscapes of water governance.

Acknowledgments

Thank you to Kent Eaton and Jonathan Fox for comments on an earlier version of this article that promoted its development. Additional gratitude is owed to the editors of this special issue and three anonymous reviewers for detailed substantive and conceptual feedback that helped to strengthen the article.

Funding

Research for this article was funded by Fulbright, the University of California Pacific Rim Research Program, the UC Santa Cruz Chicano/Latino Research Center, and the UC Santa Cruz Department of Politics.

Notes

1. CBWM regimes in the Global South began to flourish in the context of growing international financial support for water system construction starting in in the 1970s (e.g., Fresh Water Action Network Central America [FANCA] 2006; Schouten and Moriarty 2008).
2. Arguably, even cases of urban "water theft" reflect this kind of self-organization and empowerment for water access (in particular see Meehan 2013, 326).
3. Although CAPS observed for this study demonstrate the potential for residents to develop competencies for operation and maintenance (O&M), the contribution of Naiga et al. (this issue) highlights, importantly, the persistence of major O&M challenges for rural communities in the Global South.
4. Thanks to an anonymous reviewer for raising the point that legitimacy vis-à-vis residents can exist "along with disempowerment/exclusion of marginal groups in the community," something that may help to explain nonattendance and nonparticipation at assemblies.
5. As of 2010, more than 30 municipal CAPS networks had formed across the country and more than 80 municipalities had sent CAPS members to participate as representatives in the national network. While they constituted a critical mass for the purpose of political and policy interventions, only a fraction of the thousands of active CAPS members participated in national-level collective action.
6. Another CAPS member gave her interpretation of the negotiations: "I think the bottom line for ENACAL was the budget. They said that if the CAPS took [responsibility for] sanitation, it would take [from them] half of [their] national level budget. They wanted sanitation for themselves, because sanitation brings money, even from the international organizations" (interview, June 4, 2010).

References

Ackerman, J. 2004. Co-governance for accountability: Beyond 'exit' and 'voice.' *World Development* 32 (3):447–63. doi:10.1016/j.worlddev.2003.06.015

Agrawal, A., and K. Gupta. 2005. Decentralization and participation: The governance of common pool resources in Nepal's Terai. *World Development* 33 (7):1101–14. doi:10.1016/j.worlddev.2005.04.009

Avendaño, N. 2004. *Nicaragua: el proceso de la privatización del agua*. Managua, Nicaragua: Ediciones Educativas, Diseño e Impresiones S.A.

Baltodano, F., and J. Olmedo. 2001. Evaluación de la Decentralización de la UNOM en Comunidades de los Departamentos de Matagalpa y Jinotega. MA thesis, Universidad Nacional Autónoma de Nicaragua, Managua, Nicaragua.

Beccar, L., R. Boelens, and P. Hoogendam. 2002. Water rights and collective action in community irrigation. In *Water rights and empowerment*, ed. R. Boelens and P. Hoogendam 1–21. Assen, The Netherlands: Van Gorcum.

Becker, C. D., and E. Ostrom. 1995. Human ecology and resource sustainability: The importance of institutional diversity. *Annual Review of Ecology and Systematics* 26:113–33. doi:10.1146/annurev.es.26.110195.000553

Berkes, F. 2002. Cross-scale institutional linkages: Perspectives from the bottom up. In *The drama of the commons*, ed. E. Ostrom 255–321. Washington, DC: National Academy Press.

Boelens, R. 2002. Recipes and resistance: Peasants' rights building and empowerment in the Licto Irrigation System, Ecuador. In *Water rights and empowerment*, ed. R. Boelens and P. Hoogendam 144–72. Assen, The Netherlands: Van Gorcum.

Boelens, R. 2008. Water rights arenas in the Andes: Upscaling networks to strengthen local water control. *Water Alternatives* 1 (1):46–55.

Boelens, R. 2009. The politics of disciplining water rights. *Development and Change* 40 (2):307–31. doi:10.1111/j.1467-7660.2009.01516.x

Boelens, R., and B. Doornbos. 2002. The battlefield of water rights: Rule-making and empowerment in the arena of conflicting normative frameworks—Irrigation development in Ceceles, Ecuador. In *Water rights and empowerment*, ed. R. Boelens and P. Hoogendam 217–239. Assen, The Netherlands: Van Gorcum.

Boelens, R., D. Getches, and A. Guevara-Gil. 2010. Water struggles and the politics of identity. In *Out of the mainstream: Water rights, politics and identity*, 1–25. London, UK: Earthscan.

Boelens, R., and P. Hoogendam (eds). 2002. *Water rights and empowerment*. Assen, Netherlands: Van Gorcum.

Crook, R. C., and J. Manor. 1998. *Democracy and decentralisation in South Asia and West Africa: Participation, accountability, and performance*. New York, NY: Cambridge University Press.

Dobbin, K. B., and B. Sarathy. 2015. Solving rural water exclusion: Challenges and limits to co-management in Costa Rica. *Society & Natural Resources* 28:388–404. doi:10.1080/08941920.2014.948245

Donahue, J. M. 1983. The politics of health care in Nicaragua before and after the revolution of 1979. *Human Organization* 42 (3):264–72. doi:10.17730/humo.42.3.x737h47hqw3r2785

ENACAL. 2003. *La Decentralización De La Unidad Nacional De Operación y Mantenimiento*. Managua, Nicaragua: ENACAL.

ENACAL. 2008. Plan de Desarrollo Institucional de ENACAL: 2008–2012. Nicaraguan Institute of Water and Sanitation. http://www.enacal.com.ni/informacion/Wc89973b236e289.htm

Feeny, D., F. Berkes, B. J. McCay, and J. M. Acheson. 1990. The tragedy of the commons: twenty-two years later. *Human Ecology* 18:1–19. doi:10.1007/bf00889070

Fox, J. 1996. How does civil society thicken? The political construction of social capital in Rural Mexico. *World Development* 24 (6):1089–103. doi:10.1016/0305-750x(96)00025-3

Fresh Water Action Network Central America. 2006. Las Juntas de Agua en CentroAmérica: Valoración de la Gestión Local del Recurso Hídrico.

Fuys, A., and S. Dohrn. 2010. Common property regimes: Taking a closer look at resource access, authorization, and legitimacy. In *Beyond the biophysical: Knowledge, culture, and power in agriculture and natural resource management*, ed. L. German, R. Verma, and J. J. Ramisch 193–214. New York, NY: Springer.

García, N. 2008. CAPS Se Multiplican Para Saciar La Sed Rural. *El Nuevo Diario*, July 15. http://www.elnuevodiario.com.ni/contactoend/21361

Gibson, C., J. T. Williams, and E. Ostrom. 2005. Local enforcement and better forests. *World Development* 33 (2):273–84. doi:10.1016/j.worlddev.2004.07.013

Gómez, L. I., H. M. Ravnborg, and R. H. Rivas. 2007. *Institucionalidad Para La Gestión Del Agua En Nicaragua*. Managua, Nicaragua: Managua: Institución de Investigación y Desarollo Nitlapán.

Government of Nicaragua, and PAHO. 2004. *Análisis sectorial de agua potable y saneamiento de Nicaragua*. Managua, Nicaragua: Government of Nicaragua and PAHO.

Hardin, G. 1968. Tragedy of the commons. *Science* 162:1243–48.

Hoogesteger, J. 2012. Democratizing water governance from the grassroots: The development of Interjuntas-Chimorazo in the Ecuadorain Andes. *Human Organization* 71 (1):76–86. doi:10.17730/humo.71.1.b8v77j0321u28863

Hoogesteger, J. 2013. Social capital in water user organizations of the Ecuadorian highlands. *Human Organization* 72 (4):347–57. doi:10.17730/humo.72.4.jv2177g624q35253

Hoogesteger, J., and A. Verzijl 2015. Grassroots scalar politics: Insights from peasant water struggles in the Ecuadorian and Peruvian Andes. *Geoforum* 62:13–23. doi:10.1016/j.geoforum.2015.03.013

INAA. 1989. *Los Acueductos Rurales En Nicaragua*. Managua, Nicaragua: INAA.

Kreimann, R. 2010. The rural CAPS: Ensuring community access to water. *Revista Envío* 339. http://www.envio.org.ni/articulo/4197

Kull, C. A. 2002. Empowering pyromaniacs in Madagascar: Ideology and legitimacy in community-based natural resource management. *Development and Change* 33 (1):57–78. doi:10.1111/1467-7660.00240

Larson, A. 2005. Formal decentralisation and the imperative of decentralisation 'from below': A case study of natural resource management in Nicaragua. *European Journal of Development Research* 16 (1):55–70. doi:10.1080/09578810410001688734

Llano-Arias, V. 2015. Community knowledge sharing and co-production of water services: Two cases of community aqueduct associations in Colombia. *Water Alternatives* 8 (2):77–98.

Lund, C. 2006. Twilight institutions: Public authority and local politics in Africa. *Development and Change* 37 (4):685–705. doi:10.1111/j.1467-7660.2006.00497.x

Medrano, E., O. Tablada, A. Kome, F. Baltodano, N. Medina, N. Swagemakers, and W. Obando. 2007. *22 Años de experiencia recopilada sobre el trabajo de acueductos rurales.* Managua, Nicaragua. http://unicef.org.ni/publicacion/96/22-anos-de-experiencia-recopilada-sobre-el-trabajo/

Meehan, K. 2013. Disciplining de facto development: water theft and hydrosocial order in Tijuana. *Environment & Planning D* 31:319–336. doi:10.1068/d20610

Ministerio del Medio Ambiente y Recursos Naturales. 2011. Construyendo la Política del Recurso Hídrico en El Salvador hacia la Gobernabilidad en la Gestión del Agua. http://www.marn.gob.sv/phocadownload/informe_taller_politica_recursos_hidricos.pdf

Murphree, M. W. 2009. The strategic pillars of communal natural resource management: Benefit, empowerment and conservation. *Biodiversity and Conservation* 18 (10):2551–62. doi:10.1007/s10531-009-9644-0

Murtinho, F., H. Eakin, D. López-Carr, and T. M. Hayes. 2013. Does external funding help adaptation? Evidence from community-based water management in the Colombian Andes. *Environmental Management* 52:1103–14. doi:10.1007/s00267-013-0156-z

Narayan, D. 1994. Contribution of people's participation: Evidence from 121 rural water supply projects. Environmentally Sustainable Development Occasional Paper Series 1. http://documents.worldbank.org/curated/en/750421468762366856/The-contribution-of-peoples-participation-evidence-from-121-rural-water-supply-projects

Novo, P., and A. Garrido. 2010. The new Nicaraguan water law in context: Institutions and challenges for water management and governance. IFPRI Discussion Paper. http://www.ifpri.org/publication/new-nicaraguan-water-law-context

Ostrom, E. 1990. *Governing the commons: The evolution of institutions for collective action.* New York, NY: Cambridge University Press.

Ostrom, E. 2002. *The drama of the commons.* Washington, DC: National Academy Press.

Ostrom, E. 2009. A general framework for analyzing sustainability of social-ecological systems. *Science* 325:419–22. doi:10.1126/science.1172133

Ostrom, E. 2010. Polycentric systems for coping with collective action and global environmental change. *Global Environmental Change* 20:550–57. doi:10.1016/j.gloenvcha.2010.07.004

Pahl-Wostl, C. 2009. A conceptual framework for analysing adaptive capacity and multi-level learning processes in resource governance regimes. *Global Environmental Change* 19:354–65. doi:10.1016/j.gloenvcha.2009.06.001

Perreault, T. 2003. Changing places: Transnational networks, ethnic politics, and community development in the Amazon. *Political Geography* 22:61–88. doi:10.1016/s0962-6298(02)00058-6

Perreault, T. 2006. From the Guerra Del Agua to the Guerra Del Gas: Resource governance, neoliberalism and popular protest in Bolivia. *Antipode* 38 (1):150–72. doi:10.1111/j.0066-4812.2006.00569.x

Perreault, T. 2008. Custom and contradiction: Rural water governance and the politics of Usos y Costumbres in Bolivia's irrigators' movement. *Annals of the Association of American Geographers* 98 (4):834–54. doi:10.1080/00045600802013502

Ribot, J. C. 1999. Decentralisation, participation and accountability in Sahelian forestry: Legal instruments of political-administrative control. *Africa: Journal of the International African Institute* 69 (1):23–65. doi:10.2307/1161076

Ribot, J. C. 2007. Representation, citizenship and the public domain in democratic decentralization. *Development* 50 (1):43–49. doi:10.1057/palgrave.development.1100335

Ribot, J. C. 2011. Choice, recognition and democracy effects of decentralisation. Swedish International Centre for Local Democracy (Working Paper 5). https://localdemocracy.net/2011/01/01/choice-recognition-and-the-democracy-effects-of-decentralization/

Ribot, J. C., A. Agrawal, and A. Larson. 2006. Recentralizing while decentralizing: How national governments reappropriate forest resources. *World Development* 34 (11):1864–86. doi:10.1016/j.worlddev.2005.11.020

Ribot, J. C., and A. Larson. 2005. *Democratic decentralisation through a natural resource lens.* New York, NY: Routledge.

Rodríguez, F. J., J. A. Martínez, N. S. Silwany, O. A. Incer, S. Zeledón, and J. M. González. 2008. Informe de Consulta y Dictamen: Ley Especial de Comités de Agua Potable y Saneamiento. Nicaraguan National Assembly. http://legislacion.asamblea.gob.ni/SILEG/Iniciativas.nsf/0/d5fa5a48b5802a05062574ef00610db0?OpenDocument#_Section4.

Romano, S. T. 2012a. From protest to proposal: The contentious politics of the Nicaraguan anti-water privatisation social movement. *Bulletin of Latin American Research* 31 (4):499–514. doi:10.1111/j.1470-9856.2012.00700.x

Romano, S. T. 2012b. *From resource management to political activism: Civil society participation in Nicaragua's rural water governance.* PhD dissertation, University of California, Santa Cruz, CA.

Romano, S. T. 2016. Democratising discourses: Conceptions of ownership, autonomy, and 'the state' in Nicaragua's rural water governance. *Water International* 41 (1):74–90. doi:10.1080/02508060.2016.1107706

Sandier, T. 2010. Common-property resource: Privatization, centralization, and hybrid arrangements. *Public Choice* 143 (3/4):317–24. doi:10.1007/s11127-010-9620-y

Schouten, T., and P. Moriarty. 2008. *Community water, community management: From system to service in rural areas.* Warwickshire, UK: Practical Action Publishing.

Smit, S., S. P. Tamayo, V. Ibarra, J. Rojas, A. Benavidez, and V. Bey. 2012. *Gobernanza y sostenibilidad de los sistemas de agua potable y saneamiento rural en Colombia.* InterAmerican Development Bank. https://publications.iadb.org/handle/11319/3137

Thayer, M. 2010. *Making transnational feminism: Rural women, NGO activists, and northern donors in Brazil.* New York, NY: Routledge.

Trevett, A., and O. Nuñez. 1998. AHJASA: Ongoing management and maintenance support for Honduras' community water systems. *Waterlines* 16 (3):23–26. doi:10.3362/0262-8104.1998.011

Urbano Rural. 2015. Las amenazas que afectan el agua para el consumo humano en los campos Chilenos. http://elurbanorural.cl/las-amenazas-que-afectan-el-agua-para-el-consumo-humano-en-los-campos-chilenos/

Woolcock, M., and D. Narayan. 2000. Social capital: Implications for development theory, research, and policy. *The World Bank Research Observer* 15 (2):225–49. doi:10.1093/wbro/15.2.225

Water Crisis and Options for Effective Water Provision in Urban and Peri-Urban Areas in Cameroon

Lotsmart Fonjong and Violet Fokum

ABSTRACT

About 58% of inhabitants of Sub-Saharan Africa, including Cameroon, have no access to potable water. The water sector in Cameroon has undergone restructuring in the wake of public-sector reforms and privatization. This article examines the extent to which privatization of water management has impacted on water crisis in peri-urban areas. It is framed within the United Nations Millennium Development Goal of reducing by half the proportion of people without access to portable water by 2015 and on the neoliberal argument for the privatization of public goods. Primary data emanate from interviews conducted among local inhabitants and public and water authorities of five purposively selected municipalities. Findings suggest that privatization of the water sector has not improved the water problems of peri-urban inhabitants. Inhabitants are experiencing water shortages, rationing, poor coverage, and high pricing, as investments in infrastructure lag behind the rising demand for the utility. In the prevailing circumstances, public–private partnership presents a possible alternative for Cameroon.

Introduction

Water is one of the most valuable and influential natural resources because of its industrial and domestic importance. Access to safe water is essential to sustain life and indispensable for a healthy and dignified life (Kiefer and Roaf 2008, cited in Moyo 2011). Water scarcity is today a global phenomenon that affects close to 2.8 billion people worldwide, especially in developing countries (Mbua 2013). The European Union Water Framework Directive (WFD) established in 2000 observes that "water is not a commercial product like any other but, rather, a heritage which must be protected, defended and treated as such" (European Commission 2002). Both the availability and quality of water are crucial. There is a direct connect between water, water provision, and water management. That is why although 71% of the earth surface is covered by water, access to potable water is still a rare privilege to many poor households. Even during the rainy seasons in the equatorial rain forest of Africa where there is supposed to be abundant water, potable water remains a scarce utility.

At the turn of the millennium, the United Nations Millennium Development Goal (UN MDG) on environmental sustainability aimed at reducing by half the number of people

---

Color versions of one or more of the figures in the article can be found online at www.tandfonline.com/usnr.

without sustainable access to safe drinking water and improved sanitation. While improved water sources were accessible to more than 2 billion people from 1990 to 2010, Sub-Saharan Africa had the lowest drinking-water coverage compared to the other regions of the world (UNICEF and World Health Organization [WHO] 2012). Just 58% of the population in Sub-Saharan Africa enjoys access to safe drinking water, and the gap is widening as the increasingly urban population growth places a greater strain on existing service providers (Ghosh and Morella 2011). The world's urban population is predicted to increase from 3.3 billion in 2007 to 6.4 billion in 2050 (United Nations Department of Economic and Social Affairs [UNDESA] 2013), with much of the growth taking place in peri-urban and informal settlements. Providing water to these new settlements is challenging because of cost and other managerial exigencies (Olajuyibe 2010).

In the past, provision of potable water as a public utility in urban space in Sub-Saharan Africa was the traditional responsibility. Privatization that ensued from the structural adjustment program (SAP) of the 1990s in Africa brought about fundamental changes that liberalized the water sector. The sector was largely privatized, with the aim being to ensure financial viability, service quality, and coverage (Dagdeviren and Robertson 2008). Many more African countries have since then embraced privatization. In the past two decades, they have adopted private-sector water management, which has proven more effective than government in eliminating inefficiencies and other hidden costs (Ghosh and Morella 2011). Water provision and access are linked to income and urbanization, as Ghosh and Morella (2011) believe that higher income countries make safe water affordable and accessible, and that population densities associated with urbanization help to reduce the cost of expanding access to modern services. But limiting the problem of water management to water affordability alone, without an analysis of the capacity and ability of the water providers to meet the demand for water, can be misleading. This seems to be the case in Cameroon, a relatively high-income country within the subregion, where the urban and peri-urban water crisis is a governance-related malfunction of both demand and supply.

Poor governance lies at the heart of the world's water crisis (Rogers and Hall 2003). How available water resources are managed is key to achieving water security (United Nations Development Programme [UNDP] 2013). However, Rogers and Hall (2003) have indicated that the ineffectiveness of water governance by states has been the hindering factor to water security. In Cameroon, this ineffectiveness is seen in lack of appropriate institutions, bureaucratic inertia, insufficient capacity, and shortage of investment (UNDP 2013).

Cameroon is ranked second in Africa (after the Democratic Republic of Congo) in terms of quantity of available water resources (Figure 1), which is estimated to be three times the world's average of 7,000 m³ (Ako, Eyong, and Nkeng 2009), but in Cameroon access to water still remains a major problem because of inadequate management (Mafany Fantong, and Nkeng 2006) and authorities' inability to understand the pattern of urbanization for effective planning. Urban planning has to recognize that increasing urban population lives in peri-urban areas: areas within urban fringes that have both urban and rural characteristics. Urban, rural, and peri-urban areas are interlinked and operate as a system rather than as independent geographical units (Iaquinta and Drescher 2000). Peri-urban areas in Cameroon emerge spontaneously due to deficiency in planning and urbanization, and are difficult to delimit. Although their inhabitants are diverse, most are urban poor who cannot afford the cost of living in the city, and rural people who have been engulfed by urban sprawl. Peri-urban population also includes a few middle-class people either looking

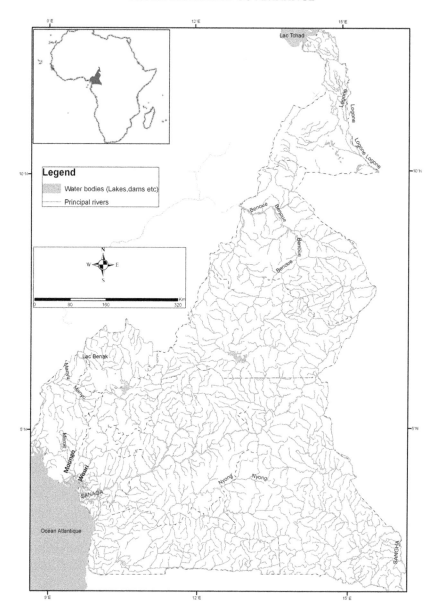

Figure 1. A sketch map of Cameroon hydrological network. (*Source*: Authors' adaptation from IRAD Hydrological Map of Cameroon, 2009.)

for space, comfort, and quiet, or escaping from the pressures of the city. Although peri-urbanism may have potential for urban development and sustainability, the absence of planning leaves its inhabitants with a number of social deprivations (roads, water, electricity, housing, schools, and other services), making living and commuting in these areas challenging.

The role of water as engine of socioeconomic development makes its management of pivotal importance. Cameroon's record in this respect falls below expectation. Statistics on the number of persons with access to water in the country vary. Otto (2014) estimates the figure to be between 42 and 74% of the population. The Global Water Partnership

(GWP 2010) states that 45.3% of Cameroonians (58% urban and 23% rural) have access to drinking water. The World Bank (2012) believes that access to drinking water is declining with increasing poverty. In 2002, for example, Société Nationale des Eaux du Cameroun (SNEC), the then principal provider of water, was present in only 35% of cities and towns in Cameroon (Tanawa et al. 2002). These trends threaten the UNICEF/WHO (2012) estimates, according to which 92% of the global population will have access to improved drinking water by 2015. Towns and cities in Cameroon during the last decade suffered a great deal from poor water services when provision was the monopoly of the state-run SNEC. SNEC's lapses led some urban centers to consume water from unsafe sources, and others, like Kumbo, to create their own water authority (for Kumbo, the Kumbo Water Authority).

What one observes in Cameroon is a mismatch between water resources, provision, and demand. In the context of perpetual water crisis and population disenchantment, SNEC was dissolved in 2005 and the exploitation and distribution of water were shared by a parastatal (CamWater) and a private company, Cameroounaise Des Eaux (CDE). This article uses examples from five municipalities to examine the state of privatization, and highlights the missing links between water privatization and the ability of the actors involved to satisfy minimal demand from a rapidly growing peri-urban clientele.

Framing of the Study

The last 30 years have witnessed a dramatic decrease in the state's role in economic activities (Newbery 1997). State monopoly in the provision of welfare services in Africa has been regarded as wasteful and inefficient (Hoexter 2007), as population numbers keep increasing. In the case of water provision, global institutions including the United Nations have warned about the likely negative impact of a growing global population and the effects of climate change on the ability of the people to access fresh water (Roberts 2008).

Two indicators were identified to measure the attainment of this target MDG target "to halve, by 2015, the proportion of people without sustainable access to safe drinking water and basic sanitation": the proportion of rural and urban population with sustainable access to improved water sources, and the proportion of those living in urban and rural settings with access to improved sanitation (United Nations 2000). UNICEF/WHO (2012) believes the world met this target ahead of this date, as more than 2 billion people gained access to improved drinking-water sources, including piped supplies and protected wells, between 1990 and 2010. The MDG indicator measuring progress in the proportion of the population with access to improved water sources and sanitation is too simplistic. It does not take into account distance from the sources and the regularity of the water. In this article, we identify pipe-borne water supply and boreholes and wells provided either by water companies or municipal authorities as improved sources of water. However, unlike the MDG indictor, we also interrogate the distance between the users and these sources, regularity of the sources, and affordability by users.

Government owned and operated most water supply systems in industrialized countries and supplied water, often at subsidized rates, to ensure universal access and safeguard public health (Bakker 2010). A similar situation existed in several Sub-Saharan African countries prior to SAP. SAP introduced privatization, which shifted the provision of some key facilities (health, education, and water) from the state to private actors. Market mechanisms were deployed to pursue social goals (Covenant on Economic, Social and Cultural Rights [CESCR] 1996). The insistence on water privatization was, however, based on alleged state inefficiency. The World Bank points to the perceived flawed management by states, and structural defects in public-sector management of water, as being responsible for the poor quality and low penetration of the water supply system (World Bank 2006; Moyo 2011). Today, water management in some African countries is privatized. The state, however, retains the responsibility for defining the framework within which private actor-providers operate (Feyter and Isa 2005; Moyo 2011). Such responsibility departs significantly from what was formerly the focus of state control in the production, management, and supply of water.

Many of these countries were easily convinced by the expected gains of privatization rooted in the neo-liberal fundamental ideology of free-market organization over the welfare state (Khan 2006). Here, the market mechanism is hailed and the private sector is inherently seen as superior to the public sector in the production of goods and services. The free market is viewed as advancement on the welfare state and social democracy, and as a provider of economic efficiency (Taylor 1983). The privatization of water in Cameroon is construed in this light, although without any concrete reasons to expect positive outcomes. Privatization of water thus expands tradable goods to include water. The water utility sector becomes a profitable venture based on demand, supply, and affordability, rather than a provider of public goods that require subsidies (Bakker 2007, cited in Moyo et al. 2013). Private investment introduces the principle of full cost recovery without subsidies, as all cost is considered when calculating the profitability of investments (Moyo 2011).

Major donors, including the World Bank, are sensitive to the principle of full cost recovery as part of the conditionality for loan in the water sector, especially in developing countries (Perry 1997). It follows that those involved should be able to recover the full costs of providing water to all users (Blumel 2004). The belief is that this would minimize inefficiencies and ensure water access to all through pricing techniques. Apart from maximizing water, higher prices avoid waste and encourage only those uses that are most valuable, thereby increasing the total volume of water for use by households (Moyo 2011). But this may not necessarily be true in Cameroon, with peri-urban neighborhoods where private companies are unwilling to extend their water networks both because of their capacity and because of the relatively low demand. In this case, privatization might not be enough to ensure access to better water sources for the majority of the population.

Context of the Study

Water commodification transforms water from a public good into a tradable commodity. This leaves water in the hands of the private individuals sector, anticipating better management. Water commodification gained prominence in the 20th century with fears of scarcity, driven by the view that public monopoly and governance of water were ineffective. Governance in the broad term includes institutions, organizations, and policies/practices that shape and manage water resources, including the delivery of water to diverse populations and industries (Olsson and Head 2015). This shift from state ownership and subsequent efforts to commodify water enable more actors to participate in decision making, thereby increasing the probability of consensual decisions, which was impossible previously under one actor, the government (Roberts 2008). The state role in environmental problems is realigned and scaled down to be positioned as just one of many stakeholders aligned along horizontal networks (Rhodes 1996). It is hoped that resource management will take place more effectively through the pooling of more knowledge and coordination between government agencies, the corporate sector, and civil society (Roberts 2008). However, commodification of water has instead created a situation whereby water provision is monopolized by a few multinational corporations, with the top two multinationals controlling approximately 75% of the industry (Simonson 2003). This robbing of the commons has amplified already existing problems of water governance. Commodification necessitates a full recovery price and the removal of subsidies to ensure free market trade. Even in South Africa with public water management, introduction of basic users' charges created disconnections of supply from thousands who could not afford it, with implications for the health and social equality of the citizens (Bond 2004). A public–private partnership (PPP) that widens the range of stakeholders in governing the water sector through networking with civil society and the public and private sectors (Durant 2004) is likely to lead to better services.

Methodology

Cameroon is generally well watered (Ako, Eyong, and Nkeng 2009), although with uneven distribution of rainfall across the country. The main wet season lasts for about 7 months, during May–November, but varies from the south to the north (Mcsweeney, New, and Lizcano 2010). Debundsha, the wettest area, located at the leeside of Mount Cameroon, receives up to 10,000 mm annual rainfall, while the semi-arid Sahel (10–12°N) counts among the driest places with 700 mm/year (GWP 2009). Available water resources are estimated at 322 billion m³; approximately 120 billion m³ of this is usable groundwater, which is spatially unevenly distributed (Mafany Fantong, and Nkeng 2006). This figure amounts to an annual available water volume of 21,000 m³ per inhabitant, which is three times higher than the 7,000-m³ world average (Otto 2014). Cameroon also has a dense, evenly distributed river network and other surface and groundwater resources, most of which are concentrated within the equatorial forest and littoral ecological zones. Cameroon has 10 political regions, which have been further subdivided into divisions and subdivisions, run respectively by appointed prefects and subprefects. Municipalities within these subdivisions are headed by elected mayors.

This is a descriptive qualitative study based on desktop review and primary data generated from semistructured interviews conducted in five municipalities drawn from two regions (Littoral and South West). The target population consists of local inhabitants and administrative and water authorities of the chosen municipalities. The five purposively chosen municipalities are Douala IV in the Littoral Region, and Buea and Kumba I, II, and III in the South West Region. The chosen municipalities are all (1) within the same ecological zone, (2) among the fastest growing municipalities in the country, and (3) naturally well watered by surface water, mainly the rivers Wouri, Mungo, and Meme and Lake Barombi, as seen in Figure 2. The names of the municipalities (Douala IV, Buea, Kumba I, II, and III) are used throughout the article to represent their peri-urban neighborhoods where field data were actually collected.

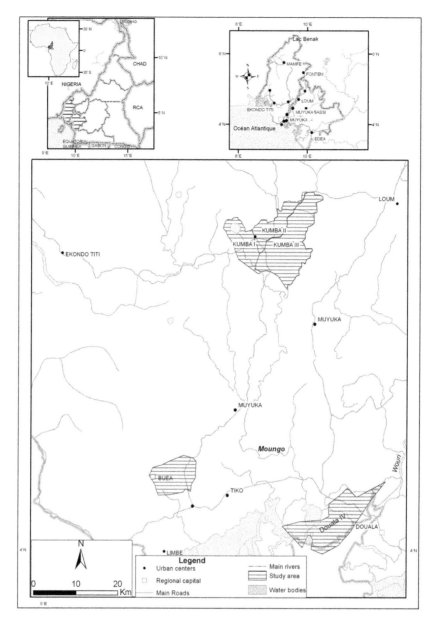

Figure 2. Sketch location map of studied areas. (*Source*: Authors' adaptation from IRAD Hydrological Map of Cameroon, 2009).

Three sets of semistructured interview guides were used for data collection in the chosen municipalities: one directed to local inhabitants, the second to government, and the third to water officials. The 15 public and water officials interviewed were mainly subprefects, mayors, divisional representatives of ministries of Water and Urban Planning, and water companies (CamWater, CDE, and defunct SNEC). These target officials are directly or indirectly responsible for local implementation of government policies relating to the provision and management of basic welfare services including water provision. Interviews with authorities focused on the current situation of water and the efforts of respective services to solve the local water puzzle. Interviews with representatives of water companies examined issues relating to water infrastructure, coverage, pricing, and challenges, among others.

Local inhabitants interviewed to corroborate literature and information gathered from public and water officials consisted of household members and owners of small/medium-size businesses. Inhabitants were purposively selected in order to ensure that a fair representation of all the socioeconomic classes of the society who have lived in the area for more than 5 years were interviewed. Each of the municipalities was broadly subdivided into major quarters, and respondents were hand picked among civil servants, business operators, poor laborers, and the middle class to ensure representativeness. Interviews focused on issues of access to water, affordability, effects of water scarcity, and shortages. Forty-nine respondents were selected in this group from four of the five municipalities (Douala IV and Kumba I, II, and III) proportionate to individual population size. As a result, 21 respondents were selected from Douala IV, 10 each from Kumba I and III, and 8 from Kumba II. Coding from interview transcripts was followed by thematic analysis of new and predefined codes derived in line with research objectives. The frequencies of some codes and themes from the sample population have been used to generate descriptive statistical tables. A quote library with direct quotes from all the transcripts was generated, and some quotes have been used to relay the voices of the respondents directly. Results obtained have been broadly related to secondary data.

Results and Discussion

The Complex Framework of Water Management in Urban Cameroon

Many structures and actors with conflicting roles are involved in managing the water sector in Cameroon. The central actor is the Ministry of Water and Energy (MINEE) through its Directorate of Water Supply and Hydrology, for both urban and rural areas (African Ministers' Council on Water [AMCOW] 2012). In principle, MINEE defines, implements, and evaluates water policies regarding production, transport, and distribution. However, the absence of clearly attributed roles and actions has allowed other public institutions like the ministries of environment, interior, finance, regional development, mines, and research to play the same role (Ako, Eyong, and Nkeng 2009; GWP 2009). Since 2005, CamWater and CDE have been the principal actors in urban areas, following a contractual agreement on water management in which CDE takes charge of water production and distribution and CamWater manages the infrastructure (AMCOW 2011).

Before the new management in 2008, urban water provision was the monopoly of SNEC, which had conducted the production, transportation, distribution, and marketing of water resources in urban and suburban areas in Cameroon since 1967. During this period, SNEC's production capacity of 450,000 m^3 per day provided drinking water in 105 urban centers with 225,000 users, representing just 1.5% of the inhabitants (CamWater 2007). CamWater manages the public water service for the urban and suburban areas in the entire country, carrying out research and infrastructural development leading to the production and distribution of water (CamWater 2013; 2014). CDE, a subsidiary of the Office National de l'Eau Potable (ONEP) from Morocco, currently has a 10-year lease to provide drinking water in 110 urban and suburban centers beginning 2008. In the process, CDE caters to the treatment, distribution, and marketing of public water, and carries out maintenance, extension, and rehabilitation on all assets. CDE is currently active in the North, South, East, West, and Central regions.

In terms of legislation, Cameroon's 1998 national water law is limited, as it was not elaborated within the framework of integrated water resource management. It fails to address some of the key principles of sustainable water resources management like management of water in hydrological basins, effective stakeholder participation, and economic value of water (Masanga 2014). Water experts believe that there is no formal national water policy for the interpretation, application, and enforcement of water legislation (Masanga 2014). As a result, despite its amorphous legal and institutional water framework, Cameroon is still unable to ensure regular and sustainable water provision to most of its citizens.

The Situation of Water Provision in Urban and Peri-urban Areas in Cameroon

Water consumption per person in Cameroon in 2009 was 37 liters per capita per day and utility coverage was between 40 to 60% (Biedler 2012). Urban and peri-urban areas depend on three main sources of water (pipe-borne, boreholes/wells, and streams/springs), excluding direct rain water. Although the MDG on water considered boreholes/wells as sources of potable water and solutions to the global water problem, these sources are not very safe in urban Cameroon due to their poor hygienic and sanitation conditions. For example, in Douala and other densely populated cities, wells/boreholes are located without due safety measures around pit toilets and marshy areas, and therefore are at the mercy of flooding and poor sewage disposal. City dwellers are increasingly turning to these unsafe sources because of very low coverage of water networks. In 1996, for example, only 5.8 million inhabitants (Yongs 2010) out of a population of more than 14 million were served by the defunct SNEC.

Field interviews (Table 1) suggest that just 39% of those living in peri-urban areas in the four municipalities have access to pipe water, of which the supply is not even regular. The high percentage (63%) for Douala IV can be attributed to the affluence of the municipality and the Sino-Cameroon water project completed in 2010 (Bainkong 2010).

A significantly high number (23%) of inhabitants interviewed, with 50% being from Kumba III alone, still depend on streams or springs, which by virtue of their urban nature are unsafe. The problems of Kumba III are similar to those of other suburban areas in Cameroon, with generalized poor public and basic infrastructure. The few inhabitants (7.4%) with water are affluent. This is not the case with the vast majority (84.6%) living away from the city. The quality of water from urban springs and streams is threatened

Table 1. Basic sources of water used by a sampled of peri-urban inhabitants around selected cities in Cameroon.

	Sources of water					
	CamWater pipe-borne water		Boreholes/wells		Streams/springs	
Municipalities	Number	%	Number	%	Number	%
Douala IV	17	63	7	27	0	0
Kumba I	4	15	4	15.4	6	37.5
Kumba II	4	15	6	23	2	12.5
Kumba III	2	7.4	9	34.6	8	50
Total	27	39	26	37	16	23

by anthropogenic pollution, including chemicals and industrial wastewater (detergents, surfactants, pharmaceuticals, polycyclic aromatic hydrocarbons [PAHs]). Besides poor availability, affordability and regularity are important to people's choices of water sources. This explains why some inhabitants have opted for more than one source for water. A male civil servant in Douala IV who has no problem with affordability but still depends on both CamWater and unsafe well/boreholes, for example, observes, "I cannot afford to depend solely on CamWater, which is not regular." Another Douala respondent (housewife) relying solely on unsafe streams says she has to because her neighborhood is not served by CamWater.

Moreover, irregularity of water supply is noted in the cities. The few homes with water installations sometimes go for days, weeks, and even months without water. Kumba had a severe water crisis in 2012/2013, going for more than 6 months without water. Public authorities reported that during this period the city suffered from cholera, diarrhea, typhoid, and poor hygiene. Hygienic and sanitation conditions in schools were seriously compromised. The absence of physical accessibility of water forced some schools to seek alternative water sources to complete the 2013/2014 academic year in Kumba (Fonkwen 2013).

Privatization of water provision in urban areas has thus been unable to ensure regular water supply in peri-urban Cameroon. More than 65% of the inhabitants blame the situation on government. Just 20% attribute the crisis to CamWater, an indication that the population sees water as a public good to be provided by its government. Local authorities of CamWater and the water and energy ministries attribute the problem to natural forces, citing the case of Buea, where seasonal fluctuations impose shortages and rationing, especially in the dry season. On this point, however, Fonjong and Ngekwe (2014) have reported cases of water shortages and rationing in Buea during the wet season, attributing the problem to human rather than natural factors. CamWater also confirmed that the water infrastructure of most cities, including Buea, cannot meet the demand.

The absence of safe water has caused 1.1 billion people globally to remain without access to improved sources of water. About 2.4 billion lack access to any form of improved sanitation services. Consequently, 2.2 million people in developing countries, mostly children, die every year from diseases associated with poor water supply and sanitation (WHO/UNICEF 2012). More than 18,300 deaths yearly in Cameroon are linked to poor hygiene and sanitation (WHO/UNICEF 2010, 106). This means current public measures for water provisioning in Cameroon are ineffective and below the WHO safe drinking water quality. This poor water situation as seen in Kumba often leads to agitation.

Effects of Privatization of the Water Sector

The general perception of the population surveyed is that privatization of the water sector has (61%) affected the sector (Table 2) in terms of water provision, coverage, and pricing. A Douala-based working -lass female respondent observed that "the privatization of this sector has done nothing to improve on the national water problem … It's a complete mess. There is poor relationship between investors and customers and no educative seminars." The 28.5% of interviewees who thought positively of privatization were mostly the rich, who could easily afford the cost of water installations and monthly payments. Such respondents live in the rich neighborhoods of Douala IV and Kumba I and are mostly wealthy

Table 2. Assessment of the privatization of the water sector by sampled population (percent).

| Municipalities | Perception of the effects of privatization of water by population | | | |
	Good	Fair	Poor	Don't know
Douala IV	16.32	8.16	14.28	4.08
Kumba I	8.16	0	12.24	0
Kumba II	4.08	0	12.24	0
Kumba III	0	0	22.44	0
Total	28.51%	8.16%	61.22%	4.08%

government officials and businessmen. Even mayors acknowledged the negative impact of privatization on their population. All the mayors were unanimous that privatization came with constant shortages, irregular supply, and high bills, making it difficult for the poor to cope. As one of the mayors of Kumba pointed out, "Water has become very expensive and irregular for everyone."

Privatization thus runs contrary to the spirit of Law 98/005 of April 14, 1998, on the water sector, which makes the state responsible for access to water by all Cameroonians. If facilitating access to water by all is a government responsibility, then access to water for domestic and personal use should be sustainable (20 liters per person per day) in the spirit of the WHO guidelines to which Cameroon generally adheres. Sufficient access to water in urban cities in Cameroon is estimated at 50 to 100 liters per person depending on the need (Smets 2000). However, these figures are rare, especially in peri-urban Douala and Kumba, where many still go without potable water.

A follow-up of the services of CamWater and CDE in urban areas produced the same mixed feelings among the interviewed inhabitants of the four municipalities as reported in Table 3.

For privatization to deliver, it has to be context specific. From Table 3, the majority of respondents judged the services of the water provider after privatization to fall between poor (28.6%) and fair (20.4%). One inhabitant from Kumba describes it "a failure," with consumers paying for poor services in "a country with no customer protection." Some 24.5% of interviewees were unable to evaluate the services of CamWater, but there is no evidence that these results were likely to be positive given the acute water crisis reported in these municipalities in Table 1. Some respondents contend that people were willing to pay for water but the company was unwilling to extend coverage to the peripheries because they are sparsely inhabited and unprofitable. Despite the precarious water situation of these areas, very few people (22.5% of interviewees) are willing to relocate. "The stress is unbearable, we travel far to buy water from water retailers at the exorbitant price of 100 F CFA (about 10 cent) a litre," observes a Douala city dweller who is thinking of relocating. Water retailing is a common phenomenon in cities in Cameroon, where those who can afford the cost of water installation retail water to the poor in their neighborhood at prices

Table 3. Sampled population evaluation of the services of water provider under privatization (percent).

| Municipalities | A sampled population assessment of the services of CamWater in relation to those of SNEC | | | | | |
	Excellent	Good	Fair	Poor	Don't know	I don't have CamWater
Douala IV	12	6	2	4	8	8.16
Kumba I	0	0	8	8	4	0
Kumba II	0	0	6	1	8	0
Kumba III	0	0	4	7	4	0
Total	12%	6%	20.4%	28.6%	24.5%	8.2%

high enough to recover their cost and even pay for their personal consumption. Those (75.5%) who have accommodated the water situation are either landlords or those unable to pay rents elsewhere.

Evidently, demand still exceeds supply, even with privatization. In the 1990s international financial institutions, other donor agencies, and regional development banks started pushing for the involvement of multinational water corporations, expecting them to bring the much-needed financing, efficiency, management skills, and technology to the water service sector (Lundqvist 1988, cited in Moyo 2011). The result from such internationally induced privatization of water exploitation in Cameroon has so far been dismal. Yaounde, the capital, for instance, has a daily demand of 350,000 m³ water, but until June 2013 CDE was only able to provide 100,000 m³ per day (Otto 2014). Totouom, Sikod, and Abba (2012) further reveal that the water challenges of urban areas have forced urban dwellers in Cameroon to rely on a diversity of water sources (boreholes, public fountains, wells), entailing additional cost on purification as reported by 10.4% of the households.

Beyond the Water Situation in Peri-Urban Areas in Cameroon

One cannot overstate the importance of water. Ever since the beginning of human civilizations around the Nile, Tigris, and Euphrates rivers, population growth and distribution have been linked to the availability of fresh water for food production and a variety of industrial processes (Sherbinin 1997). The emergence of new settlement patterns and the expansion of existing ones increase human intervention in natural aquifers, rivers, springs, and other sources, creating delays in the water cycle. In the 21st century, population growth and urbanization, together with changes in production and consumption patterns, have placed unprecedented demands on water and other resources. Existing figures suggest that inhabitants of rural and urban areas use more than 50% of all accessible water runoff. This proportion is expected to increase to 70% by 2025, thereby reducing the quantity and quality of water available for aquatic ecosystems (Postel, Daily, and Ehrlich 1996). Yet new settlements and new water needs are springing up almost every day. The nature of water governance is thus pertinent and makes rethinking even more relevant. Should water be the sole responsibility of government? Left in the hands of private investors, or run as a public–private partnership?

The perilous water situation in Cameroonian cities is a policy and management problem that falls squarely on imperfections in governance. Popular opinion in the studied cities holds that government has not done enough in its responsibility of providing this public amenity. As Figure 3 illustrates, government policy of privatization is judged by more than half of respondents to be responsible for the present predicament. This is likely because privatization entails a change in the role and responsibility of the state rather than simply a change of ownership (Chirwa 2004a, 2004b, cited in Moyo 2013). Interestingly, although the population is unhappy with the services of the corporate companies managing water, people do not lay the blame on those companies but on the state that privatized the utility in the first instance. This blame on government resonates with Shiva (2002), who argues that water is a free gift of nature that cannot be bought but the government sold it to corporate individuals.

Some public authorities of Kumba agree with the population that the privatization of urban water was a bad policy: "In my opinion, a sector like water should never be given

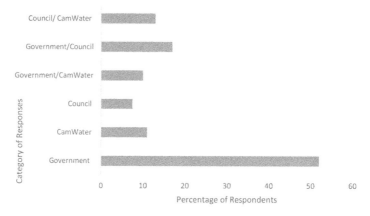

Figure 3. Perception of a sample of population on those responsible for water crisis in peri-urban areas.

to individuals or foreigners to manage ... the current problem with water coverage in the city will continue since expending coverage to neighborhoods without water may not be profitable to the companies," observed one of the mayors interviewed. Privatizing without subsidies makes water expensive to the poor, since every private initiative aims at full cost recovery (Dagdeviren and Robertson 2008). Moreover, interviewees of the three Kumba municipalities, even without consuming water, continued to receive bills, a practice that increased public animosity against CamWater and the state. The type of public animosity in Kumba confirms the Taylor and Sonnenfeld (2017) analysis that water crises create social conflicts. Kumba inhabitants paid for what they did not consume because they were powerless before powerful investors. In 2012 a local nongovernmental organization (NGO) and a law firm, in collaboration with INTERIGHTS–London and Human Rights Watch, challenged the practice in a legal suit. Only then was it discontinued. CamWater and CDE do not seem to have long-term investment plans in Cameroon.

Since the private takeover, there has been neither visible investment in maintenance nor development of water infrastructure to satisfy the growing cities. Cities like Buea still depend on colonial water infrastructures designed for smaller populations before 1960. Furthermore, keeping councils out of water management does not seem a smart move, for it also excludes them from basic maintenance. CDE and CamWater are still relying on infrastructure inherited from SNEC, which needs major investment and renovation to meet current demands. As one subprefect of Kumba observes, "The people of the municipality are exploited by CamWater with high water bills. The corporation is disgruntled and unwilling to assist even the local councils to develop alternative water sources." This is why Taylor and Sonnenfeld (2017) noted that the water crisis will weaken effective governance and collaboration.

A keen analysis of opinions of affected sampled populations, especially those in Figure 3, suggests that the direct intervention of government and local councils in water management is paramount in solving the water puzzle. Involving local councils in the public–private partnership (PPP) is no surprise, as Law 762/PJL/AN 2004 on decentralization makes elected councilors accountable to the electorate. As Ako, Eyong, and Nkeng (2009) explain, councils have the institutional responsibility of basic service provision to communities, including the management of water resources. Public–private partnership addresses some of the limits of water-sector privatization. CamWater/CDE seems unwilling to make the kind of investment in network extension that will lead to improvement in access to water, especially in poor vicinities. Bakker (2010) has also upheld PPP. Moyo (2011), believes that efficient water management enables dignified living standards and facilitates social inclusiveness and participation in public life. But Hayev (1944) and Friedman (1962) oppose this somewhat Keynesian approach as inefficient, dishonest, and demoralizing for hard workers.

Obviously, the challenge of universal access to safe water sources can be understood as both a supply and a demand problem (Ghosh and Morella 2011): as the recurrent problem of inadequate infrastructure and investments in the water sector versus the demand of constantly increasing populations and cities. Here, "available water networks may not have the carrying capacity required to service all residents in a particular area without further investment and upgrading" (Ghosh and Morella 2011, 40). Cameroonians, for example, lack proper services because not enough is invested in new infrastructure or in maintaining existing and often overstretched supply systems. Water agencies and authorities still depend on obsolete equipment, with some dating back to the colonial period. Olajuyibe (2010) attributes this situation, common in Sub-Saharan Africa, to poor government and private-sector investment, and lack of capacity and financial resources. Cain and Mulenga (2009) corroborate this view, citing the case of Nigeria, where public efforts at water provision fell short because of inability to upgrade existing infrastructure. The Department of Water and Sanitation in South Africa also highlighted similar financial and human resource capacities challenges in implementing its water policy (Förster, Downsborough, and Machaya 2017).

Conclusion

Access to potable water has since 2010 been considered by the UN as a basic human right. More than 1 billion people in the world today are still deprived of this right, among whom are the vast majority of inhabitants of urban and peri-urban areas of Cameroon. Paradoxically, the UN is celebrating the attainment of the MDG of reducing the number of people without access to safe water at a time when the reality in Cameroon and in other Sub-Saharan African countries is proving the contrary. This article highlights the extent of the urban water crisis in Cameroon and reveals it as a human-created problem that can be fixed by adopting the right policy approaches. Privatization reduced hidden economic cost of water provision and increased social cost without carrying out necessary investments to transform obsolete water infrastructures and increase network coverage. Therefore, it has not increased water accessibility of inhabitants in peri-urban areas.

Local critiques of privatization are quick to label it as a failure to be associated with dry taps and price exploitation. Privatization itself might not be the problem in Cameroon, but rather the quality and viability of investors entrusted with water management. One would expect every business enterprise to expand the water coverage and network to peri-urban areas in Douala where there is demand. But this is not happening and so calls in question the investment capacities of CamWater and CDE. We are inclined to argue that the persistent water crisis in Cameroon is fundamentally a public- and private-sector governance issue, where the former lacks clearly defined sectoral objectives to direct public resources to priority sectors like water. In the case of the latter, it is the result of inadequate managerial and financial capacities of the private sector on the one hand, and on the other the fact that investors are driven by profit motives not compatible with the social objective of providing water to all as a human right.

Caught in this quagmire, inhabitants are advocating for public intervention in water exploitation and distribution, with local councils playing a central role. This is not asking for free water but for a tariff rationalization that reflects income stratification that is currently not practiced in Cameroon. Reducing imperfections in water management by private investors and guaranteeing water to all citizens by governments are both important objectives. This means that state investment cannot be completely substituted in the process of water provision in Cameroon, particularly in the current context of rapidly growing population and challenges in water regimes from climate change. Water provision requires huge investments that cannot be supported by private capital alone. Public–private partnership is a possible alternative that combines public and private resources, with the civil society acting as watchdog for efficient water delivery. The PPP, unlike private water companies, has the potential to be transparent, fair, and accountable, and to conduct business. Nonetheless, the PPP will not just happen without government taking the lead in building a strong framework, knowing that the PPP is only as good as its organization and resources.

Funding

Funding for this study was obtained from the Faculty of Social and Management sciences grant of the University of Buea.

References

African Ministers' Council on Water. 2011. Water supply and sanitation in Cameroon. Turning finance into services for 2015 and beyond. https://www.wsp.org/sites/wsp.org/files/publications/CSO-Cameroon.pdf (accessed June 8, 2015).

African Ministers' Council on Water. 2012. A snapshot of drinking water and sanitation in Africa. 2012 Update. Prepared for AMCOW as a contribution to Fourth Africa Water Week Cairo, Egypt, May 14–15. http://www.wssinfo.org/fileadmin/user_upload/resources/Africa-AMCOW-Snapshot-2012-English-Final.pdf

Ako, A., G. Eyong, and G. Nkeng. 2009. Water resources management and integrated water resources management in Cameroon. *Water Resources Management* 24 (5):871–88. doi:10.1007/s11269-009-9476-4

Bainkong, G. 2010. China–Africa cooperation: The case of Cameroon—China reduces potable water scarcity in Douala. *Cameroon Tribune.* https://www.cameroon-tribune.cm/index.php? (accessed May 7, 2015).

Bakker, K. 2007. The "commons" versus the "commodity": alter globalization, anti-privatization and the human right to water in the global south. *Antipode* 39 (3): 430–455.

Bakker, K. 2010. *Privatising water: Governance failure and the world's urban water crisis.* Ithaca, NY: Cornell University Press.

Blumel, E. 2004. Implications of formulating human right to water. *Ecology Law Quarterly* 31: 957–1006.

Biedler, M. 2012. *Integrated urban water management for Douala; Cameroon.* Background report. Washington, DC: World Bank.

Bond, P. 2004. Water commodification and decommodification narratives: Pricing, policy debates from Johannesburg to Kyoto to Cancun and Back. *Capitalism Nature Socialism* 15:7–19.

Cain, A., and M. Mulenga. 2009. Water service provision for the peri-urban poor in post-conflict Angola. Human Settlements Working Paper Series: Water, No. 6. London, UK: International Institute for Environment and Development.

CamWater. 2007. Invest in the sector of providing portable water in Cameroon. http://www.camwater.cm/partenaires/coopération-financiere (accessed February 10, 2014).

CamWater. 2013. Des mesures transitoires d'urgence. http://www.camwater.cm (accessed March 25, 2015).

Hayev, F. A. 1944. The Road to Serfdom. Chicago, IL: University of Chicago Press.

CamWater. 2014. Urgent transitory measures. http://www.camwater.cm (accessed February 10, 2014).

Chirwa, D. 2004a. The doctrine of state responsibility as a potential means of holding private actors accountable for human rights. *Melbourne Journal of International Law* 5:1–36.

Chirwa, D. 2004b. Water privatisation and socio-economic rights in South Africa. *Law, Democracy & Development* 8:18–206.

Covenant on Economic, Social, and Cultural Rights. 1996. International covenant on economic, social and cultural rights. Adopted by General Assembly resolution 2200A (XXI) of December 16, 1966. http://www.refworld.org/docid/3ae6b36c0.html (accessed December 2, 2014).

Dagdeviren, H., and S. Robertson. 2008. *Reforming without resourcing: The case of the urban water supply in Zambia.* Policy 8. Brasilia, Brazil: International Poverty Centre.

Durant, R. 2004. Reconnecting with stakeholders. In *Environmental governance reconsidered: Challenges, choices, and opportunities,* eds. R. Durant, D. Fiorino, and R. O'Leary, 177–182. Cambridge, MA: MIT Press.

European Commission. 2002. Water is life water framework directive. http://ec.europa.eu/environment/water/water-framework/pdf/waterislife_en.pdf (accessed February 13, 2015).

Feyter, K., and G. Isa eds. 2005. *Privatization and human rights in the age of globalization.* Antwerp, Belgium: Intersentia.

Fonjong, L., and M. Ngekwe 2014. Challenges of water crisis on women's socio-economic activities in the Buea Municipality, Cameroon. *Journal of Geography and Geology* 6 (4):122–33. doi:10.5539/jgg.v6n4p122

Fonkwen, M. 2013. Schools hard hit, as Kumba water crisis intensify. *Cameroon Post* online. http://www.cameroonpostline.com/schools-hard-hit-as-kumba-water-crisis-intensify/ (accessed May 11, 2015).

Förster, J., L. Downsborough, and C. Machaya. 2017. When policy hits practice: Structure, agency and power in South African water governance. *Society & Natural Resources* 30 (4).

Friedman, M. 1962. *Capitalism and freedom.* Chicago, IL: University of Chicago Press.

Ghosh, B., and E. Morella. 2011. *Africa's water and sanitation infrastructure: Access, affordability, and alternatives.* Washington, DC: World Bank.

Global Water Partnership. 2009. National action plan for the integrated management of water resources (PANGIRE) in the financial, economic and social sectors, vol. 3, 163.

Global Water Partnership. 2010. *Partnerships for African's water development: Planning for integrated water resources management and development in Cameroon.* Yaoundé, Cameroon: Global Water Partnership Central Africa.

Hayev, F. A. 1944. *The road to serfdom.* Chicago, IL: University of Chicago Press.

Hoexter, C. 2007. *Administrative law in South Africa.* Wetton, South Africa: Juta Legal & Co.

Iaquinta, D., and A. Drescher. 2000. Defining the peri-urban: Rural–urban linkages and institutional connections. http://portal.geographie.uni-freiburg.de/forschungsprojekte/indigenoveg/Background1 PeriurbanTypology.pdf (accessed August 5, 2016).

Khan, I. 2006. Public vs private sector an examination of neo-liberal ideology: Managing the privatisation debate. http://www.mpra.ub.uni-muenchen.de/13443 (accessed March 23, 2010).

Kiefer, T., and V. Roaf. 2008. The human right to water and sanitation-benefits and limitations. In *The human right to water–current situation and future challenges,* ed. M. Mancisidor, 127–150. Barcelona: Icaria.

Lundqvist, L. 1988. Privatisation: Towards a concept for comparative policy analysis. *Journal of Public Policy* 8:1–19.

Mafany, G., W. Fantong, and G. Nkeng. 2006. Groundwater quality in Cameroon and its vulnerability to pollution. In *Groundwater pollution in Africa,* ed. Y. Xu and B. Usher, 47–57. London, UK: Taylor & Francis.

Masanga. 2014. Economic adaptation, water security and climate resilient development in Africa. WACDEP/GWP capacity development in Africa. http://www.gwp.org/Global/WCDP%20Images/Capacity%20building%20UNDP%20GWP%20Africa_final.pdf (accessed August 2, 2014).

Mbua, L. 2013. *Water supply in Buea, Cameroon: Analysis and the possibility of rainwater harvesting to stabilize the water demand.* BrandenburgischenTechnischen, Universität Cottbus-Senftenberg, Senftenberg, Germany.

Mcsweeney, C., M. New, and G. Lizcano. 2010. UNDP climate change country profiles, Cameroon. *American Methodological Society*, 179–166.

Moyo, K. 2011. Privatisation of the commons: Water as a right; Water as a commodity. *Stellenbosch Law Review* 22 (3):804–22.

Moyo, P., L. Chapungu, and B. Mudzengi. 2013. Effectiveness of water hyacinth (Eichhornia Crassipes) in remediating polluted water. The case of Shagashe river in Masvingo, Zimbabwe. *Advances in Applied Research* 4 (4):55–62.

Newbery, D. 1997. Privatisation and liberalisation of network utilities. *European Economic Review* 37:357–83. doi:10.1016/s0014-2921(97)00010-x

Olajuyibe, A. 2010. Sustainable water service delivery: An assessment of water agency in a rapidly urbanizing city in Nigeria. *Journal of Sustainable Development* 3 (4):210–19. doi:10.5539/jsd.v3n4p210

Olsson, L., and B. Head. 2015. Urban water governance in times of multiple stressors: An editorial. *Ecology and Society* 20 (1):27. doi:10.5751/es-07300-200127

Otto, W. 2014. *Access to drinking water and stakeholder action—Drinking water governance in Cameroon from a political–ecological perspective case study. Upper Mefou Watershed, Cameroon.* Department for Geographical Development Studies Freie Universität Berlin, Berlin, Germany.,

Perry, C. 1997. Water as an economic good: A solution, or a problem? http://www.irre.eng.k/Papers/report14.pdf (accessed March 23, 2011).

Postel, S., G. C. Daily, and P. Ehrlich. 1996. Human appropriation of renewable fresh water. *Science, New Series* 271 (5250):785–88. doi:10.1126/science.271.5250.785

Rhodes, R. 1996. The new governance: Governing without government. *Political Studies* 54:652–67. doi:10.1111/j.1467-9248.1996.tb01747.x

Roberts, A. 2008. Privatizing social reproduction: The primitive accumulation of water in an era of neoliberalism. *Antipode* 4 (40):535–60. doi:10.1111/j.1467-8330.2008.00623.x

Rogers, P., and A. Hall. 2003. Effective water governance. Global Water Partnership 7, Sweden. http://www.gwp.org/global/toolbox/publications/background%20papers/07%20effective%20water%20governance%20(2003)%20english.pdf

Sherbinin, A. 1997. *Water and population dynamics: Local approaches to global challenges.* Washington, DC: IUCN and PRB.

Shiva, V. 2002. *Water wars; Privatization, pollution and profit.* Cambridge, UK: South End Press.

Simonson, K. 2003. *The global water crisis: NGO and civil society perspectives.* Geneva, Switzerland: CASIN.

Smets, H. 2000. The right to water as a human right. *Environmental Policy and Law* 30:248–50.

Tanawa, E., H. B. D. Tchapnga, E. Ngnikam, E. Temgoua, and J. Siakeu. 2002. Habitat and protection of water resources in suburban areas in African cities. *Building and Environment* 37:269–75. doi:10.1016/s0360-1323(01)00024-5

Taylor, L. 1983. *Structuralist macroeconomics, applicable models for the third world.* New York, NY: Basic Books.

Taylor, P., and D. Sonnenfeld. 2017. Editors' note: Special issue on water crises and institutions: governance challenges in an era of uncertainty. *Society & Natural Resources* 30 (4).

Totouom, A., F. Sikod, and I. Abba. 2012. Household choice of purifying drinking water in Cameroon. *Environmental Management and Sustainable Development* 1 (2):108. doi:10.5296/emsd.v1i2.1642

UNICEF, and World Health Organization. 2012. *Progress on drinking water and sanitation: 2012 update.* New York, NY: UNICEF and World Health Organization.

UNICEF/WHO. 2012. Millennium development goal drinking water target met. Joint news release. http://www.who.int/mediacentre/news/releases/2012/drinking_water_20120306/en/ (accessed March 27, 2015).

United Nations. 2000. United Nations Millennium Declaration 55/2. Resolution adopted by the General Assembly. http://www.un.org/millennium/declaration/ares552e.pdf (accessed May 15, 2015).

United Nations Department of Economic, and Social Affairs. 2013. International decade for action, "Water for life" 2005–2015. http://www.un.org/waterforlifedecade/background.shtml (accessed May 5, 2014).

United Nations Development Programme. 2013. *User's guide on assessing water governance*. Oslo and Stockholm, Sweden: UNDP.

World Health Organization/UNICEF. 2010. *Progress on sanitation and*

World Bank. 2006. *Approaches to private participation in water services*. Toolkits. Washington, DC: World Bank.

World Bank. 2012. *Cameroon – The path to fiscal decentralization: opportunities and challenges*. Washington, DC: World Bank.

drinking-water: 2010 *Update*. Geneva, Switzerland: World Health Organization and UNICEF. http://www.wssinfo.org/fi (accessed July 5, 2011).

Yongs, H. 2010. Suffering for water, suffering from water: Access to drinking-water and associated health risks in Cameroon. *Journal of Health Population and Nutrition* 28 (5):424–35. doi:10.3329/jhpn.v28i5.6150

Women's Crucial Role in Collective Operation and Maintenance of Drinking Water Infrastructure in Rural Uganda

Resty Naiga, Marianne Penker, and Karl Hogl

ABSTRACT

Operation and maintenance of communally owned water sources in Uganda still pose challenges despite the devolution of water management from the state to user communities. Using a mixed-methods approach and a gender-sensitive collective action analytical framework, this article quantifies the role of women in drinking-water governance and identifies barriers to women's participation. The findings show that women not only are more willing to contribute but have also stated higher actual contribution than their male counterparts. The article outlines the institutional and individual attributes constraining women's effective participation in water management and suggests how to enhance women's participation in water governance. We argue that a strategy built on water users' collective action in Uganda has to be built on women's participation through effective rules and monitoring mechanisms, as well as on long-term sensitization and awareness creation on gender stereotypes that hitherto hinder women's participation.

Introduction

Continued water supply scarcity has been widely attributed to poor water governance (Global Water Partnership [GWP] 2002; Mugumya 2013; Fonjong and Fokum, this issue). Water governance is defined as the range of political, social, economic, and administrative systems that are in place to regulate the development and management of water resources and the provision of water services at different levels of society (GWP 2002). Owing to the fact that women and men assume distinct responsibilities in using and managing water systems, establishing appropriate linkages with gender has been recommended globally as a means of addressing the water governance crisis and achieveing sustainable water resource management (Cleaver 1998; International Conference on Freshwater [ICF] 2001).

In Uganda, as in many developing countries, women and children collect water for household use (Asingwire 2008; Asiimwe and Naiga 2015; Baker et al. 2015; Mpalanyi, Kabonesa, and Staines 2015; Van Houweling 2015). Cognizant of the central role women play in the provision, management, and safeguarding of water, the Ministerial Declaration adopted at the International Conference on Freshwater (2001) in Bonn highlighted that "water resources management should be based on a participatory approach. Both women and men should be involved and have an equal voice in managing the sustainable use of water resources and sharing the benefits."

To enhance the participation of major stakeholders in decision making, the government of Uganda adopted an integrated water resources management framework. The framework provides for the decentralization of water governance to the local level to involve water users in the planning and implementation of water projects (Romano, this issue; Förster et al., this issue; International Conference on Water and the Environment [ICWE] 1992; ICF 2001). These changes culminated in a paradigm shift from a supply-driven approach to a demand-driven approach to water provision in Uganda. While water provision was largely the responsibility of the government in the supply-driven approach, there are sets of conditions to be fulfilled by water users in the demand-driven approach. The conditions and responsibilities include the expression of demand for water through a formal application to the district stating the choice of technology, providing a list of elected Water User Committee[1] (WUC) members for each point water source,[2] and paying 5% of the construction costs as well as operation and maintenance (O&M) plan of the water infrastructure (Directorate of Water Development [DWD] 2011b). Multilateral and bilateral agencies support the demand-driven approach as being pro-poor and gender sensitive (World Bank 1999).

In rural Uganda, five main types of water sources are generally used (DWD 2011a), all of which are represented in the study areas: traditional water sources (ponds/open wells), which are considered as unsafe, and improved point water sources, such as boreholes, shallow wells, protected springs, and gravity-flow tap stands. Improved water access ranges from 33 to 76% in the study areas, with the distance to the nearest safe water source ranging from 0.5 to 5 km (DWD 2011a; Naiga and Penker 2014; Naiga, Penker, and Hogl 2015). In case of water source breakdown or inability to walk a long distance to the nearest improved water source, users resort to unsafe water sources.

With the shift from a supply to a demand-driven approach since the 1990s, access to safe water has improved slightly in rural areas of Uganda. However, O&M still pose great challenges, accounting for the nonfunctionality of more than 50% of the water infrastructure (DWD 2011a). O&M challenges have also been documented for demand-driven water governance in Bolivia, Peru, and Ghana (Whittington et al. 2008). As in Uganda, the O&M challenges in Bolivia, Peru, and Ghana are largely attributed to a lack of collective action, such as unwillingness to contribute user fees that can be used for repairs and spare parts (Whittington et al. 2008; Naiga and Penker 2014; Naiga, Penker, and Hogl 2015).

Point water sources in rural Uganda are collectively owned, used, and managed. They yield a limited amount of water prompting user rivalry. It is also difficult to exclude unauthorized users, which triggers common-pool resources problems such as overuse and free riding (Poteete, Janssen, and Ostrom 2010). Collective action and local self-governance are key to organizing and mobilizing resources to operate and maintain the infrastructure (Baland and Platteau 1999; World Bank 1999).

Women's roles in collective action in general and water management specifically have been widely documented (Meinzen-Dick and Zwarteveen 1998; Agarwal 2000; Poteete and Ostrom 2004; Pandolfelli, Meinzen-Dick, and Dohrn 2008; Singh 2008; Sultana and Thompson 2008). Despite the considerable rhetoric about women's participation and roles, less attention has been paid to the differences between women and men's contributions and needs regarding the local organization of the operation and maintenance of water infra-structure. With this article, we wish to contribute to this gap of empirical evidence regard-ing the roles that women play in the collective operation and maintenance of water infrastructure (Meinzen-Dick and Zwarteveen 1998; Pandolfelli, Meinzen-Dick, and Dohrn 2008).

Most of the literature on local water governance is built around single-case or small-*N* studies (Eberhard, this issue; Poteete, Janssen, and Ostrom 2010). While this literature pro-vides interesting insights, the explanatory value of the role played by women in operation and maintenance is unclear. In Uganda, too, there is a need for quantitative data regarding the women's roles within demand-driven water governance (Asingwire 2008; Nkonya, Pen-der, and Kato 2008; DWD 2011a; Nakano and Otsuka 2011; Mugumya 2013).

To narrow this gap, we analyze from an institutional perspective how responsibilities for the operation and maintenance of drinking water infrastructure are shared within local communities. The following questions guide this article: (1) What role do women play in operation and maintenance of a common drinking-water infrastructure? (2) What are the barriers to women's participation? The major contribution of this article is the quanti-fication of women's contributions to the operation and maintenance of drinking-water infrastructure in rural Uganda.

Water Governance and Gender in Uganda

In rural Uganda, the role of safe water provision at the household level is primarily played by women and girls. Females protect and maintain water sources and determine water storage and use, which affect the health of children and other family members (Upadhyay 2004; Asingwire 2008; Mugumya 2013; Asiimwe and Naiga 2015; Mpalanyi, Kabonesa, and Staines 2015). Compared to men, women in Uganda bear the brunt of inadequate water access, as they are not only expected to walk long distances in search for water, which puts their safety at risk, but are also expected to care for the sick family members as a result of waterborne diseases on top of their other domestic tasks (Mugumya 2013; Mpalanyi, Kabonesa, and Staines 2015). Men's role in water management relates mostly to purchase of household water containers and fetching water for commercial purposes (such as making bricks) and for their animals. Therefore, men are less concerned about water quality (Mpalanyi, Kabonesa, and Staines 2015; Naiga, Penker, and Hogl 2015). Financial and in-kind contributions toward safe water infrastructure determine whether women and children can access water (Mpalanyi, Kabonesa, and Staines 2015). However, in terms of paying O&M water user fees, men tend to abdicate the responsibility to their female household members (Asiimwe and Naiga 2015; Naiga, Penker, and Hogl 2015).

Cognizant of women's pivotal role in water management, Uganda has established a legal framework to encourage women's participation at all levels of governance. The Govern-ment of Uganda [GoU] (1999) is complemented by the Government of Uganda [GoU] (1997), and these provide for the participation of women in development activities, includ-ing water, sanitation, and hygiene. The legal framework is operationalized by an operation and maintenance strategy that emphasizes community responsibility for the maintenance of rural water supplies (DWD 2011b). Water User Committees are the executive organs of the local water user groups. In an effort to promote the participation of different user groups, women are supposed to occupy half of WUC positions, including key positions, such as chairpersons, vice-chairpersons, secretaries, or treasurers (DWD 2011b). While WUCs are charged with managing water sources on behalf of their communities, they are not registered. Also, their mandates, roles, liabilities, and responsibilities are not clearly defined and are hardly monitored.

In addition to the 5% contribution toward capital costs of new water infrastructure, water users are also expected to participate in major decisions such as making an application for water, selecting a type of technology, selecting the water source location, electing Water User Committee members, and collectively engaging into O&M-related activities such as payment of user fees and labor toward water source protection (DWD 2011a). To ensure long-term access to safe water, the Water User Committees are expected to collect water user fees, hire hand pump mechanics, and ensure that water users contribute labor toward the protection of the catchment area (DWD 2011a, 2011b). Without the water users' willingness to engage in collective action for operation and maintenance, long-term access to safe water in rural Uganda will remain elusive.

Analytical Framework

We applied a gender-sensitive collective action analytical framework (Meinzen-Dick et al. 2006) (see Figure 1), which builds on the Institutional Analysis and Development

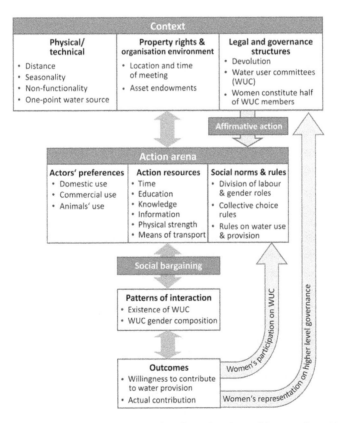

Figure 1. Gender and collective action framework (adapted with modification from Meinzen-Dick et al. 2006).

framework (Ostrom, Gardner, and Walker 1994; Ostrom 2011). We consider the framework suitable for analyzing the roles of women and the barriers that women face in collective action for water provision due to its focus on the institutions and actors that create gendered patterns of interactions and outcomes. To adapt this framework to the context of water governance in rural Uganda, we kept its basic first- and second-tier variables (Context: physical/technical, property rights and organizational environment, legal and governance structures; Action Arena: actors' preferences, action resources, rules and social bargaining; Patterns of Interaction; Outcomes) and added the "affirmative action" variable to take into account past and current policies and actions to support women's participation. Drawing from previous studies (Naiga and Penker 2014; Naiga, Penker, and Hogl 2015),we derived two feedback mechanisms, defined as women's participation in Water User Committees and women's representation in higher level governance.

According to our framework (Figure 1), the physical, technical, property rights, policy, and governance conditions present the context, which entails different constraints and opportunities for men and women in water access and management. Central to the framework is the action situation, defined as the social place where actors interact, make decisions, solve problems, or fight (Ostrom 2007). Women and men interact with different preferences, information, capabilities, asset endowments and power resources. Each action situation is also shaped by social norms and rules about gender-specific behavior, resource use, and decision-making mechanisms. Finally, actions and patterns of interaction lead to outcomes such as gender-specific willingness to contribute to the operation and maintenance of a common water infrastructure.

Study Area and Methods

Study Area Selection, Sampling, and Data Collection

We used a mixed-method approach comprising of both quantitative and qualitative methods. With the support of experts from the Ministry of Water and Environment and data on the variation in water source technologies, local water governance, and water source functionality rates, we selected the district of Isingiro as the worst and the district of Sheema as the best practice examples of local governance, and one subcounty[3] per district[4] (Masha in Isingiro and Kigarama in Sheema) to include a broad variety of technologies and variation in functionality rates (see DWD 2011a; Naiga and Penker 2014; Naiga, Penker, and Hogl 2015).

The data were collected in three phases. The first phase consisted of a total of 19 key-informant interviews (KI) and 11 focus-group discussions (FGD) at the community level (April to December 2012). National (KIn), district (KId), and community (KIc) level key informants were purposively selected based on their roles, experience and knowledge of rural water governance regimes, such as officials from the Ministry of Water and Environment and the Ministry of Gender and Social Development, district water officials in Isingiro and Sheema, and technical support officers at the Mbarara Water Regional Support Unit. Three focus-group discussions were conducted with WUC members (FGDwuc) and eight with water users—four with both men and women (FGDmx), two with men only (FGDm), and two with women only (FGDw). The interviews provided context-specific knowledge for adapting the analytical framework to the study areas.

The second phase involved quantitative data collection (January to April 2013). This phase was vital for applying the explanatory variables identified in qualitative interviews to a larger sample to quantify their explanatory value.

We used simple random sampling to select four villages[5] in Masha and five villages in Kigarama. Based on lists of households obtained from local leaders, we randomly selected 100 households in each of the 4 villages in Masha and 80 households in each of the 5 villages in Kigarama, except 1 village in Kigarama where 82 households were interviewed. Utilizing a callback[6] approach, the response rate was 100%, yielding 802 household questionnaires with closed-ended questions.

We also interviewed 50 WUC members from the 9 villages, 25 in each subcounty (Masha and Kigarama), using closed- and open-ended questions. Each of the four selected villages in Masha had one point water source, and contrary to the official guidelines (DWD 2011b) stipulating a minimum of seven members per WUC, one of the WUCs in Masha had only four members. Therefore, all 25 WUC members in Masha were interviewed. In Kigarama, each of the five villages had two point water sources. Two to three members from each of the WUCs were interviewed, which also added up to 25 WUC members in Kigarama.

Feedback loops from the expert discussions and pretests to the interview schedules and questionnaires were helpful in cross-checking for content, clarity, consistency, and ambiguous or overlapping categories and for testing the applicability of the questionnaires in the study areas.

The third phase of field work involved seven participatory workshops at the national (PWn) and the community (PWc) level held in March and April 2014 to present and validate the results of previous steps. At this stage we also discussed barriers to women's participation and how to overcome them with stakeholders from all levels. These discussions supported the interpretation of the study results and co-learning about the scope of needed action.

Overall, we were able to refer to 802 household interviews, 50 WUC interviews, 19 key informant interviews, 11 focus-group discussions, and 7 participatory workshops in our analysis. The purpose of this selection design and data collection phases was, inter alia, to enable diverse groups of women and men to express their views without fear or intimidation from their counterparts or from higher level authorities.

Methods of Data Analysis

After comparing the characteristics of the study sample with those of the country to judge the representativeness of the sample (see later discussion), we used a binary logit model to quantify the effects of gender and other explanatory variables on the probability of users' willingness to contribute toward water infrastructure O&M (see Table 1). Using a Pearson's chi-squared test, we established the relationship between the two categorical variables, sex and actual contribution (Table 2). Furthermore, a content analysis of the interview transcripts was conducted to understand gender-specific roles in O&M, to derive challenges encountered by women, and to obtain suggestions of how to overcome them but also to triangulate the quantitative results.

Before the analyses, the quantitative data were crosschecked for the basic requirement for the chi-squared test and logistic regression (e.g., expected counts ≥5 per cell, tolerance values >0.4, VIF values <2.5, distribution of eigenvalues).

Table 1. Binominal logistic regression—Water users' willingness to contribute to water provision (yes/no).

				95% Confidence interval for exp(B)	
Explanatory variables	B	S.E.	Exp(B)	Lower	Upper
Female on water user committee*	1.010	.415	2.745	1.217	6.193
Lack of community participation**	−1.545	.441	.213	.090	.507
Unawareness of water user roles***	−1.316	.350	.268	.135	.533
Mistrust of water user committee*	−.935	.356	.393	.196	.789
Sex of the respondent (female)***	1.424	.335	4.152	2.166	7.960
Distance (less than one kilometer)*	.904	.424	2.471	1.077	5.668
Constant	4.382	1.110	80.015		

Note. Significance: *p < .05, **p < .01, ***p < .001; nonsignificant predictors are not included: lack of training, water not considered suitable for drinking/cooking/washing/animals, existence of water user rules, age of respondent, education level of respondent, source of income, reliability of the water source.

Demographic Characteristics of the 802 Household Interviewees

The demographic characteristics of the 802 household interviewees are comparable to the characteristics of the general population in rural Uganda. The slight bias toward a higher share of female interviewees of 59% in our sample compared to 51% at the national level can partly be explained by a comparatively high share of women in the study areas (53% females). Women also tend to work at or near their homes, which rendered them more available for interviews.

Regarding the educational level, 19% of interviewees had no formal education, compared with the national average of 17%. The higher share of agricultural sources of income of 56% in our sample, compared to the 46% observed at the national level, is typical for rural Uganda. Although the study sample is small, it seems to be demographically representative.

Results

Gender and Willingness to Contribute to Water Provision

The logistic regression presents the variables explaining water users' willingness to contribute to water provision in the study areas (Table 1). Overall, the underlying regression model predicts 92.1% of the 802 households correctly. In the equation, we see two gender-specific variables: the household respondent's sex, and the existence of female WUC members. The logistic regression shows that interviewed female water users are four times more willing to contribute to water provision than their male counterparts (p < .001). The household respondent's sex has the highest positive effect recorded.

The existence of female WUC members increased the likelihood of the willingness to contribute by 2.7 times compared to water users who were not represented by female

Table 2. Sex and actual contribution cross tabulation ($\chi^2 = 32.133, p < .001$).

	Sex		
	Female	Male	Total
In the last six months, have you regularly contributed your water user fee?			
Yes	300	143	443
No	172	187	359
Total	472	330	802

members ($p < .05$). Hence, although women represented fewer than the stipulated half of the members (see later discussion), the result indicates a positive effect of female WUC members on water users' willingness to contribute to water provision in the study areas.

The variable with the most negative effect on the respondents' willingness to contribute to water provision was a lack of community participation in water-related decisions. It reduced the interviewed users' probability of contributing by 0.213 ($p < .001$). Many water users indicated that they had not participated in water-related decisions before water infrastructure installation, although the law provides for users' participation in both the pre and post water infrastructure installation activities such as the selection of the technology type, the decision on the location of the water infrastructure, the election of the WUC members and O&M activities (DWD 2011a).

Under the decentralized governance, districts are expected to carry out sensitization, including fostering awareness of water user roles and responsibilities at the community level. In the survey, we also asked water users whether they were ever sensitized and made aware of their roles and responsibilities in water provision. Users' lack of awareness of their roles and responsibilities reduced the likelihood of contributing by 0.268 ($p < .001$).

Mistrust of WUC also reduced the likelihood of contributing by 0.393 ($p < .01$). According to the O&M framework, one of the means to ascertain both downward and upward accountability as well as transparency of WUC activities is the public availability of books of accounts and bank accounts. However, none of the 14 WUCs analyzed did keep books of accounts or bank accounts.

Another significant variable is the distance to the water source. Interviewees were asked to indicate the distance they walked to the nearest safe water source (less than 1 km, 1 to 2 km, or more than 2 km). Household respondents with a shorter distance (below 1 km) from the water source were significantly more willing to contribute ($p < .05$). According to the odds ratio, users closest to the water source are 2.5 times more willing to contribute to water provision than those more than 2 km away.

Gender and Actual Contributions to Water Provision

Table 2 presents the cross tabulation of the dichotomous variables "actual contribution" and "sex." A Pearson's chi-squared test showed a significant relationship between the two variables ($\chi^2 = 32.133$, $p < .001$). Based on the odds ratio, the likelihood of a female interviewee reporting an actual contribution is 2.3 times higher than that of a male interviewee.

In addition to financial contributions, household respondents were also asked about in-kind contributions. When asked about the labor contributed toward cleaning and protecting the water source within the last 6 months, 45% of women reported contributing, compared to 34% of males. Regarding in-kind contribution, key informants and workshop participants confirmed that since women and children bear the brunt of water scarcity at a household level, they feel obliged to ensure that the water source is not overgrown with vegetation (PWcmx; KId44 m; KIc10w; FGDwuc Kigarama). Interviewees further explained that building and mending fences was a male responsibility (PWcmx, FGDmx, KId44 m; KIc10w; FGDwuc Kigarama). Interviewees also reported men using the water sources mainly for watering their animals and commercial purposes, especially fetching water for sale and making bricks. This, too, might explain their labor contribution toward O&M of the water infrastructure (PWcmx; KId44 m; KIc10w; FGDwuc Kigarama).

Furthermore, focus-group discussions at the community level recognized women's contribution in terms of community mobilization and sensitization on water-related matters. As a male participant explained, "Women in our village play a leading role in mobilizing community members to make their financial contributions, especially in cases of water source breakdown" (FGDm Kigarama). Another male participant observed, "It does not matter whether a woman is a WUC member or not, they always remind us about water user rules" (FGDwuc Rubeho). The quantitative results further indicated that 75% of female interviewees were aware of the existing water user rules compared to 39% of males, which also confirms women's potential informal role in local water management.

The quantitative analysis indicated that 32% of female interviewees attended a meeting convened by a WUC within the last year (compared to 27% of male interviewees). In contrast to this quantitative information, several interviewees argued that women are more likely to miss information, as they tend to be confined to their homes (PWcmx, FGDmx, Rubeho, FGDm, Kabaare, FGDw, Masheruka, KIcm2). As a female participant observed, "There is a tendency by the district officials to target men during training programs on water-related activities" (FGDw, Maseruka). A male Key Informant at district level confirmed this by stating, "We target men mostly, since they are household heads and decision makers" (KInm2).

Women's Participation in Water User Committees

Women are supposed to constitute half of the WUC members and should also occupy influential positions (e.g., chair, vice-chair, secretary, or treasurer) (DWD 2011b). However, in all the 14 WUCs analyzed, women represented less than one-third of members and only 3 WUC had a woman in a leadership position (2 WUCs in Isingiro had female treasurers, while Sheema had 1 WUC with a female secretary). A male key informant confirmed, "The law providing for women participation on WUC is rarely adhered to" (KIcm5).

Lack of higher level representation was also reported as a challenge to effective WUC performance and women participation. Interviewees expressed the need for WUC representation at district and national level as a means of minimizing delays and distortions of water related issues (KIcf7; KInm3 and FGDmx, Rubeho).

The national- and community-level interviewees attributed female underrepresentation on WUCs to a lack of awareness about the rules and to a lack of capacity at the district level to foster awareness and monitor water related activities. A male district key informant confirmed: "At the district level we are aware that in some cases, WUC composition is not 'right,' but since the demand-driven approach is relatively new, it requires effective monitoring mechanisms and continuous awareness creation in communities but districts lack capacities and funds to effectively carry out these roles. Software[7] activities, though important, receive the smallest budget share" (KInm1). Women's underrepresentation on WUCs and limited influence on water related decisions were also attributed to their limited control over land (FGDw, PWn, PWc, KInm1), which is an important in-kind contribution toward water infrastructure installation and O&M related decisions (KInw11, KIcw8, KIcw5, FDGwuc, FGDw, PWn, PWc,).

Women's participation requires engagement in the public domain, including attending meetings, trainings, and mobilization and sensitization activities. But gender stereotypes and a gendered division of labor tend to confine women to the private domain (PWn, PWc, FGDmx, Rubeho, FGDmx Nyarubungo, KInw11, KIcw8, KIcw5, FDGwuc Masheruka). A male participant noted that women who chair meetings are labeled "impossible women" (FGDm Nyarubungo). A female key informant at the national level confirmed that a woman who aspires to public participation is labeled "macho." This attitude toward women's participation discourages participation in and aspiration to community service.

Some women cannot take up key WUC positions due to low literacy levels (KInm2, FGDwuc, FGDmx, KIcm5, KIcm3). Although literacy levels are generally low in Uganda, women were found to be more disadvantaged than men in terms of education. Another explanation provided was a lack of physical strength, which was seen as constraining women's participation as hand pump mechanics, who have to carry the heavy kits over long distances when carrying out water infrastructure repairs (KInm2, FGDwuc, FGDw, KIcm5, KIcm3). Participation was also affected by a lack of confidence, inexperience and low self-esteem, which limits women's ability to speak in public (FGDm Rubeho, FGDmx, Kabutsye PWc, PWn, KInm1, KInw4).

Despite the institutional and cultural challenges to female WUC membership, 85.3% of the household respondents considered their formal and informal participation crucial. We examined the cross tabulation of the "trust in WUC" variable and whether women were members of the WUC and controlled for the influence of the interviewees' sex using a log-linear analysis of the three categorical variables: sex of interviewee, women on WUC, and trust of WUC (Figure 2). The results indicate a significant higher order interaction among the three variables ($\chi^2 = 4.973$, $p < .05$). Compared to a WUC without female members, the likelihood of a female interviewee trusting a WUC with female members is 2.4 [(253/87)/(73/59)] times higher, while for male interviewees it is reduced to 0.3 [(104/147)/(326/146)]. In other words, males are less likely to trust a WUC with female members.

The qualitative results, however, did not help to explain this gender bias in the trust of female WUC membership. The arguments for trusting women on WUCs came from both men and women and included that women do not smoke or drink, have stronger feelings of shame, lead by example, have water "at heart," and value water more than men (FGDmx, Rubeho; FGDwuc Nyarubungo; KIcw8; KIcm1; KIcm5;KIcm3; KIcm9; FGDw Runyinya).

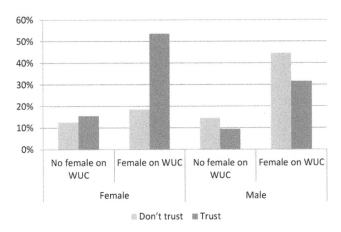

Figure 2. Sex of interviewee, female on water user committee, and trust in the water user committee.

We discussed all the results presented here with stakeholders at all levels in follow-up participatory workshops (already described) for validation, co-learning, and determining the scope of needed action. There was broad agreement that women's participation was predominantly hindered by the sociocultural norms and gender stereotypes, which should be addressed through intensified sensitization and awareness creation at the household and community levels. Further measures proposed by stakeholders at the national, district, and community levels include:

- Provision of further quantitative data, such as cost–benefit analyses of involving women in water management (PWn, KIcm10, KInw11, FGDm Masheruka). Evidence on potential benefits of involving women could help to slowly overcome gender stereoptypes.
- Provision of low-cost technologies for reducing drudgery at the household level (FGDmx Kabutsye, KIdw3, KIdm2, PWcmx, KIcw6). This would help women to free further time from domestic-related work to participate in water-related decision-making processes.
- Government policies to ensure that girls are enrolled and kept in school to completion (FGDw Rubeho, KInm1, KIdw7, PWnmx) and adult literacy campaigns (PWcmx, KIc5, KIn12, FGDm, Kabaare). Education of girls and women, but also of boys and men, to reflect on implications of the traditional gender roles and stereotypes on water resources management and outcomes. Education could also help to build capacity and self-esteem of women to take up key roles in water management and advocate for their interests in public space and at home.

Discussion

Discussion of Results

The combined results from the 802 household and 50 WUC member interviews indicate that women reported not only significantly higher willingness to contribute but also higher actual contributions to water provision compared to male interviewees. These findings contrast with developing countries literature arguing that financial contributions are a male domain mainly because women tend to be poorer on average than their male counterparts (Ellis 2000). In Kenya, Crow, Swallow, and Asamba (2012) noted that financial contributions are male responsibilities, and in India, Singh (2007) found that operations and maintenance of water infrastructure are male responsibilities. According to our results, a gendered division of labor and women's higher dependence on clean drinking water as a means of survival and source of livelihood might explain the observed increased women's willingness to contribute and actual contribution to water provision. Men's failure to pay O&M water fees has been attributed to their limited cultural roles in domestic water privision (Mpalanyi, Kabonesa, and Staines 2015).

Our quantitative results further indicate that female water users are more likely to trust in WUCs than men. Lack of trust was identified as an obstacle to water policy reforms elsewhere (such as in South Africa by Goldin 2010) and as explanatory factor for water users' reluctance to contribute water user fees in Uganda (Naiga and Penker 2014). Our gender-sensitive analysis showed that female WUC members positively influenced female water users' trust in the WUC but reduced that of males. However, during the structured interviews and focus group discussions, men did not refer to mistrust in women WUC members, but rather pointed out female characteristics they considered beneficial for WUC membership. The correlation between males' mistrust in WUC and WUC gender composition might, however, show that males do not like the idea of women holding public positions. This is underlined by interviewees referring to women in public positions as "impossible women" or "macho." How socially ascribed characteristics of a "good" or "bad" wife and mother shape water use practices was analyzed before (see O'Reilly 2006; Van Houweling 2015).

According to our results, men might prefer informal participation of women in water governance, as pointed out by a male focus-group participant who stressed that it did not matter whether a woman is a WUC member or not. The affirmative action by the government and the legal requirements supporting female WUC membership can also be interpreted as a mission to reshape women's role from traditional and informal domestic water managers and "good" mothers to formal public representatives and water managers (O'Reilly 2006). Therefore, gender roles and gender–nature interrelations do not only impact on the local water governance, but water-related policies can also challenge traditional gender roles.

Both men and women interviewees at all levels argued for strengthening affirmative action and overcoming sociocultural norms and stereotypes, which are hindering women's formal participation in water governance. This rhethoric for more formal participation might be explained by the fact that interviewees were aware that the national goals of female participation, in terms of the quantity and quality of positions, have often not been met. Faulty female participation in WUCs in terms of both quality and quantity was also reported for Kenya (Wambu and Kindiki 2015), in a study on 121 rural water supply projects in developing countries (Narayan 1995) and for India (Prokopy 2004). Our quantitative results on women's higher willingness to contribute to O&M and their higher trust in WUCs with female members also support the calls for further affirmative action.

Discussion of the Analytic Framework

To our knowledge, no empirical study had applied the gender-sensitive collective action framework to quantify women's contribution to O&M of water infrastructure in Uganda or elsewhere. And as water governance institutions are context sensitive, the authors opted for a research design that was open enough to include aspects that were not covered by the framework. The gender-sensitive collective action framework helped structure our results. The first part of the framework (context) was useful for identifying key aspects of the environment that influence collective action outcomes and for determining how these contextual aspects differ in importance for men and women (e.g., the distance to water sources). The elements of the second part (the action arena) helped to identify the different action resources required for women's effective participation in WUCs, which in turn can have a long-term impact on changing the conditions for women participation in local water-related decisions and in other public domains (see preceding discussion and O'Reilly 2006). Being aware that women are not a homogeneous group and remaining cautious of transferring an analytic lens from one place to another, we used the structure of the framework to examine how each element (of the context, the action arena, patterns of interaction, and outcomes) is shaped and influenced by the context-specific gender differences in the study areas. While the analytical framework has proven useful in these regards and despite its broad applicability, the dynamic processes associated with the policy reform, such as the uncertainty created by the rapid transition from supply to demand-driven water governance, inefficiency of state bureaucray, and inadequate government funding and capacity, were difficult to grasp within this framework. Romano (this issue) and Fonjong and Fokum (this issue) discuss different challenges of state failure for water provision in Nicaragua and Cameroon.

Conclusions

This study provides much needed quantitative information about the pivotal role of women in the collective operation and maintenance of drinking water infrastructure in the context of devolution in Uganda. Compared to male interviewees, female respondents were four times more willing to contribute water user fees, and they were more likely to trust WUCs, particularly those with female members. The willingness to contribute and trust in local governance organizations are key for an effective implementation of the demand-driven approach that depends on financial and in-kind contribution from water users. Women have much higher stakes in the long-term access to safe water than men. Therefore, a strategy that aims to increase the likelihood of water user contributions to the operation and maintenance of water infrastructure has to be built on formal and informal participation of women in local water governance.

Notes

1. Committee elected by users at the community level to oversee operations and maintenance.
2. These include boreholes, shallow wells, protected springs, and gravity-flow systems.
3. "Subcounty" is the level below district and is made up of a number of parishes.
4. "District" is the highest level of the local government administrative structures.
5. "Village" is the lowest administrative unit, consisting of neighboring households.
6. In the case when nobody was at home in the ramdomly selected households, the research team would make several visits until they found the interviewee.
7. Here used as an umbrella term that refers to a package of activities involving awareness raising, community mobilization, postconstruction follow-up, and community support.

Funding

We thank all the interviewees for their valuable information and the anonymous reviewers for their valuable comments. We acknowledge the OeAD-APPEAR partnership program for the funding that enabled this research. The support from the Institute for Sustainable Economic Development and Institute of Forest, Environmental and Natural Resource Policy at the University of Natural Resources and Life Sciences Vienna (BOKU), Austria, is gratefully appreciated.

References

Agarwal, B. 2000. Conceptualising environmental collective action: Why gender matters. *Cambridge Journal of Economics* 42 (3):283–10. doi:10.1093/cje/24.3.283

Asiimwe, G. B., and R. Naiga. 2015. Towards understanding challenges to water access in Uganda. In *Water is life*, ed. S. Linnane, K. G. McGuigan, H. Fagan, and A. Rugumayo 59–72. Rugby, UK: Practical Action Publishing.

Asingwire, N. 2008. Shifting paradigms in social policy reform: A case of demand versus supply-driven approaches to safe water supply in Uganda. PhD dissertation, Makerere University, Kampala, Uganda.

Baker, T. J., B. Cullen, L. Debevec, and Y. Abebe. 2015. A socio-hydrological approach for incorporating gender into biophysical models and implications for water resources research. *Applied Geography* 62:325–38. doi:10.1016/j.apgeog.2015.05.008

Baland, J. M., and J. P. Platteau. 1999. The ambiguous impact of inequality on local resource management. *World Development* 27 (5):773–88. doi:10.1016/s0305-750x(99)00026-1

Cleaver, F. 1998. Choice, complexity, and change: Gendered livelihoods and the management of water. *Agriculture and Human Values* 15:293–99.

Crow, B., B. Swallow, and I. Asamba. 2012. Community organised household water increases not only rural incomes, but also men's work. *World Development* 40 (3):528–41. doi:10.1016/j.worlddev.2011.08.002

Directorate of Water Development. 2011a. *Assessment of the effectiveness of the community-based maintenance system for rural water supply facilities.* Kampala, Uganda: DWD.

Directorate of Water Development. 2011b. *Updated national framework for operation and maintenance of rural water supplies in Uganda.* Kampala, Uganda: DWD.

Ellis, F. 2000. *Rural livelihoods and diversity in developing countries.* New York, NY: Oxford University Press.

Global Water Partnership. 2002. *Dialogue on effective water governance.* Stockholm, Sweden: Global Water Partnership.

Goldin, J. A. 2010. Water policy in South Africa: Trust and knowledge as obstacles to reform. *Review of Radical Political Economics* 422:195–212. doi:10.1177/0486613410368496

Government of Uganda. 1997. *The national gender policy.* Kampala, Uganda: Ministry of Gender, Labour and Social Development.

Government of Uganda. 1999. *National water policy.* Kampala, Uganda: Ministry of Water and Environment.

International Conference on Freshwater. 2001. Conference report, Bonn, Germany, December 3–7. www.Water-2001.de (accessed September 22, 2015).

International Conference on Water, and the Environment. 1992. *Development issues for the 21st century. The Dublin statement report.* Janurary 26–31. Dublin, Ireland: ICWE.

Meinzen-Dick, R., L. Pandolfelli, S. Dohrn, and J. Athens. 2006. Gender and collective action: A conceptual framework for analysis. Paper presented at the 11th Biennial Conference of the International Association for the Study of Common Property (IASCP), June 19–23, Bali, Indonesia.

Meinzen-Dick, R., and M. Zwarteveen. 1998. Gendered participation in water management: Issues and illustrations from users' associations in South Asia. *Agriculture and Human Values* 15:337–45.

Mpalanyi, M. J., C. Kabonesa, and A. Staines. 2015. Lived experiences of women as principal gatekeepers of water management in rural Uganda. In *Water is life*, ed. S. Linnane, K. G. McGuigan, H. Fagan, and A. Rugumayo 31–42. Rugby, UK: Practical Action Publishing.

Mugumya, F. 2013. Enabling community-based water management systems: Governance and sustainability of rural point-water facilities in Uganda. PhD dissertation, Dublin City University, Dublin, Ireland.

Naiga, R., and M. Penker. 2014. Determinants of users' willingness to contribute to safe water provision in rural Uganda. *Lex Localis-Journal of Local Self-Government* 12 (3):695–714. doi:10.4335/12.3.695-714(2014)

Naiga, R., M. Penker, and K. Hogl. 2015. Challenging pathways to safe water access in rural Uganda: From supply to demand-driven water governance. *International Journal of the Commons* 9 (1):237–60. doi:10.18352/bmgn-lchr.480

Nakano, Y., and K. Otsuka. 2011. Determinants of household contributions to collective irrigation management: The case of the Doho Rice Scheme in Uganda. *Environment and Development Economics* 16:527–51. doi:10.1017/s1355770x11000167

Narayan, D. 1995. The contribution of people's participation: Evidence from 121 rural water supply projects. ESD occasional paper series no. 1. World Bank, Washington, DC.

Nkonya, E., J. Pender, and E. Kato. 2008. Who know, who cares? The determinants of enactment, awareness, and compliance with community natural resources management regulations in Uganda. *Environment and Development Economics* 13:79–101. doi:10.1017/s1355770x0700407x

O'Reilly, K. 2006. "Traditional" women, "modern" water: Linking gender and commodification in Rajasthan, India. *Geoforum* 37:958–72. doi:10.1016/j.geoforum.2006.05.008

Ostrom, E. 1990. *Governing the commons: The evolution of institutions for collective action*. New York, NY: Cambridge University Press.

Ostrom, E. 2007. Going beyond panaceas, Special feature: A diagnostic approach for going beyond panaceas. *Proceedings of the National Academy of Sciences* 104 (39):15181–87.

Ostrom, E. 2011. Background on the institutional analysis and development framework. *Policy Studies Journal* 39 (1):7–27. doi:10.1111/j.1541-0072.2010.00394.x

Ostrom, E., R. Gardner, and J. Walker. 1994. *Rules, games, and common-pool resources*. Ann Arbor, MI: University of Michigan Press.

Pandolfelli, L., R. Meinzen-Dick, and S. Dohrn. 2008. Gender and collective action: Motivations, effectiveness and impact. *Journal of International Development* 20:1–11. doi:10.1002/jid.1424

Poteete, A. R., M. A. Janssen, and E. Ostrom. 2010. *Working together: Collective action, the commons, and multiple methods in practice*. Princeton, NJ: Princeton University Press.

Poteete, A. R., and E. Ostrom. 2004. Heterogeneity, group size and collective action: The role of institutions in forest management. *Development and Change* 35 (3):435–61. doi:10.1111/j.1467-7660.2004.00360.x

Prokopy, L. S. 2004. Women's participation in rural water supply projects in India: Is it moving beyond tokenism and does it matter? *Water Policy* 6:727–56.

Singh, N. 2007. Women's participation in local water governance: Understanding institutional contradictions. *Gender, Technology and Development* 10 (1):61–76. doi:10.1177/097185240501000104

Singh, N. 2008. Equitable gender participation in local water governance: An insight into institutional paradoxes. *Water Resources Management* 22:925–42. doi:10.1007/s11269-007-9202-z

Sultana, P., and P. Thompson. 2008. Gender and local floodplain management institutions: A case study from Bangladesh. *Journal of International Development* 20:53–68. doi:10.1002/jid.1427

Upadhyay, B. 2004. Gender roles and multiple uses of water in North Gujarat. Working paper 70. International Water Management Institute (IWMI), Colombo, Sri Lanka.

Van Houweling, E. 2015. "A good wife brings her husband bath water": Gender roles and water practices in Nampula, Mozambique. *Society & Natural Resources* 29 (9):1065–78. doi:10.1080/08941920.2015.1095377

Wambu, C. K., and M. Kindiki. 2015. Gender disparities in water resources management projects in Njoro Sub-county, Kenya. *International Journal of Social Sciences Studies* 3 (2):123–29. doi:10.11114/ijsss.v3i2.703

Whittington, D., J. Davis, L. Prokopy, K. Komives, R. Thorstens, H. Lukacs, A. Bakalian, and W. Wakeman. 2008. How well is the demand-driven, community management model for rural water supply systems doing? Evidence from Bolivia, Peru, and Ghana. Brooks World Poverty Institute (BWPI) Working Paper 22. University of Manchester, Manchester, UK.

World Bank. 1999. *Decentralisation: Critical implementation issues for rural water supply and sanitation sub-sector in Uganda. A consultancy report*. Washington, DC: World Bank.

When Policy Hits Practice: Structure, Agency, and Power in South African Water Governance

Jan Janosch Förster, Linda Downsborough, and Machaya Jeff Chomba

ABSTRACT

A new water governance framework with the aim of overcoming past racial inequalities in water access and addressing the critical challenges of water security in the country was developed by the post-Apartheid South African government in the years following 1994. The adoption of ideas of collaborative governance and institutional devolution associated with integrated water resources management (IWRM) are central to this framework. Using social theory, this study examines structural and agential dimensions of power manifested during the establishment process of a water user association in the Northwest Province of South Africa. Portraying that the establishment process of this new institution was flawed due to power asymmetries of interacting actors, this article unmasks supposedly collective decision-making processes in collaborative water governance. As the establishment of water user associations in South Africa is an ongoing political process, our findings have societal relevance for the country's future water policy implementation.

Introduction

The racial policies of societal segregation of the white South African Apartheid regime (1948–1994), in which race, gender, and class were the dominant factors in South African society, mirrored water access in the country (van Koppen, Schreiner, and Fakir 2011). Accordingly, water access was highly unequal. Thus, at the heart of the new water policy framework of the post-Apartheid South African government lies the idea of redressing past inequalities of water access through a formal institutional mechanism of collaborative water governance on the local level—the water user association. In this article, however, we argue that the formal structure of policy and law including the idea of collaborative water governance in newly established institutions might be articulated on paper, but that existing agential capabilities on all levels of South African water governance in practice are not fit for the successful implementation of such policy.

South Africa, along with several other African nations (African Ministers' Council on Water [AMCOW] 2012), has embraced the ideas of integrated water resources management (IWRM), which promotes concepts of devolution of water management competencies to newly established institutions on regional and local levels and stakeholder participation in decision making (Braid and Goergens 2010). Water user associations

(WUAs) were envisaged as institutional vehicles for collaborative water governance on a local level.[1] In the South African National Water Act of 1998 (NWA 1998; Department of Water Affairs [DWA] 1998) they are defined as "cooperative associations of individual water users who wish to undertake water related activities for their mutual benefit." Through negotiated and deliberative processes within newly established WUAs the access to water for productive purposes was anticipated to be "radically transformed" (National Water Policy Review [NWPR]: DWS 2014).

However, IWRM has been criticized for delivering results that often fall short of promises and that water problems "continue unabated or even worsen" (Ingram 2013, xv). Lautze et al. (2011, 6), for example, point out that "IWRM is more prescriptive in nature, having largely pre-defined outcome goals," whereas real-world societal action is coined by a multitude of social processes with rather uncertain outcomes. Institutional approaches to collaborative natural resource governance in many instances face the same inherent problems (Sabatier et al. 2005). They often do not lead to beneficial social outcomes like increased distributive justice. Decision making, sharing responsibilities, and creating accountability (Bloomquist and Schlager 2005), the embeddedness into larger and inflexible governance bureaucracies (Ananda and Proctor 2013), and also a lack of fit between the newly established institutions and the socioecological processes that they try to govern (Bixler 2014) are often highlighted when explaining the misfit between goals of a policy and the outcomes of its implementation in practice. Indeed, what has been internationally defined as "good outcomes" of IWRM-based policy of collaborative[2] governance through local water institutions, or simply as "good governance," does not necessarily reflect outcomes generated in practice (Franks and Cleaver 2007; Lankford and Hepworth 2010).

Another factor underlying this misfit is power (Brisbois and de Loe 2015; May 2015). Power is among the most fundamental ideas in social sciences and social theory (Haugaard and Clegg 2009). Despite that, power analyses building on social theory are highly underrepresented in the field of water governance (Mollinga et al. 2010; Brisbois 2015). Although power has recently found its way back into mainstream academic discourses around water governance (Swyngedouw 2006), it had long been coated by a sweet icing of IWRM and its supporting lobbies and developmental agendas of mainly Western organizations and governments (Molle 2008; Cherlet and Venot 2013).

It is therefore essential to apply a theoretical lens that builds on social theory and incorporates issues of power to understand real-world hydro-social complexities of water governance. In this article, we consider water governance as the outcome of structural and agential factors within the various spectra of sociopolitical processes on the macro level of policy formulation and coordination, the meso level of institutional implementation, and the micro level of social dynamics around water (Saravanan 2010). As such, water governance is the coordination of societal action around water (Benz et al. 2007).

WUAs are the local "linchpin" of South Africa's water governance framework; empirical studies exploring their implementation and operation are rare (Meissner et al. 2013). Within the limited amount of international and South African literature that exists, a common finding is that both still prove to be a huge challenge (Schreiner 2013). Orne-Gliemann (2008, 9), for example, found that limited recognition of local diversities and a misplaced focus on institutional design rather than on social realities has led to a lack of "sustainability, participation and institutional autonomy." Faysse and Gumbo (2004) similarly portray constraints to the participatory inclusion of small-scale water users, as well as access to information and different degrees of organization around water issues of traditional communities and commercial farmers as problematic in praxis. More recently, in a case study of a WUA establishment in the Thukela river basin in South Africa, Kemerink et al. (2013) found that immense challenges in terms of inclusion and representation exist. They identified degrees of experience and collective identities around water issues, as well as different normative mind sets of commercial farmers of European decent, and rather traditional communities and emerging farmers, as hindering factors towards effective WUA implementation (Kemerink et al. 2013). The studies just mentioned hold value for the future of South African WUAs in practice. However, they are theoretically and practically void of addressing the fundamental social dynamic underlying the challenges of collaborative water governance, namely, power.

This article contributes to an improved understanding of structural as well as agential factors of power in situations of collaborative water governance in South Africa. It does so by first introducing a theory frame[3] (Rueschemeyer 2009) for exploring collaborative water governance that focuses on power, while drawing on social theories of structure and agency. Second, it applies this frame to an empirical case-based study of a WUA establishment in the Groot Marico catchment in South Africa.

The insights derived from the empirical evidence hold value beyond the South African context by demonstrating the role of structural and especially agential factors of power in the process of establishing new institutions of water governance. In order to improve the future implementation of WUAs in South Africa and worldwide, it is crucial to understand the role of power in that process and the factors that constitute such power. This article contributes to such improved understanding. Using social theory and theories of power we also provide a fresh theoretical perspective on water governance through WUAs, which, we hope, might spark scholarly discussions on formal institutional governance in the future.

Theory Frame: Structural and Agential Factors of Power

Social action is shaped by structural and agential factors within certain contexts (Giddens 1984; Barbalet 1987). Within this "symbiotic interplay of structure and agency" (Harvey 2009, 32), power relations play a central role (Haugaard and Clegg 2009). As power is central to contextual social interaction (Bressers and de Boer 2013), and social actions are (to a certain degree) shaped by societal structures, such as formal legal (and informal) rules (Diermeier and Krehbiel 2003), a theoretical perspective focusing on social theory of structural and agential factors of power is essential for understanding collaborative water governance among heterogeneous actors (Swyngedouw 2006; Cleaver 2012).

There are several ways in which the operation of power can be thought of: for example, a rather linear understanding of power as domination or "power-over," in which instance, according to Dahl (1957), A forces B to do what B would not otherwise do; or power understood as "A affects B in a manner contrary to B's interests" (Lukes 1974, 27). These are certainly expressions of power, but are not the only possible manifestations of it. In this article we focus on power as "power-to" (Morris 2006). This refers to a perspective of power as capacity for action (power-to), which stems from the use of resources and capabilities available to a person or group (Morris 2006).

Adopting such a perspective enables us to effectively analyze differences in the resource and capability endowments among actors and how powerful agents use such power to influence the establishment process of a WUA to their advantage.

Structure and Power

We adopt Giddens's (1984) notion that rules, as societal structures, are best understood as "procedures of action, aspects of praxis" (Giddens 1984, 21). This implies that rules have the potential to guide social action, including the control of power relations among agents or actors by other agents enforcing such rules (Saar 2010). However, we also acknowledge that legal rules and guidelines can be a source of power. This is what Barbalet (1987, 1) calls "structural resources" and is evidenced by the notion that powerful agents might be able to "play the game" of supposedly collaborative water governance more skillfully, because they have sound knowledge of how to use the rules of the "game" to their advantage (Saravanan 2010).

However, rules are viewed by Giddens (1984) as both constitutional and regulative. Subsequently, rules in this article not only describe codified laws that constitute, for example, what kind of legal entity a WUA is and what its mandated functions are, but, more importantly, address regulative rules for establishing a WUA in the first place. As such, these regulative rules are the codes of conduct for sociopolitical processes; in other words, they constitute procedural rules.

Agential Power

Drawing on social theory, we conceptualize agents as actors endowed with resources and capabilities to act in a certain way. In this sense, agency in this article does not refer "to the intentions people have in doing things, but to their capability of doing those things in the first place" (Giddens 1984, 15; see also Saar 2010). "Correspondingly, agency relates to action" and "action depends upon the capability of the individual to 'make a difference' to a pre-existing state of affairs or course of events" (Giddens 1984, 14). In other words, agency is related to power, and such power depends on the strategic deployment of a combination of resources and capabilities in a certain context.

We propose a resource as a materialized or socially derived something that actors can draw upon to achieve a desired outcome. These resources can be financial (money) and physical (e.g., a computer, means of transport) (Ribot and Peluso 2003; De Haan and Zoomers 2005). Another important physical resource in the South African context is land, because the access to land often still determines access to water. Furthermore, we suggest that social connectedness (degree of organization around issues of water amongst a group of actors) is a socially derived resource, because it enables actors in collaborative water governance to pool their resources strategically before and within negotiations around water access (see Saravanan 2010). Capability in this article describes a physical or cognitive ability to act (Franks and Cleaver 2007; Sen 2009). Knowledge is the central cognitive ability of individuals and groups in decision-making procedures around water, as the existence or nonexistence of knowledge may enable or constrain meaningful action like stakeholder collaboration (Goldin 2010).

Such an eclectic understanding of power is necessary, because "the operation of power takes place in many different ways" (Saar 2010, 9), and it is the "multiplicity of force relations" (Foucault 1978, 9) that reduces the explanatory weight of any mono-causational concept of power. To conceptually cater for this notion, we suggest that power is highly contextual and that to "exercise power is to create conditions or control circumstances in which others are implicated" (Barbalet 1987, 31). Influencing the context in which other actors act is thus a form of power (Bressers and De Boer 2013).

Methods

A systematic document analysis (Gough, Oliver, and Thomas 2012) was conducted on the National Water Act 1998 (NWA) and the National Water Resource Strategy 2 (NWRS 2) as the overarching guidelines, setting out the constitutional and procedural rules for the establishment of WUAs in South Africa. Our article thus builds on methods of textual and thematic analysis (du Plooy-Cilliers, Davis, and Bezuidenhhout 2014). Field research was carried out between January and April 2011 with additional site visits in 2015. Data was collected through semistructured and focus-group interviews with 48 participants living in the area of the proposed WUA. These data were enriched by personal observations based on field notes and transect walks with key participants in the study area. As such, data were gathered and analyzed, drawing on methods common in sociology and social anthropology within a qualitative case-based research approach (Ragin 2008).

Interview participants were chosen using purposive sampling and snowball sampling (Babbie 2014) and traversed macro, meso, and micro levels of water governance. These included four local commercial farmers (CF) of European decent, four emerging farmers (EF), and 18 participants from the local community (LC) and research participants from civil society organizations, like South African Universities, agricultural development projects, commercial farmers associations, and community-led agricultural development projects.

We present the findings of this research under the headings of macro, meso, and micro levels of water governance. The micro-level findings are presented in the form of a short narrative and afterward are analytically reflected upon. We support our initial argument that in South Africa sound structures for water governance exist, but that a huge lack of agency on all levels of water governance hinders successful implementation, with empirical findings from the ground. As such, the following background to the study area is already interlaced with empirical evidence.

Background to the Study Area

The case study is located in a subcatchment of the Crocodile (West)–Marico river system in the Northwest Province of South Africa. The area experiences mean annual rainfall of 400–800 mm and has one of the lowest conversion rates of rainfall to surface water in the world—only 8% (Middleton and Bailey 2009). The Crocodile (West)–Marico Water Management Area (WMA)[4] contributes 22% of the national gross domestic product (GDP), but accounts for merely 4% of the overall water availability (Muller et al. 2009), illustrating the great importance of distributive governance arrangements for water resources. The legacy of Apartheid (van Koppen, Schreiner, and Fakir 2011) is still clearly visible. Twenty-one years after the end of Apartheid, land claim struggles between commercial farmers and traditional communities are still ongoing (Interview, LC 2011,

2015). Large white-owned commercial irrigation farms of between 30 and 200 ha are located in between and around poor black communities of sometimes 3,000–5,000 inhabitants. The only source of water (besides limited groundwater abstractions) for productive purposes for commercial farmers and emerging farmers is the Marico–Bosveld Dam with a storage capacity of 27 million m³, which is fed mainly by runoff from the Groot Marico River and rainwater. A distribution infrastructure of open canals built in the 1950s transports this water to the commercial irrigation farms. This system is operated by the Department of Water and Sanitation local office next to the dam; however, it does not extend to traditional communities in the study area.

There, people of the Bahurudshe tribe face a daily struggle to access water for productive purposes; they currently use the water supplied to them by the local municipality for drinking purposes to also water their subsistence food gardens and cattle (Interview, LC 2015). Most water entitlements from the Apartheid period to commercial farmers of European decent are still valid by law. This is called existing lawful use and relates to the amount of productive water used in between the period of 1996–1998. As per National Water Act 1998 these water abstractions[5] are still lawful today and do not require a new license until specifically requested by DWS or a CMA. In the study area, water for productive purposes from the Marico–Bosveld dam is related to property and is allocated per hectare of irrigated land.

Subsequently, water allocations for productive purposes are still tied to land ownership despite the intentions of the NWA 1998 to separate the two and end the system of riparian rights, which advantaged the white minority of commercial irrigation farmers. That in turn means that without the acquisition of land,[6] black rural communities (or emerging farmers) are practically not able get access to water from the Marico–Bosveld dam for productive purposes, despite their repeatedly expressed intentions to increase their food security through small-scale subsistence agriculture (Interview, LC 2011, 2015). However, the authority to govern and ultimately distribute the dam water would have been mandated to the proposed WUA once established.[7] As such, the access to the WUA means access to the collaborative decision-making procedures about the largest source of productive water in the study area.

Employing the theory frame of structural and agential power as proposed in the preceding fits this context. Using the empirical evidence accumulated during this research, we portray that the establishment process of the WUA was flawed due to power asymmetries of interacting agents and actors. A WUA established in such manner would have created an institution defeating the purpose of establishing it in the first place—collaboration of different water users to undertake water management for their mutual benefit.

Macro Level

Structure consists of constitutional and procedural (regulative) rules. As they pertain to WUAs, the two central pieces[8] of such structure in South Africa are the NWA 1998 (DWA 1998) and the National Water Resource Strategy 2 (NWRS 2) (DWA 2013; see also Pegram et al. 2006). The NWA is the primary piece of legislation of South African water governance; it is a formal macro-level structure of constitutive rules. The NWA makes provisions for the establishment of institutions for water governance, including catchment management agencies and WUAs, whereas the NWRS 2 is described as "a manual of how to do things according to the Act" (Interview, DWS 2015). As such, the NWRS 2 provides the procedural rules for implementing the NWA in the country. While the authors recognize the significance of the constitutive rules, the procedural rules in the form of the WUA establishment guidelines (DWAF 2007) are more important for this research. It should also be noted that the study area currently does not have a functioning catchment management agency and this article reports on the attempts to establish a WUA. For the procedural rules of establishment meetings, critical excerpts from these guidelines include the importance of information sharing; knowledge building; representativeness; local inputs; and auditing within a debate to "foster a spirit of joint and participative decision-making," especially in terms of water for agricultural purposes (Department of Water Affairs and Forestry [DWAF] 2007, 8). For achieving effective outcomes "facilitators must explain the Act, its aims and their role and function as a WUA." Facilitators further-more "must ensure that all interest groups are represented and that one group does not dominate" (DWAF 2007, 8).

The DWS, whose core functions are water-sector policy, support, and regulation, as well as coordination and oversight of WUAs, faces huge agential challenges in terms of financial resources and human capabilities to perform various tasks of implementing its own water policy (Interview, DWS 2015; see also Schreiner 2013). Interviews with the DWS in Pretoria (2015) corroborated these findings: "No, we do not have the capacity to do what would be required by the Act."

Meso Level

The regional office of the DWS is supposed to function as the regional authority of water management in the area (in the absence of a regional CMA structure) and was mandated with the establishment of WUAs in the broader study area (Interview, regional office 2011). However, during the interviews it became clear that the regional office of DWS in Mafikeng was understaffed and did not appear to have the capacity for the challenging task of building capabilities like knowledge that may enable meaningful collaboration amongst stakeholders (Goldin 2010). "Human resources and finances are the biggest challenges" and "for additional staff members we do not have the budget" (Interview, regional office 2011). At the time of conducting this research, there were only two staff members in the regional office responsible for WUA implementation in the whole Northwest Province (Interview, regional office 2011), home to approximately 3.6 million people on 104,882 km^2 of land (Statistics South Africa 2014). A senior South African researcher (2011) told us during interviews that government actors from all levels of South African water governance are at a point "where they just cannot implement their own Act."

Micro Level

Giddens (1984) reminds us that the relationship between structure and agency is one of mutual influence. Structure and "structural resources" we have asserted as the rules and guidelines to be followed in the WUA establishment process. Furthermore, we have con-ceptualized agency as the ability to utilize resources and capabilities in order to access and influence the WUA establishment, but also with the resources and capabilities of agents facilitating the establishment process according to the guidelines set out by the DWS. As such, this section of the article is concerned with the interplay of structural and agential factors of power in the final meeting of the WUA establishment process. The lead author attended the final establishment meeting of the WUA in 2011 (but meetings have taken place prior to this one) in the study area and documented the following narrative. It is important to note at this stage that the establishment of this WUA to date has not been successful.

Besides 20 commercial irrigation farmers of European decent, two officials from the national DWS, and two officials from the regional office who were supposed to facilitate the meeting, only three small-scale emerging farmers were present and no representatives of the local, rural communities attended. During field interviews members of local communities and other local emerging farmers expressed their interest in becoming members of the new WUA, but they did not attend this meeting as they had no knowledge of it (Interviews, EFs, LC 2011, 2015). The invitations were sent out via e-mail 1 day prior to the meeting by the operator of the local irrigation scheme of the DWS (Interview, CFs 2011). People from local communities and emerging farmers might have an e-mail address, but they do not have the technological means to access their e-mail accounts regularly; in fact, most of them did not know how to use such technology or could not read or write (Interviews, LC, EFs 2011, 2015).

The meeting took place at a venue on a hillside overlooking the area, but out of reach of any major taxi route. Local taxis are a vital mode of transport in South Africa, as the country has no public transport system; most of the emerging farmers and members of local communities have no other means of transport. One of the commercial farmers indicated that "the meeting was held there, because we said so" (Interview, CF 2015). This created a situation in which emerging farmers and members of the local community living in the area of proposed WUA responsibility were not present and thus could not engage in major decisions regarding their representation on the decision-making board of the WUA that was voted for in this final meeting. Additionally, they could not engage in the process of discussing the WUA's proposed constitution.

The meeting was held in English, and the topics discussed included the hydrological and legal boundaries of WUA and some other legal and technical details. The language used had a legal character concerning statues and paragraphs of the constitution that was supposed to be debated in the meeting. During the meeting the three emerging farmers openly voiced their concerns of not being able to follow of "what is going on here" (Interview, EF 2011) due to their limited understanding of the English language. This caused the facilitators from the national DWS to conduct a half-hour knowledge-building session in the mother tongue of the members after the meeting. Therefore, decisions that would affect these emerging farmers' livelihoods were explained to them only after the meeting occurred. The spokesman of the commercial farmers dominated the course of events by systematically going through the points on his agenda. However, the constitution of the WUA, as a set of self-imposed constitutive and procedural rules, was never part of the voting agenda and was not debated. A commercial farmer told us: "We farmers started the process. We had elections amongst the farmers. When it started we had the farmers union—Buure vereniging [Boer association]—and among other committees, we also have a water committee. And out of that water committee all the farmers selected other farmers as members of the WUA" (Interview, CF 2015).

The three emerging farmers present had no part in writing this constitution, although their names appeared in the final document (Interviews, CFs, EFs 2015). In turn, this constitution would provide the procedural rules for the operation of the WUA. Moreover, when it came to the elections of the management committee that would take all major decisions regarding water management in the future, it became obvious that commercial farmers had already agreed on positions of president, vice-president, and treasurer up front and were now using their majority vote in attendance to instate them. The meeting was closed by the DWS official with an agreement that the DWS would present the constitution to be signed off by the Minister of Water Affairs for potential gazetting and report back to the spokesperson of the commercial farmers.

This specific scenario is illustrative of asymmetry in "power-to" despite proper structural and regulatory measures being potentially available. Collaboration and engagement are hampered because of huge differences in the endowment with resources and capabilities to meaningfully engage and influence the "course of events" during and the circumstances of that meeting. The power asymmetries and their consequences are discussed in the following.

Asymmetrical Agential Power

Government Facilitators

The WUA establishment guidelines clearly state a process in which facilitators are required to set an agenda that has been collaboratively compiled and explains all structural and legal procedures. During the meeting just described, the DWS officials did not lead the process by an agenda that was set up with the input of all actors involved. The facilitators did not read the Act and did not explain what the purpose of a WUA was, as set out in the establishment guides of DWS (DWAF 2007). Accordingly, no opportunity for "local input" was provided, and no "audit" by the DWS was undertaken.

The "structural resources" that the DWS representatives could have used to steer the power dynamics of the meetings were not used. Moreover, the procedural rules stipulated in the WUA establishment guides and the NWRS 2 were largely ignored. The facilitators from the regional offices were not adequately trained for the purposes of creating collaborative platforms of shared decision making. Equal representativeness was never ensured before the meeting commenced; the demographics were highly skewed in favor of the commercial farmers.

During the meeting the DWS should also have facilitated a discussion of the WUA constitution. However, it became clear during the meeting that the commercial farmers had written the constitution without the participation of other stakeholders: "We took a constitution from another WUA and made some minor changes. ... Meetings in the last 5 years were held amongst us [commercial] farmers" (Interview, CFs 2015). Local rural communities or emerging farmers were not included in the WUA development process: "Honestly, what do they need more water for? We are running the show here" (Interview, CF 2011).

This shows how collaborative decision making was totally absent and how the lack of power of government facilitators to conduct the meeting according to the procedural rules allowed the establishment proceedings to be dominated by commercial farmers, and (historically) marginalized people who were initially targeted by the new water policy were notably absent. This presents the inverse of what was anticipated by policy, law, and WUA establishment guidelines on paper, but was the reality of social dynamics in practice. This was also the reason for the DWS to not approve the previous three applications for a WUA establishment within the last 10 years (Interview, DWS 2015).

Commercial Farmers

The lack of government capacity to facilitate the WUA establishment meeting had a number of beneficial outcomes for commercial farmers, who had the power to influence the circumstances and the course of events of that meeting by influencing the venue chosen for the meeting, as well as setting the agenda while excluding emerging farmers and local communities into the meetings prior to the final meeting. This shows that commercial farmers were much better organized; they had a very high degree of historically grown, social connectedness with each other.

The historical context of the racist Apartheid era is a central factor in current water governance in South Africa. During the Apartheid era the white agro-farming businesses were protected and supported by a large regulatory apparatus within the government (du Toit 2004). This has led to the establishment of many other institutional support structures that continue to exist today. In the study area commercial farmers were organized into local farmers associations; into agricultural lobby organizations like Agri-Northwest as part of the national Agri-SA organization; and into the South African Association for Water User Associations (Interview, SAAFWUA 2015), a large lobby group with "73 members from WUAs and still existing Irrigation Boards representing a combined 1.2 million hectares in South Africa" (Interview, SAAFWUA 2015). Accordingly, the resources and capabilities of members of this white agricultural elite (education, knowledge, and the experience of being organized in formal institutions relevant to water management, as well as their degree of social connectedness to government actors) were thus not surprisingly more advanced than those of the historically exploited and marginalized emerging farmers or local communities (van Koppen, Schreiner, and Fakir 2011). Commercial farmers had significantly more power to "play the institutional game of water" to their advantage.

Confirming this, a senior representative from the DWS commented in 2015 on the power asymmetries between the DWS facilitators and commercial farmers in practice of water governance:

> They will even tell the representatives of the Department something he doesn't know and then take out the Act and point to the paragraph and section. Some of them were even part of drafting the NWA by the time before 1994; they know this law better than we do. And they also know more about the local conditions than our Department officials, because we don't have enough officials to go to the ground. These guys know how to play the game.

Emerging Farmers and Local Communities

The three emerging farmers who participated in the meeting had no knowledge about the legal framework of the NWA or institutional structure of water governance of WUAs and CMAs, or about the procedural rules for the establishment of the WUA (Interview, EFs 2011). During their participation in the research project, it was only the first or second time that they had heard about a WUA to be established in the area: "No one came to speak to us, and so we did not know" (Interview, EFs 2011).

In addition, they mentioned that a lack of transport to physically reach the venue of the meetings and limited financial resources to pay for a local taxi were huge obstacles to attending and participating in the meetings even if they had known about it (Interview, EFs, LC 2011). "Access to technology and also equipment is also a problem. We don't have the computers here that can help us to get information. We also don't have transport" (Interviews, LC 2011, 2015).

Discussion

Policy travels a long institutional way until it hits reality (Mollinga 2010). The ambitious structures of South African water governance that were put in place by the post-Apartheid government have not found sufficient agential power in practice to successfully implement new collaborative institutions of water governance. Theoretically, situations of negotiated decision making over collaborative natural resource governance have also been labeled as collective action. Collective action theorists and related institutionalist approaches (see Olson 1965; North 1990; Ostrom 1993) tend to assume that "outcomes of collective action would benefit the group as a whole and that members of a group share a common understanding of desired outcomes" (Epstein et al. 2014, 112). Such thinking about institutions and actors most often ignores underlying power asymmetries among heterogeneous actors in institutions. Similarly, Rachel et al. (this issue, XX–XX) argue that rather than being a platform for building consensus, negotiations often "resemble strategic 'policy games' between powerful stakeholders." In that light, our research confirms the findings of Kemerink et al. (2013), Faysse and Gumbo (2004), and Orne-Gliemann (2008) mentioned earlier in terms of problems of participation and inclusion and a lack of collaborative action (see also Berry n.d.). However, we draw different conclusions.

Theoretically, we have asserted that power depends on the strategic deployment of a combination of resources and capabilities to influence a "course of events" within certain circumstances. We have shown that commercial farmers possessed a greater degree of what Giddens (1984) describes as "defining properties" for action, and thus they held greater power to control the "circumstances" (Barbalet 1987) and influence the "course of events." This was reinforced by the limited power of the government actors to facilitate the meeting according to the structure of procedural rules. As a result, the (maybe naïve) idea of redressing of past inequalities of water access through participatory and discursive means within WUAs "has not really happened" (Interview, DWS 2015).

However, our findings suggest that in environments of asymmetrical agential power relations collaborative governance tends to be not very collaborative at all. The functionalist idea of just having to design the right kind of institution, with socially beneficial collaborative (or collective) action following, is thus often rightly criticized as overly simplistic and avoiding the conceptual shallows of power (Epstein et al. 2014). Similarly, Huang and Xu (this issue) highlight that power is a critical determinant of success of water governance arrangements. In our example, the emerging farmers and members of local communities possessed very limited power to access the meeting in the first place or to influence the circumstances or the course of events. Our results thus reveal that while policy and law are crucial for setting out structural factors of collaborative water governance, it is agential factors that largely determine its outcomes in practice. In particular, agential factors on the micro level should be thoroughly understood prior to the formulation and implementation of any form of collaborative water governance. In the same light, it must also be noted that real-world social complexities and the seemingly simple solutions of IWRM are often at odds with each other (Halbe et al. 2013). Considering the inherent flaws in the facilitation of the final WUA establishment meeting and the vast power asymmetries among involved actors, it seems questionable whether a WUA established in such a manner would have fulfilled the ideas of redress of historical inequalities of water access anyway. In other words, if a water policy does not build on the specific contextual realities in practice, it is likely not to achieve its goals. Such policy is likely to crumble when it hits practice.

Concluding Remarks

For the future of South African water governance it is therefore imperative to strengthen agential powers on all levels of water governance. First and foremost this is crucial for those who were initially targeted by the new water policy—the historically (and today's) marginalized people. From a structural perspective it is first imperative to pay greater attention to the enforcement of procedural rules by powerful agents and, second, to rethink the appropriateness of IWRM-based water policy approach with WUAs as vehicles for collaborative water governance in South Africa. A legal and practical separation of land ownership and water entitlements seems inevitable. However, without developing resources and capabilities of involved actors prior to the establishment of new institutions, enabling involved actors to meet on equal footing of power, collaborative processes of decision making over contested and scarce resources tend not to be collaborative at all. This is an enormous task for the DWS to overcome in light of the already existing agential deficits regarding financial resources and human capabilities. But at the same time it is the *conditio sine qua non* for improving the outcomes of supposedly transformative water governance in South Africa.

Acknowledgments

We are grateful to Dr. Bruce Missingham, Dr. Bimo Nkhata, Dr. Rose-Marie Bezuidenhout, Dr. James Patterson, Garth Barnes, and Dr. Charles Breen for their helpful comments on this article. We also thank the International Water Security Network, funded by Lloyd's Register Foundation. We are furthermore grateful to *Society & Natural Resources* editors Peter Leigh Taylor and Dr. David Sonnenfeld and three anonymous reviewers for their invaluable comments and suggestions.

Notes

1. Catchment management agencies (CMAs) as river basin organizations were supposed to take up a similar role on regional, provincial level, but 18 years after the enactment of the NWA 1998 only two CMAs are fully operational in South Africa. CMAs and WUAs were supposed to manage water across provincial and local scale in a cooperative way (Department of Water and Sanitation [DWS] 2014).
2. We agree with Berry (n.d., 2) in considering collaboration as a "somewhat more active notion of participation in which individuals or groups (usually referred to as stakeholders) debate, consult, and make decisions associated with an endeavor."
3. The idea of a "theory frame" refers to an analytical frame as analytical concept that emphasizes (among other criteria) the importance of past research for present theory, the fact that theory is clustered and is often presented in a nested set of frames, and that theory frames are context dependent (Rueschemeyer 2009).

4. This WMA is now merged with other areas to form the Limpopo–Northwest WMA. However, at the time of the research the area was called Crocodile (West)–Marico WMA.

5. The National Water Act 1998 of South Africa specifies existing lawful use (ELU) in Chapter 4, Section 22 and Chapter 4, Sections 32–35. A process called validation and verification with the aim of transferring ELU into new licenses adjusted in terms of the allocated volume in relation to the actual water use has been initiated. This has, however, been largely delayed due to existing human and financial capacity deficits (Mochotli 2010).

6. The de facto connection between land ownership and entitlements to productive water has been a contested issue in South Africa since 1994. Mochotli (2010) and Misibi and Dlamini (2011) provide useful insights into this matter, including the African National Congress (ANC) government's limited progress in its Water Allocation Reform (WAR).

7. This WUA would have constituted a new institution, as commercial farmers in the area have not been previously organized into so-called irrigation boards (see Department of Water Affairs and Forestry [DWAF] 2007).

8. The Constitution of the Republic of South Africa surely provides another central piece of legislation in terms of water governance and property of land and water, especially Section 25 of the Constitution. However, due to the limited publication-related latitude, it does not play a major role in this article.

References

Ananda, J., and W. Proctor. 2013. Collaborative approaches to water management and planning: An institutional perspective. *Ecological Economics* 86:97–106. doi:10.1016/j.ecolecon.2012.10.018

African Ministers' Council on Water. 2012. Status report on the application of integrated approaches to water resources management in Africa. http://www.amcow-online.org/index.php?lang=en (accessed May 4, 2015).

Babbie, E. 2014. *The basics of social research*, 6th ed., international edition. Wadsworth, UK: Cengage Learning.

Barbalet, J. M. 1987. Power, structural resources and agency. *Current Perspectives in Social Theory* 8:1–24.

Benz, A., S. Lutz, U. Schimank, and G. Simonis ed. 2007. *Handbuch governance. theoretische grundlagen und empirische anwendungsfelder [Handbook governance: Theoretical foundations and empirical applications]*. Wiesbaden, Germany: Verlag für Sozialwissenschaften [Publishing House for the Social Sciences].

Berry, K. A. n.d. Challenges to broadening participation: Definition, representation, and power relations. White paper for the AAG's Retreat on Catalyzing Research on Geographies of Broadening Participation, University of Nevada, Reno. http://www.aag.org/galleries/project-programs-files/Berry.pdf (accessed August 3, 2016).

Bixler, R. P. 2014. From community forest management to polycentric governance: Assessing evidence from the bottom up. *Society & Natural Resources* 27 (2):155–69. doi:10.1080/08941920.2013.840021

Blomquist, W., and E. Schlager. 2005. Political pitfalls of integrated watershed management. *Society & Natural Resources* 18 (2):101–117.

Braid, S., and A. Goergens. 2010. Towards the development of IWRM implementation indicators in South Africa. Water Research Commission Report No 1839/10. http://www.wrc.org.za/Pages/DisplayItem.aspx?ItemID=9027&FromURL=%2fPages%2fKH_AdvancedSearch.aspx%3fdt%3d%26ms%3d%26d%3dTowards+the+development+of+IWRM+implementation+indicators+in+South+Africa%26start%3d1 (accessed January 10, 2017).

Bressers, H., and C. De Boer. 2013. Contextual interaction theory for assessing water governance, policy and knowledge transfer. In *Water governance, policy and knowledge transfer*, ed. C. de Boer, J. Vinke-de Kruif, G. Özerol, and H. Bressers. New York, NY: Routledge.

Brisbois, M. C. 2015. Natural resource industries and the state in collaborative approaches to water governance: A power-based analysis. PhD dissertation, University of Waterloo, Waterloo, ON, Canada.

Brisbois, M. C., and R. de Loe. 2015. Power in collaborative approaches to governance for water: A systematic review. *Society & Natural Resources* 29 (7):775–90. doi:10.1080/08941920.2015.1080339

Cherlet, J., and J. P. Venot. 2013. Structure and agency: Understanding water policy changes in West Africa. *Water Policy* 15:479–95. doi:10.2166/wp.2013.086

Cleaver, F. 2012. *Development through bricolage. Rethinking institutions for natural resources governance*. New York, NY: Earthscan, Routledge.

Dahl, R. 1957. The concept of power. *Behavioural Science* 2 (3):201–15.

de Haan, L., and A. Zoomers. 2005. Exploring the frontiers of livelihoods research. *Development and Change* 36 (1):27–47. doi:10.1111/j.0012-155x.2005.00401.x

du Toit, A. 2004. Forgotten by the highway: Globalisation, adverse incorporation and chronic poverty in a commercial farming district of South Africa. CPRC working paper 49, PLAAS chronic poverty and development policy series no. 4, Chronic Poverty Research Centre, University of Western Cape, Cape Town, South Africa.

Department of Water Affairs. 1998. National water act 1998. http://www.info.gov.za/view/DownloadFileAction?id=70693, (accessed February 04, 2011).

Department of Water Affairs. 2013. *National water resource strategy*, 2nd ed., June. https://www.dwa.gov.za/documents/Other/Strategic%20Plan/NWRS2-Final-email-version.pdf (accessed September 22, 2013).

Department of Water Affairs, and Forestry. 2007. Guidelines for the establishment and operation of a developmental water user association. https://www.dwaf.gov.za/IO/Docs/WUA/WUA%20Establishment%20Guide/ApprovedGuideonestablishmentoperationofAgriculturalWUAs.pdf (accessed January 04, 2011).

Department of Water, and Sanitation. 2014. National water policy review (NWPR 2013). Parliamentary Monitoring Group. http://www.pmg.org.za/calls-for-comment/national-water-policy-review-nwpr (accessed January 01, 2015).

Diermeier, D., and K. Krehbiel. 2003. Institutionalism as a methodology. *Journal of Theoretical Politics* 15 (2):123–144. doi:10.1177/0951629803015002645

du Plooy-Cilliers, F., C. Davis, and R.-M. Bezuidenhhout. 2014. *Research matters*. Cape Town, South Africa: Juta.

Epstein, G. 2014. Studying power within the social-ecological-systems framework. In *When policy meets reality*, ed. P. Mollinga, A. Bhat, and V. S. Saravanan, 111–35. Bonn, Germany: ZEF Development Studies.

Faysse, N., and J. Gumbo. 2004. *The transformation of irrigation boards into water user associations in South Africa: Case studies of the Umlaas, Komati, Lomati and Hereford irrigation boards. Volume 2. Working Paper 73*. Colombo, Sri Lanka: International Water Management Institute.

Foucault, M. 1978. *The history of sexuality, vol. 1: An introduction*. New York, NY: Vintage.

Franks, T., and F. Cleaver. 2007. Water governance and poverty: A framework for analysis. *Progress in Development Studies* 7 (4):291–306. doi:10.1177/146499340700700402

Giddens, A. 1984. *The constitution of society: Outline of the theory of structuration*. Los Angeles: University of California Press.

Goldin, J. A. 2010. Water policy in South Africa: Trust and knowledge as obstacles to reform. *Review of Radical Political Economics* 42 (2):195–212. doi:10.1177/0486613410368496

Gough, D., S. Oliver, and J. Thomas. 2012. *An introduction to systematic reviews*. London, UK: Sage

Halbe, J., C. Pahl-Wostl, J. Sendzimir, and J. Adamowski. 2013. Towards adaptive and integrated management paradigms to meet the challenges of water governance. *Water Science & Technology* 67 (11):2651–60.

Harvey, D. 2009. Complexity and case. In *The Sage handbook of case-based methods*, ed. D. Byrne and C. Ragin. Thousand Oaks, CA: Thousand Oaks.

Haugaard, M., and S. Clegg. 2009. Introduction: Why power is the central concept of the social sciences. In *The Sage handbook of power*, ed. S. Clegg and M. Haugaard 1–24. Thousand Oaks, CA: Sage.

Ingram, H. 2013. Doing better and delivering worse: Pathology of water experts. In *Water governance, policy and knowledge transfer*, ed. C. de Boer, J. Vinke-de Kruif, G. Özerol, and H. Bressers. New York, NY: Routledge.

Kemerink, J. S., L. E. Méndez, R. Ahlers, P. Wester, and P. van der Zaag. 2013. The question of inclusion and representation in rural South Africa: Challenging the concept of water user associations as a vehicle for transformation. *Water Policy* 15 (2):243–57. doi:10.2166/wp.2012.127

Lankford, B., and N. Hepworth. 2010. The cathedral and the bazaar: Monocentric and polycentric river basin management. *Water Alternatives* 3 (1):82–101.

Lautze, J., S. de Silva, M. Giordano, and L. Sanford. 2011. Putting the cart before the horse: Water governance and IWRM. *Natural Resources Forum* 35:1–8. doi:10.1111/j.1477-8947.2010.01339.x

Lukes, S. 1974. *Power: A radical view*. London, UK: Macmillan.

May, C. K. 2015. Visibility and invisibility: Structural, differential and embedded power in collaborative governance of fisheries. *Society & Natural Resources* 29 (7):759–74. doi:10.1080/08941920.2015.1072257

Meissner, R., N. Funke, S. Nienaber, and C. Ntombela. 2013. Status quo of research on South Africa's water resource management institutions. *Water SA* 15 (5):721–31.

Middleton, B. J., and A. K. Bailey. 2009. Water resources of South Africa—2005 Study. WRC Report Number TT 380/08, Water Research Commission. http://www.wrc.org.za/Pages/KH_Advanced Search.aspx?k=Middleton&start=1&o=1&ww=1&as=1 (accessed January 1, 2009).

Misibi, I. M., and P. Z. Dlamini. 2011. Water allocation reform in South Africa: History, processes and prospects for future implementation. Water Research Commission Report No. 1855/1/11, vi–xv. Pretoria, South Africa: Water Research Commission of South Africa.

Mochotli, D. 2010. Emergency response plan for the eradication of water use authorisations applications backlog: LETSEMA. Presentation to the Portfolio Committee: Water & Environmental Affairs, Pretoria, South Africa, November 3, 2010. http://www.wrc.org.za/Pages/DisplayItem. aspx?ItemID=3760&FromURL=%2fPages%2fKH_AdvancedSearch.aspx%3fdt%3d%26ms%3d% 26d%3dStrategic+review+of+current+and+emerging+governance+systems+related+to+water+in +the+environment+in+South+Africa%26start%3d1 (accessed January 2, 2017).

Molle, F. 2008. Nirvana concepts, narratives and policy models: Insight from the water sector. *Water Alternatives* 1 (1):131–56.

Mollinga, P. P., A. Bhat, and V. S. Saravanan. 2010. *When policy meets reality. Political dynamics and the practice of integration in water resources management reform*. ZEF Development Studies, vol. 13, Bonn, Germany: LIT (Center for Development Studies, ZEF).

Morris, P. M. 2006. Steven Lukes on the concept of power. *Political Studies Review* 4 (2):124–35. doi:10.1111/j.1478-9299.2006.000104.x

Muller, M., B. Schreiner, L. Smith, B. van Koppen, H. Sally, M. Aliber, B. Cousins, B. Tapela, M. van der Merwe-Botha, E. Karar, and K. Pietersen. 2009. Water security in South Africa. Development planning division, working paper series No. 12, Development Bank of Southern Africa DBSA, Midrand, South Africa, 5–39.

North, D. 1990. *Institutions, institutional change and economic performance*. Cambridge, UK: Cambridge University Press.

Olson, M. 1965. *The logic of collective action. Public goods and the theory of groups*. Cambridge, MA: Harvard University Press.

Orne-Gliemann, M. 2008. Water user associations in South Africa: Balancing flexibility and clarity. http://www.ceepa.co.za/index.php/63 (accessed February 3, 2011).

Ostrom, E. 1993. Design principles in long-enduring irrigation institutions. *Water Resources Research* 29 (7):1907–19. doi:10.1029/92wr02991

Pegram, G., G. Mazibuko, B. Hollingworth, and E. Anderson. 2006. Strategic Review of current and emerging governance systems related to water in the environment in South Africa. Water Research Commission (WRC) Report No. 1514/1/06.

Ragin, C. C. 2008. *Redesigning social inquiry. Fuzzy sets and beyond*. Chicago, IL: University of Chicago Press.

Ribot, J., and N. L. Peluso. 2003. A theory of access. *Rural Sociology* 68 (2):153–81.

Rueschemeyer, D. 2009. *Usable theory. Analytic tools for social and political research*. Princeton, NJ: Princeton University Press.

Saar, M. 2010. Power and critique. *Journal of Political Power* 3 (1):7–20.

Sabatier, P. A., W. Focht, M. Lubell, Z. Trachtenberg, A. Vedlitz, and M. Matlock. 2005. *Swimming upstream: Collaborative approaches to watershed management*. Cambridge, MA: MIT Press.

Saravanan, V. S. 2010. Movers, shakers and power brokers. Agents in negotiated water management in the Indian Himalayas. In *When policy meets reality. Political dynamics and the practice of integration in water resources management reform*, ed. P. P. Mollinga, A. Bhat, and V. S. Saravanan. ZEF Development Studies, vol. 13, 27–61. Bonn, Germany: LIT.

Schreiner, B. 2013. Viewpoint—Why has the South African national water act been so difficult to implement? *Water Alternatives* 6 (2):239–45.

Sen, A. 2009. *The idea of justice*. Cambridge, MA: Allan Lane and Harvard University Press.

Statistics South Africa. 2014. StatsSA, Yearly archives. http://www.statssa.gov.za/?m=2014 (accessed April 14, 2015).

Swyngedouw, E. 2006. Power, water and money: Exploring the nexus. Background paper: UNDP, Human Development Report. https://www.researchgate.net/publication/254419655 (accessed June 23, 2016).

van Koppen, B., B. Schreiner, and S. Fakir. 2011. The political and economic context and changing water policy in South Africa post-1994. In *Transforming water management in South Africa. Designing and implementing a new policy framework*, ed. B. Schreiner and R. Hassan 1–17. Global Issues in Water Policy 2. Berlin, Germany: Springer.

Standing Up for Inherent Rights: The Role of Indigenous-Led Activism in Protecting Sacred Waters and Ways of Life

Emma S. Norman

ABSTRACT

Time and time again, Indigenous people throughout the world are faced with the need to reassert their way of life, and to "buck" political and social systems that continually marginalize their treaty rights. In this article, I explore the role of Indigenous activism at different scales—personal, tribal, and collective—to intervene in key moments to uphold treaty rights and protect Indigenous ways of life. In defending treaty rights, Indigenous peoples have become leaders in the social and environmental justice movement, particularly in relation to climate justice and fishing rights. The article recounts three ethnographies that illustrate how access to rights is wrapped up in geopolitics and the political economy. Highlighting these acts of resilience and leadership in the face of crisis is the central work of this article. The article concludes with a call to fundamentally rethink governance mechanisms and structures, to protect ecological and human health.

Introduction

It is hard to imagine that a simple act of fishing or pulling a canoe could be seen as an act of resistance. Yet time and time again, Indigenous Peoples throughout the world are faced with the need to reassert their way of life, and to "buck" mainstream political and social systems that structurally marginalize their traditional way of life (La Duke 1999; Mirosa and Harris 2012; Holifield 2013; Norman 2014; Whyte 2016). Given structural injustice of settler-colonial systems, practicing everyday acts of survival—such as fishing—can now be wrapped up in acts of resistance, activism, and even heroism. A central factor in this disconnect is the tension between fixity and mobility (Biolisl 2005; Norman, Cook, and Bakker 2015). That is, fixed (and policed) jurisdictions established through North American settler-colonial reservation and nation-state systems are in direct opposition to the intricate and reflexive relationships that Indigenous communities have with the natural world (Cajete 2000). The very cosmology of Indigenous Peoples is built on the intricate knowledge of and connection to their ancestral land—and all its relations, including its animals, plants, and water (Cajete 2000; Grossman, Parker, and Frank 2012). Thus, the act of dislocating peoples from their traditional territories and limiting access to their ancestral land and waters has significant impacts on the social, political, economic, and spiritual systems of Indigenous People in North America and throughout the world (Ayana 2004; Whyte 2016). That said: Indigenous Peoples have a long history of resilience and strategies to overcome hardship, whether the hardships springs from colonialism or from environmental change. In fact, Indigenous People around the world are taking leading roles in important issues like global climate justice and water protection. Highlighting these acts of resilience and leadership in the face of crisis is the central work of this article and of other articles in this issue, such as those of Naiga and Förster et al.

While treaties were established during the settler–colonial times in North America to grant access to traditional hunting and fishing grounds through what is called "usual and accustomed" rights, the onus continues to be placed on Indigenous Peoples to reassert these rights, and to re-remind the United States government (and mainstream society) of treaty trust responsibilities and Indigenous sovereign rights status (Grossman, Parker, and Frank 2012; Whyte 2015). Perhaps most shocking is the frequency in which these rights are dismissed, challenged, and forgotten, and the ongoing need to reactivate, resist, and re-remind dominant society of these rights—which we are seeing yet again with the Standing Rock Sioux Tribe and the water protector movement in North Dakota.

The affronts are many and complex. As the cases in this article highlight, the circumstances change—whether wrapped up in geopolitics (post 9/11), political economy and capital accumulation, or the accumulating impacts of global climate change. As such, in this article I explore the role of Indigenous activism at different scales—personal, tribal, and collective—to intervene in key moments to uphold treaty rights and protect Indigenous ways of life, including connections to waterways. I show that as tribes and Indigenous actors take leading roles to uphold treaty rights, Indigenous Peoples have become leaders in the social and environmental justice movement, particularly in relation to climate justice and fishing rights. To illustrate this leadership, I recount three vignettes—or moments in time—when the connection to and protection of the natural world have been challenged through complex geopolitical and economic situations and the subsequent acts of resistance through Indigenous communities demonstrating their leadership capacity to respond to these crises.

These acts of resistance and political and social activism are happening the world over. However, this work engages the geography with which I am most familiar, the Salish Sea Basin in the coastal Pacific of North American between Canada and the United States (see Figure 1a).

I use narrative to illustrate the tensions between the fixity of jurisdiction and power dynamics associated with bounding, and the impacts these have on water governance and traditional ways of life. The vignettes, or ethnographies, illustrate how access to rights is wrapped up in geopolitics and the political economy. First, I recount a story shared with me by a Lummi community member, Tyson Oreiro, about how a day of crabbing became wrapped up in geopolitics and jurisdictional tension post 9/11. I then illustrate how challenges to treaty rights continue with proposals to build a large-scale deep-water transport terminal in a traditional fishing area of the Lummi Nation. Lastly, I show how groups are mobilizing to protest fossil fuel extraction and the continued acceleration of global climate change, through defining moments such as the protests of the Polar Pioneer in the waters off of Seattle, WA. I historicize these events by showing how fighting for fishing rights has been ongoing since the signing of the Point Elliot Treaty of 1855. I engage in these complex issues by weaving together Indigenous research methodology, standpoint theory, critical geography, climate justice, and Indigenous activism.

Indigenous Activism and Social, Environmental, and Climate Injustice

A growing body of scholarship has helped to identify the role of Indigenous activism in combatting systemic social, environmental, and climate injustice. This scholarship contributes to a clearer understanding of how structural racism, which is often invisible in mainstream society and governments, severely impacts marginalized groups and Indigenous peoples. For example, the works of Darren Ranco, Kyle Powl Whyte, Roxanne Ornelas, Daniel Wildcat, Zoltan Grossman, Ryan Holifield, Noriko Ishiyama, and Beth Rose Middleton (among others) all provide important contributions to advocating for

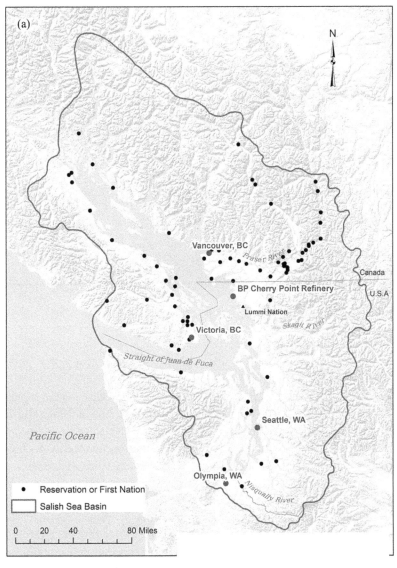

Figure 1. (a) Map of the Salish Sea Basin. (b) Photo of check burning: Lummi Nation Treaty Rights are Not for Sale! (c) Photo of No Coal sign on Cherry Point. (d) ShellNO kayaktivists protesting oil drilling in the Arctic, May 2015.

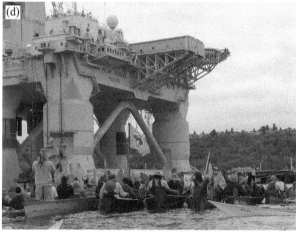

Figure 1. Continued.

Indigenous rights in a wide range of disciplines, including geography, environmental justice, Indigenous studies, political ecology, and philosophy.

Middleton's (2011) scholarship, for example, engages in a wide range of topics related to Indigenous environmental justice, intergenerational trauma and healing, and Indigenous Peoples' roles in climate change discourse. Most recently, her work in re-envisioning land conservancies through an Indigenous lens provides important insights on how strategic partnerships can help protect access to culturally significant lands and waterways—topics emerging in the Salish Sea.

Similarly, scholars such as Whyte, Wildcat, Grossman, and Parker provide important contributions related to climate justice and Indigenous peoples. Grossman, Parker, and Frank (2012) show how Indigenous Nations are asserting their resilience through strategic alliance building, using powerful testimony, and intervening in key public moments. Whyte powerfully situates the impacts of global climate change at a personal level. As a member of the Citizen Potawatomi Nation, he skillfully grounds the impacts of global climate change to specific harvesting and cultural practices that significantly impact his community. He refers to climate injustice as another iteration of the impacts of colonization—referring to the current environmental injustices as colonial déjà vu (Whyte 2015). Similarly, works by Ornelas help to push disciplinary boundaries by focusing on the geographies of Indigenous peoples with an emphasis on the protection of sacred lands and waters, role of Indigenous women in environmental activism, leadership, environmental justice, and human rights (Ornelas 2011; 2014).

Scholars of Native American Studies and Native Environmental Law, such as Ranco and Suagee (2007), have helped draw the connections between tribal environmental sovereignty and due process in the context of environmental regulation. Linking self-regulation, self-determination, and tribal sovereignty is an important strategy to combat structural racism and environmental and social injustices that put tribes in a position to continually defend or hold the line on treaty rights. This work builds on the prolific scholarship of public land law, water law, and Federal Indian law by legal scholar and Native rights activist Wilkinson (2006), and on Ishiyama's (2003) important contribution to *Antipode*, which explicitly link environmental justice and tribal sovereignty.

Geographers such as Holifield (2013) build on the environmental law scholarship by locating the tension between Indigenous knowledge systems and mainstream science, and data, and how this influences regulatory agencies. Thus, at its foundation, mainstream regulatory agencies are excluding certain foundational belief systems that are central to Indigenous communities. Regulation is wrapped up in power dynamics and dominant narratives that are largely invisible to the mainstream agencies and public. This conflict, as Taylor and Sonnefield describe in the introduction to this special issue, relates to asymmetrical power exercised by social actors. Similarly, Naiga and Förster et al. (this issue) show how these power imbalances are materialized as social injustices in different geographies and across different waterscapes.

The scholarship around Indigenous activism differs from other scholarship related to activism, environmental justice, and race, largely because of the unifying theme of deep and sustained connection to place and the role of Traditional Ecological Knowledge and Native Science. Other genres, such as environmental history and critical geography, helped to provide counternarratives to mainstream discourse related to the colonial-settler experience and the impacts on Indigenous Peoples and the natural world. For example, Taylor (1999) and Evenden (2004) provide important contributions to the environmental history of First Peoples, water, and fisheries in the Salish Sea Basin.

Decolonizing Research Methods and the Politics of Positionality

My methodology is part of a standpoint-theory approach, which utilizes narrative form to participate in a decolonizing research methodology and pedagogy. I am inspired and informed by Indigenous knowledges and theories—particularly drawing on the work of Cajete (2000), Wilson (2009), Kovach (2010), and Smith (2012), who strive to include research practices as part of wider projects of decolonization. Each of these scholars shows how inserting Indigenous Ways of Knowing into research practices can help identify alternative and multiple ways of seeing problems and identifying solutions. For me, these insights translate into a deep appreciation for place and an understanding of the relationships between humans and their environment over a sustained period of time.

Overall, my methodology employs a triangulation approach, where I employ ethnography, storytelling, and participant observation, in conjunction with analyzing primary and secondary sources. Additionally, following Indigenous research methodology (Smith 2012), self-location is also used as a guiding framework.

In many scientific traditions, objectivity is fiercely defended. Like many other scholars (particularly those involved in the feminist tradition, Indigenous research, and critical geography), I view this objectivity as an illusion. Although one can—and should—strive to enter into work in an unbiased fashion, positioning oneself within one's work provides transparency, which is particularly salient when one is working with issues surrounding power and justice.

Certainly, my positionality (i.e., as a researcher trained at the University of British Columbia, my role as a faculty member at Northwest Indian College, and my roles as mother, partner, sister, daughter, colleague, teacher, and friend) influences my dealings with people in the field. For example, my role in the Native Environmental Science Department introduced me to several Indigenous leaders who have generously provided comments and insight into this long-term project. In addition, the many hours of conversations with students, colleagues, and friends throughout Northwest Indian College and the Salish Sea Basin, in general, have helped me to see border politics through a more informed, nuanced, and critical lens.

A key consideration as I enter into my research is how (and whether) my work contributes to wider goals in the communities within which I work. In this case, disrupting a dominant narrative and locating power dynamics comprise an important contribution that, in the end, serves wider goals of Indigenous self-determination and, ultimately, healthier and more resilient cultures and ecosystems. The cases that follow help illustrate the ongoing work towards these goals.

Situating the Geopolitical Landscape of the Salish Sea—The Promised Rights of the Coast Salish Peoples—Exercising Treaty Rights at Risk

For Coast Salish communities of the Salish Sea, fishing is not just for economic gain or sustenance; it is a fundamental way of life integral to cultural identity. Access to First Foods such as salmon, crab, and shellfish, as well as waterfowl and edible plants, is central to maintaining this way of life. During precolonial times, the rich ecosystem provided all of the needs of the Coast Salish peoples. In fact, oral accounts speak of salmon runs so large that water was no longer visible—only the backs of the silvery salmon were visible as the salmon migrated upstream by the millions (Nugent 1982).

Post-contact, however, Coast Salish communities, like Indigenous communities around the world, have experienced tremendous affronts to their natural world and social–political–cultural structures. These compromises have come in various forms: land disposition, physical acts of violence, forced assimilation through boarding schools, outlawing of cultural events such as potlatch and other cultural practices, and degraded or decimated ecosystems (Whyte 2015).

The physical act of dispossessing land continues to have huge impacts on Indigenous communities, given the important role connections to and relationships with ancestral lands and waters have in maintaining a traditional way of life. Fragmenting communities through colonial bounding and displacing people from traditional territory onto small parcels of lands—reserves in Canada and reservations in the United States—had and continues to have severe impacts on Indigenous cultures (Miller 1997; 2006).

The signing of the Point Elliot Treaty on January 12, 1855, between U.S. Governor Isaac Stevens and Coast Salish tribal leaders marked a new relationship between the U.S. government and the coastal Pacific Tribes. The treaty acknowledges the Lummi Nation (and the other signatories) as an independent and self-governing people, whose traditional homelands extend throughout the Salish Sea, north into the Fraser River (in what is now British Columbia, Canada) and south into the neighborhoods of Seattle, WA.

The treaty established reservations and access rights to usual and accustomed areas for tribal communities throughout the U.S. side of the Coast Salish territory, and these were upheld through the Boldt decision (*United States v. Washington* 1974). The usual and accustomed territory is an important aspect of the Point Elliot Treaty, because it indicates the priority that the Coast Salish peoples have in maintaining a fishing tradition. It shows that fishing is not just about food or economy. Rather, fishing is a way of life and integral to cultural self-identity. These priorities are reflected in the treaty itself. Article 1 ceded the majority of the Coast Salish traditional territory to the settler community; Article 2 established "reserves" or reservations; and Article 5 established usual and accustomed fishing rights. Article 5 of the Point Elliot Treaty states:

> The right of taking fish at usual and accustomed grounds and stations is further secured to said Indians in common with all citizens of the Territory, and of erecting temporary houses for the purpose of curing, together with the privilege of hunting and gathering roots and berries on open and unclaimed lands. (Governor's Office of Indian Affairs [GOIA] 2015)

The priority of the coastal tribes to maintain a fishing tradition is indicated both by the location of the reservations, which are often at the mouth of rivers or other significant hunting grounds, and by their decision to prioritize access to these waters over larger land mass. Undoubtedly, the tribes were burdened with a difficult decision in 1855, when faced with the signing of the Point Elliot Treaty. Certainly, the decision was made in a time of duress, as populations were weakened by disease and other techniques of cultural genocide (Harris 2002; Thrush 2008). In fact, some tribes—including Nisqually—even question whether the "x" marking the tribal representative was even valid; oral histories indicate that, in fact, it was Territorial Governor Isaac Stevens who signed the "x" for the tribal representative (Wilkinson 2006). Despite the untenable circumstances that clouded the Point Elliot Treaty, it is important to stress the incredible resilience of the Coast Salish tribes and the foresight of the leaders when negotiating the treaty terms. The significance of Article 5 of the treaty, in maintaining fishing rights in traditional territory, is not to be underestimated. Essentially, the tribes relinquished millions of acres of land for the right to maintain access to fishing and hunting grounds, demonstrating what was—and remains—a priority for tribes. Yet fragmented governance systems (federal, state, tribal, county, city, citizen, etc.) and dominant narratives continually place the burden of maintaining these rights on the tribes themselves.

A key point is that with the signing of the treaties, the United States promised to uphold the treaty trust responsibilities. However, historically, the U.S. government has a spotty record in upholding the treaty trust responsibility. Only in recent years has federal leadership taken this responsibility more seriously. Time after time, the onus has been placed on tribes to reassert and actively defend these rights (which, it should be noted, are historically inherent rather than acquired rights).

In Washington state, the need to assert these rights grew significantly after World War II, when the economic gains made through commercial fishing and the industrializing of canneries led the state of Washington to, essentially, turn its back on the treaty and Indigenous fishing rights. The conflict came to a head during what is known as the "fishing wars" in the 1960s, when traditional fishing areas became racialized spaces and areas of violence. The fishing wars involved events when Indigenous People were harassed, beaten, and arrested for fishing in their own territory (Taylor 1999). During this infamous era, it was not uncommon for Indigenous People to face gunfire while they were trying to fish (Wilkinson 2006).

During this era, Indigenous fisherpeople had to fight for the right to fish in their traditional territories. The 6-mile bank of the Nisqually River known as Frank's Landing became the center of this controversy, as state game wardens consistently targeted fishermen. It took acts of civil disobedience and "fish-ins" led by famed Indigenous rights activists Billy Frank, Jr., and Hank Adams and high-profile allies—including Hollywood actors such as Marlon Brando—to help raise public consciousness and ignite a public conversation regarding maintaining tribal sovereignty. The violence became so heated that Hank Adams himself was shot in the stomach while protesting on the banks of the Nisqually River (Wilkinson 2006). The high-profile protests and escalating violence ultimately led the courts to intervene.

The fishing rights to usual and accustomed areas were upheld in 1974, in the historic legal case, when U.S. District Judge George Boldt interpreted "in common with" to mean "sharing equally the opportunity to take fish" between treaty and nontreaty fisherpeople (*United States v. Washington* 1974). A central aspect of the Boldt decision in the context of the Lummi Nation is not only the fixed allocation, but also the right of the tribes to manage their share (Boxberger 1989), which led to the development of the Northwest Indian Fisheries Commission.

However, as Terry Williams, a Tulalip Tribal member and policy representative of the Tulalip Natural Resources, often says, "The Boldt decision means nothing, if we have no fish—fifty percent of nothing is nothing." The affronts to the fish are many—habitat loss, upland deforestation, increased siltation in rivers, over-harvesting, invasive predators, and blocked passage through dam constructions. Salmon, crab, and shellfish numbers have declined drastically through multiple affronts: upstream degradation, deforestation, siltation, overharvesting, commercial fishing, and now—the latest affront—warmed waters through global climate change.

Global climate change is having severe consequences on fish reproduction. The increased warming of rivers and the subsequent ocean acidification process are impacting the survival rates of salmon eggs and juvenile salmon. The range of temperatures for salmon fry to survive is very small. In general, salmon eggs need river temperatures 56°F or lower to survive. The increased temperatures associated with global climate change include river temperatures reaching 60°F and higher in many Pacific Northwest river systems. This is impacting not only the salmon runs—it also has impacts on the entire marine ecosystem, including shellfish and sea star decline. Even the iconic (and culturally significant) orca whales, which rely on the salmon for survival, are compromised. The southern resident pods in the waters around San Juan Island, for example, are starving to death. Since 2010, they have been listed as endangered species, and the numbers have reached a dangerously low 70.

Although the Boldt decision reaffirmed the need for state governments to uphold treaty rights, Indigenous Peoples are still in the position of necessarily fighting for their treaty rights. Examples of the ongoing need to maintain/assert treaty rights include the Makah whale hunt off of the Olympic Peninsula (Cote 2010) and the right to fish in traditional (usual and accustomed) waters. It is the disruption, and subsequent assertion, of these rights that I describe in the next three sections—through the politics of fear produced through 9/11, the proposed shipping terminal, and the ongoing threats of environmental degradation and global climate change.

The Line in the Sea: Traditional Fishing Practices and Geopolitics Post 9/11

It was a perfect day to go crabbing. The skies were blue and the water was calm. Tyson, a young man from a long line of fisherpeople from the Coast Salish Lummi Tribe, prepared for a day on the water as generations before him had done. In the early morning calm, he made his way to one of his favorite crabbing spots in the traditional territory of his people. He prepared his gear and dropped his pots, waiting for the bounty of the sea to provide for him and his family. For many Indigenous tribes of the Coastal Pacific, it is widely known that people do not go after food (such as fish or crab); rather, food comes to them. The work that they do (and their ancestors before them have done) to protect the waters and the habitat is part of a form of reciprocity—where the sea provides for you, if you protect and care for the environment. This reciprocity (in addition to the intricate knowledge of the geography and marine environment) has worked for thousands of years, as bountiful salmon runs filled rivers in ways that are now hard to fathom.

The declining numbers, however, are not stopping the cultural traditions, nor did it stop Tyson from going crabbing that morning, 15 years ago. He went crabbing for no other reason than that, as a Lummi community member, harvesting from the sea is part of his way of life. The calm that morning provided time for reflection—time to reconnect with the waters and his ancestral home. It was time for the daily troubles to wash away and to be in the moment.

The moment was abruptly disrupted, however, when a screeching speedboat—U.S. Department of Homeland Security—approached the small fishing boat. The authorities had mounted a 50-calibre machine gun, manned and pointed directly at Tyson's boat. Screaming over the loud motor, the officers ordered Tyson to leave the area immediately or be fired upon and considered a threat to national security.

When the Homeland Security boat approached, Tyson was in the same place that he—and his ancestors before him—had always crabbed. But in a post 9/11 era, this sacred space became wrapped up in wider geopolitics of fear. It became a place of heightened interest for those in charge of securing the nations peripheries and "at risk targets," such as the oil refinery that was built at Cherry Point (on Lummi traditional territory). This heightened security meant that the traditional waters that his community had occupied for thousands of years now became—unexpectedly—"illegal" to access. This very peaceful moment quickly turned to one of violent affront as Tyson was told to leave in no uncertain terms or face violent action. Tyson explained to the officers that he was a member of the Lummi Nation, and that he had both inherent and acquired treaty rights to fish in his ancestral land. However, in the months and years following the 9/11 tragedy, the heightened sense of "security" and "defense" made the defensible lines even more pronounced and the areas that characterized "security risks" became intertwined with national interests.

In this case, the "invisible" line that was drawn in the waters was based on how close the Office of Homeland Security (located on the opposite side of the country of the waters in question) deemed as being too close to areas that are in "high risk" of security breach. This tradition of fishing in sacred, ancestral waters was thereby launched into a geopolitics nexus that is interwoven with narratives of terrorism and fear. In this case, the extended lines of proximity to oil refineries—which were deemed as a high risk for terrorist activity—had direct and immediate impacts on very local, ancestral waters for Indigenous Peoples who have been fishing since time immemorial. Although Tyson, under pressure, retreated that day, Lummi Nation's work to advocate for inherent and acquired treaty rights continues. This work is part of an ongoing responsibility to protect the waters for the next generations and to protect the right to engage in cultural practices and ways of life that are guaranteed through treaty trust responsibilities.

Treaty Rights are Not for Sale! Protecting Xwe'chieXen, Upholding Treaty, and Maintaining a Way of Life

Fifteen years after the Homeland Security incident and the tightened security associated with 9/11, fishing rights in the Salish Sea were threatened once again. This time, it came through a proposal to build what would have been the largest deep-water marine terminal in the United States, on Lummi's ancestral territory, Xwe'chieXen (Cherry Point). The threat, once again, put Coast Salish tribes in the position to defend their way of life and their treaty rights.

The Gateway Pacific Terminal was designed to export up to 54 million dry metric tons per year of bulk commodities, mostly coal. The construction of the terminal raised significant concern for the Lummi Nation. The construction would not only harm the immediate fishing and spawning grounds at the pier, but it would also result in increased shipping traffic and risks of tanker spills; this would also contribute to the global fossil fuel economy and subsequent global climate change. In addition, the construction of the marina is on sacred ancestral territory of the Lummi People, which falls north of the reservation. Given the negative impacts on fishing rights, constructing the terminal would have been a violation of the usual and accustomed fishing rights outlined in Article 5 of the 1855 Treaty of Point Elliot and reaffirmed through the Boldt decision. More poignantly, it would impact a traditional way of life.

Lummi Nation's position against the terminal was launched onto the national stage, on September 21, 2012, when dozens of Coast Salish community members gathered on the shores of Xwe'chieXen to protest the development of the proposed terminal. The Lummi leaders and their Coast Salish relatives gathered in solidarity against what was yet another affront on their traditional territory and sacred fishing grounds. In the backdrop were the crystal blue waters of the Salish Sea, glistening with the autumn sun, spotted with "No coal" signs on the beach. The speakers, wrapped in Pendleton blankets and wearing cedar hats, spoke powerfully about the ongoing need to protect sacred lands and the home of their ancestors, and to protect their home for future generations.

After the elders shared their words, a pivotal moment occurred when Lummi Nation Councilman Jay Julius held up a poster-sized proxy check—made out to Lummi Nation for a million dollars—with the words "NON-NEGOTIABLE" stamped across it. Jay took the check, held it high for the public to see, and then in a powerful gesture, placed it on an open fire, letting it burn to ashes in front of the crowd. This moment came to symbolize Lummi's position, which had the ongoing message: "Our Treaty rights are not for sale!"

By design, the protest occurred before the board meeting of one of the biggest financial bankers of the SSA Marine project. When news of the protest hit the pages of *New York Times* on October 11, 2012, coupled with a powerful testimony by Councilman Julius at the annual board meeting, the New York financier quietly backed out of the deal, starting a slow decline in the terminal project. This event marked one of many strategic moves that Lummi Nation conceived to block the development of the terminal (see Figures 1b and 1c).

The Gateway Pacific Terminal was originally presented to the Lummi Nation and local citizens as an economic development plan to build jobs and grow tax bases. SSA Marine Executive Director Bob Watters maintained that the "Gateway Pacific Terminal and tribal interest can be harmonized if good faith discussions can take place." However, the Lummi Nation disagreed with this perspective and took a firm stand against the terminal. The chairman of the Lummi Indian Business Council, Timothy Ballew II, and his predecessor, Cliff Cultee, maintained that the shipping terminal would violate the terms of the Point Elliot Treaty, and would impact the Lummi People's ability to maintain their sovereign right to participate in the act of fishing—which is at the center of Lummi cultural identity. This was directly linked to maintaining and fostering a healthy ecosystem, which would provide for the return of the sacred salmon.

The proposed construction of the shipping terminal was also opposed by environmental, citizen, and faith-based groups in the neighboring town of Bellingham, WA. The groups largely rallied against the project because of the wider implications for the contribution to global climate change. Launching a "power past coal" campaign, the groups became an educational platform for wider environmental issues. Although the local groups had a unified and strong voice, they did not have the political clout to stop the project. It was Lummi Nation's sovereign status and the treaty trust responsibilities for which the federal government had to account that ultimately made the difference.

The battle to protect Cherry Point ended on May 9, 2016. In the crowded chambers room of the Lummi Indian Business Council, Chairman Ballew played a recorded message of the conversation he had with Colonel Buck of the Army Corps of Engineers earlier that morning. In the message, Colonel Buck announced that after a careful review, the Army Corps decided to issue a permit denial by the applicant—SSA Marine. With the announcement, the room exploded with cheers, tears, and sighs of relief.

Witnesses in the room, turned to social media, posting the news, and within minutes "#TreatyWin" reached thousands of friends and allies across the world. This announcement marked a decisive win in the battle to protect Lummi Nation's inherent and acquired fishing rights. Although it was a joyous moment, Chairman Ballew and the Council members cautioned people not to let their guard down. As Chairman Ballew commented after the historic win: "The need to protect the sacred waters and land of our ancestors is ongoing. Although we won this battle today, we know that we need to stay strong and be ready for the next battle." It is this continuous need for Indigenous Communities to "hold the line"/"defend the line" of treaty trust responsibilities that this article calls into question.

ShellNo Protests—Indigenous Activists and Greenpeace Uniting Against Arctic Drilling

I close the narratives with one last vignette—the ShellNo Protests in Seattle, WA, in which my family and I participated on May 16, 2015. This protest was a "David and Goliath" scene, wherein hundreds of activists in kayaks and traditional Northwest tribal canoes came out to demonstrate against arctic drilling in Alaska by floating alongside a massive, multistory drill rig.

When news came that a massive oil rig, the *Polar Pioneer*, was aimed to dock in Seattle, WA, before heading up to the Chukchi Sea in the Arctic to commence drilling, people throughout the region mobilized. This time, it was traditional Indigenous Coast Salish canoes and contemporary kayaks that tried to stop the massive oil-drilling rig from contributing to even more release of fossil fuels.

The *Polar Pioneer* made its way to the Port of Seattle on May 15, 2015, despite massive outcries from the community and a last-minute order from the mayor and the Port Authority to delay its arrival. The rig—owned and operated by Royal Shell—proceeded into the Port of Seattle, with its people stating that they "would be in and out of the port before any legal action could stop them." The fee—upward of $150 a day—had no impact on this multi-billion-dollar company.

The *Polar Pioneer* has come to symbolize the disconnect between a scientific understanding of global climate change, and the economic and political frameworks that continue to contribute to environmental degradation. The concerns from the communities, particularly the Indigenous Coast Salish communities of the Salish Sea, are that the impacts of oil extraction and associated global climate change have disproportionate impacts on coastal communities and communities that are reliant on subsistence diets such as fisheries. Thousands of activists—both on land and on water—protested the *Polar Pioneer* and called for greater attention to this issue of social and environmental justice. The protestors included "kayactivists" organized though Greenpeace, Coast Salish Canoe Families in traditional dugout canoes, and a group of Indigenous activists through the Idle No More movement. The range of protestors "pulling together" for ecosystem protection and against environmental and social injustice was central to the strength of the grass-roots movement. The canoes and kayaks paddled together in the industrial Duwamish Bay in the Port of Seattle to show solidarity and to let Shell and the wider world know that they have reached a tipping point. Expanding oil drilling into the Arctic flies against all scientific recommendations for reduction of fossil fuels—and it does so in an incredibly ecologically fragile environment.

The rally to band together in protest was to show the public and Shell that "business as usual" is no longer viable in a world where the latest Intergovernmental Panel on Climate Change (IPCC) estimates sea-level rise upward of 3 feet by 2100. Because of the slow response time for parts of the climate system, the IPCC estimates are already committed to a sea-level rise of approximately 2.3 m (7.5 ft) for each degree Celsius of temperature for the next 2,000 years (IPCC 2014). Sea-level rise will impact a large portion of the world's population, but Indigenous Peoples are acutely affected by the impacts, as their ability to go "somewhere else" is limited.

Sea-level rise, of course, is only one issue associated with climate change—the massive decline of fisheries (due to warmed water) and shellfish (due to ocean acidification) contributes to a loss of ecological integrity, the integrity that provides the base for a traditional way of life for coastal Indigenous people. The loss of fish represents a loss of way of life and tradition. More than that, it represents systemic, institutional, and governance failures at protecting and sustaining life. The lack of connection between "rights" and "responsibilities" in dominant governance systems becomes a moral imperative. As mentioned in the first case, in traditional Coast Salish culture—like many Indigenous cultures—rights to "taking" something like fish or timber go hand-in-hand with the responsibilities of providing for its long-term protection. Through jurisdictional fragmentation and political economic pressures, the responsibilities are not built into governance systems and mechanisms (see Figure 1d).

The high profile of this politically charged event was telling. Overnight, the news of the "unwelcome" massive oil exploration rig circulated throughout international news, all over social media, and continued to widen the conversations related to environmental and social justice. In fact, since the Seattle event in 2015, hundreds of spin-off protests against the Royal Shell oil company have occurred throughout North America and in Europe and have been highlighted on mainstream news programs and shows such as the *Rachel Maddow Show*. The media attention followed the rig as it left Seattle and slowly made its way up through the Chukchi Sea, with warnings that the public eye was "watching" the company.

When the *Polar Pioneer*—dubbed the "Death Star" by activists—left the Seattle docks on June 15, protestors again took to their canoes and kayaks to show resistance. The early-morning departure of the rig marked the start of a 3-week journey to explore for oil in the Chukchi Sea. A leader of the resistance movement was a Coast Salish Canoe Skipper, the late Justin Finkbonner, who led the Lummi Youth Canoe Families through the protests. As Finkbonner noted in one of dozens of interviews after the protests: "I stood in my canoe with a drum and sang an honor song to the Salish Sea and asking forgiveness … I sang a warrior song to encourage the activists to work together and be brave" (Hopper 2015).

The confrontations of the canoe and kayak activists and the police were strikingly similar to earlier accounts, including the "fish-ins" in the 1960s with the famed Billy Frank, Jr., and reminiscent of the accounts already given in this article. Witnesses recall that as the *Polar Pioneer* left its moorings and approached the blockade, police boats nearly collided with the canoes, telling the crew they were too close and would be arrested for violating the protest agreement. Finkbonner countered, informing them that they were the ones at fault for protecting an illegal action by Shell that violated the 1855 Treaty of Point Elliott by invading waters where Indigenous Peoples had been granted the right to fish and gather natural resources.

"It seemed to work," the captain noted. Holding a banner reading "Save the Arctic," the Lummi Youth Canoe Family paddled ahead of the kayaktivists, keeping in front of the rig, where they spun ahead of the rig with a warrior spirit. As reported in *Indian Times Today*, "We must have paddled for three hours on the water, maneuvering in front of the drilling platform and tugboats to keep them from getting away" (Hopper 2015).

The Coast Guard and police boats removed slow-moving kayakers one by one, pulling out the occupants and relocating them to the Coast Guard base at Pier 36, where they were issued violation notices and fines. Seattle City Council member Mike O'Brian was one of the protesters fined. "There was nothing we could do to save them but to keep paddling," Finkbonner said. In total, 24 activists were taken into custody. "After about three miles, law enforcement boats succeeded in blocking the Lummi canoe, allowing the oil rig to speed up and outpace them. Eventually, the canoe fell silent as the rig and the tugboats retreated into the distance. Finkbonner stood and told his canoe family they had done well and should keep an open mind and a strong heart" (Hopper 2015).

These acts of resistance are both exhausting and exhilarating. Time after time, citizen groups and Indigenous activists are taking stands against dominant society, bucking political, social, and economic systems that systematically marginalize Indigenous communities. In the end, Royal Shell did not pursue the drilling in the Chukchi Sea—announcing that there was not enough oil to make the endeavor financially worthwhile. It is only speculative as to whether the protests and digital watchdogs following the process had a role in the Royal Shell decision. The take-home, however, is that the protestors are calling for system-wide change, and until ecological and cultural loss is considered more thoroughly in the daily decisions of political, economic, and social choices, the political and economic engines will continue to be motivated by profits at the expense of environmental and human health. The fact that Shell received permits to explore the possibility from the U.S. Environmental Protection Agency shows a system failure in protecting our basic needs.

What this means for long-term transitions away from fuel-based economies and toward sustainable energies is unclear. However, increasing the discourse that links environmental degradation to social and environmental justice is an important step.

Conclusion: The Role of Indigenous Leadership in Reframing Water Governance

In this article, I explored the role of Indigenous activism at different scales—personal, tribal, and collective—to intervene in key moments to uphold treaty rights and protect Indigenous ways of life. I showed that as tribes and Indigenous actors take leading roles to uphold treaty rights, Indigenous Peoples have become leaders in the social and environmental justice movement, particularly in relation to climate justice and fishing rights.

This article illustrates how time after time Indigenous Peoples have positioned themselves to respond to affronts to their rights to fish (as in the Boldt Decision), and in protecting habitat to ensure that the habitat supports viable fish runs (as with the ShellNo Protests and rejection of the SSA terminal). Building on work by noted critical scholars such as Middleton, Ornelas, Whyte, Grossman, and Parker, this article contributes to the growing literature on environmental and social justice, climate change, and Indigenous activism. Specifically, the role of alliance building is central to the ongoing work to maintain a way of life that relies on intact ecosystems for survival. The role of tribes to assure that the federal government upholds the treaty trust responsibilities is critical in the work for environmental and social justice movements.

The success of Indigenous activist movements described in this article—in addition to other movements such as Idle No More and Standing Rock—is monumental. The recent wins could be the mark of a new era, when Indigenous nations are more visible in the public eye and influential in national and international politics. My hope with this new visibility is that tribes will no longer need to "hold the line" for what was promised to them, and that the onus to continuously remind governing officials of their trust responsibilities will be lifted from Indigenous people. Although the tribes have won recent battles, the proverbial war is not over. Developers will continue to seek to develop ancestral lands, climate change will continue to degrade ecosystems, and individuals will continue to confront structural racism. However, it is my hope that allies and governments alike will step up to reduce these affronts—to stop these developments earlier, to curb the impacts of climate change sooner, to eliminate structural racism altogether. Standing with Indigenous people to maintain their way of life could possibly be the magic bullet that will address chronic environmental and social justice issues.

This change will require a paradigm shift from reactive to proactive. It will require planning for seven generations rather than the next election cycle. It will also require thinking beyond fragmented jurisdictions delineated through colonial acts. This new paradigm will directly address social and environmental justice, embrace collectivism rather than individualism, and foster diverse worldviews. This shift will also require an educational system that deals honestly with its own history, one that looks closely at its own past, institutes appropriate changes to create and foster citizens that celebrate diversity, and respects and honors all life forms. In short, although there is a long road ahead, the pathways are there for structural change that will not only protect Indigenous rights, but will protect our waterways for generations to come.

Acknowledgments

First and foremost, I thank those who shared their harrowing and inspiring stories that are the inspiration for this article: Thank you to Timothy Ballew II, Tyson Oreiro, and the late Justin Finkbonner, all of Lummi Nation. Thanks also to Northwest Indian College for providing an institutional home and support to undertake this work. Specifically, I appreciate Northwest Indian College's Institutional Review Board's review of this article and the helpful and encouraging comments provided by Dr. William Freeman and Dave Oreiro. In addition, sincere thanks to Lynda Jenson for editorial assistance, Sylvie Arques for creating the map of the Salish Sea Basin (Figure 1a), Julia Orloff-Duffy for the generous use of her photographs (Figures 1b and 1c), and Chad Norman for capturing what has become an iconic image of the ShellNo protest (Figure 1d). Thank you to Parker Norman and Luke Norman for reviewing the narratives and providing insightful comments on the flow of the vignettes. Lastly, a sincere thanks to the anonymous reviewers and the editors-in-chief, Dr. Peter Leigh Taylor and David A. Sonnenfeld, whose insightful comments strengthened this article.

Funding

Funding for this study came from the National Science Foundation (grant 1540675).

References

Ayana, J. 2004. *Indigenous peoples in international law.* New York, NY: Oxford University Press.

Biolisl, T. 2005. Imagined geographies; Sovereignty, indigenous space, and American Indian struggle. *American Ethnologist* 32 (2):239–59. doi:10.1525/ae.2005.32.2.239

Boxberger, D. 1989. *To fish in common: The ethnohistory of Lummi Indian salmon fishing.* Seattle, WA: University of Washington Press.

Cajete, G. 2000. *Native Science: Natural laws of interdependence.* Sante Fe, NM: Clear Light Publishers.

Cote, C. 2010. *Revitalizing Makah and Nuu-chah-nulth traditions spirits of our whaling ancestors.* Seattle, WA: University of Washington Press.

Evenden, M. D. 2004. *Fish versus power: an environmental history of the Fraser River*. New York, NY: Cambridge University Press.

Governor's Office of Indian Affairs. 2015. Treaty of Point Elliot, 1855. Governor's Office of Indian Affairs. http://www.goia.wa.gov/treaties/treaties/pointelliot.htm (accessed July 23, 2015).

Grossman, Z., Parker, A., and B. Frank. 2012. *Asserting native resilience: Pacific Rim indigenous nations face the climate crisis*. Corvallis, OR: Oregon State University Press.

Harris, C. 2002. *Making native space: Colonialism, resistance, and reserves in British Columbia*. Vancouver, BC, Canada: UBC Press.

Holifield, R. 2013. Environmental justice as recognition and participation in risk assessment: Negotiating and translating health risk at a superfund site in Indian country. *Annals of the Association of American Geographers* 102:591–613. doi:10.1080/00045608.2011.641892

Hopper, F. 2015. Planning for the arctic: Lummi canoe leads kayaktivists against 'Death Star' oil rig. *Indian Times Today*. http://indiancountrytodaymedianetwork.com/2015/06/29/battling-arctic-lummi-canoe-leads-kayaktivists-against-death-star-oil-rig-160887

Intergovernmental Panel on Climate Change. 2014. *Climate change 2014: Synthesis report. Contribution of working groups I, II and III to the fifth assessment report of the intergovernmental panel on climate change* [Core Writing Team, R. K. Pachauri and L. A. Meyer, eds.], 151. Geneva, Switzerland: IPCC.

Ishiyama, N. 2003. Environmental justice and American Indian tribal sovereignty: Case study of a land-use conflict in Skull Alley, Utah. *Antipode* 35:119–39. doi:10.1111/1467-8330.00305

Kovach, M. 2010. *Indigenous methodologies: Characteristics, conversations, and contexts*. Toronto, ON, Canada: University of Toronto Press.

La Duke W. 1999. *All our relations: Native struggles for land and life*. Cambridge, MA: South End Press.

Middleton, B. R. 2011. *Trust in the land: New directions in tribal conservation*. First Peoples: New Directions in Indigenous Studies. Tucson: University of Arizona Press.

Miller, B. 1997. The "really real" border and the divided Salish community. *BC Studies: The British Columbian Quarterly* 112:63–79.

Miller, B. 2006. Conceptual and practical boundaries: West Coast Indians/First nations on the border of contagion in the post-9/11 era. In *The borderlands of the American and Canadian Wests: Essays on the regional history of the 49th parallel*, ed. S. Evans 299–308. Lincoln: University of Nebraska Press.

Mirosa, O. and L. Harris. 2012. Human right to water: Contemporary challenges and contours of a global debate. *Antipode* 44:932–49. doi:10.1111/j.1467-8330.2011.00929.x

Norman, E. S. 2014. *Governing transboundary waters: Canada, the United States and indigenous communities*. London, UK: Routledge.

Norman, E. S., C. Cook, and K. Bakker eds. 2015. *Negotiating water governance: Why the politics of scale matters*. London, UK: Ashgate.

Nugent, A. 1982. *Lummi elders speak*. Bellingham, WA: Lummi Education Center.

Ornelas, R. T. 2011. Managing the sacred lands of Native America. *The International Indigenous Policy Journal*, 2:1–16. http://ir.lib.uwo.ca/iipj/vol2/iss4/6 doi:10.18584/iipj.2011.2.4.6

Ornelas, R. T. 2014. Implementing the policy of the U.N. declaration on the rights of indigenous peoples. *International Indigenous Policy Journal* 5 (1):1–13. http://ir.lib.uwo.ca/iipj/vol5/iss1/4 doi:10.18584/iipj.2014.5.1.4

Ranco, D., and D. Suagee 2007. Tribal sovereignty and the problem of difference in environmental regulation: Observations on 'Measured Separatism' in Indian Country." *Antipode* 39:691–707. doi:10.1111/j.1467-8330.2007.00547.x

Smith, L. T. 2012 *Decolonizing methodologies: Research and indigenous peoples*, 2nd ed. New York, NY: Zed Books.

Taylor, J. 1999 *Making salmon: An environmental history of the northwest fisheries crisis*. Seattle: University of Washington Press.

Thrush, C. 2008. *Native Seattle: Histories from the Crossing-Over Place*. Seattle: University of Washington Press.

United States v. Washington. 1974. 384 F. Supp. 312 (W.D. Wash. 1974).

Whyte, K. 2015. Indigenous food systems, environmental justice and settler-industrial states. In *Global food, global justice: Essays on eating under globalization*, ed. M. Rawlinson and C. Ward, 143–56. Cambridge, UK: Scholars Publishing.

Whyte, K. 2016. Is it colonial déjà vu? Indigenous peoples and climate injustice. In *Humanities for the environment: Integrating knowledges, forging new constellations of practice*, ed. J. Adamson M. Davis and H. Huang, 1–22. London, UK: Earthscan.

Wilkinson, C. 2006. *Message from Frank's landing: A life of Billy Frank, Jr.* Seattle: University of Washington Press.

Wilson, S. 2009. *Research is ceremony: Indigenous research methods.* Winnipeg, AB, Canada: Fernwood Publishing.

Crises, Uncertainty and Water Governance for Sustainable Futures

Peter Leigh Taylor and David A. Sonnenfeld

Introduction

Providing and governing water in sufficient quantity and quality for growing human and environmental needs increasingly is in crisis around the world today. To echo Rittel and Webber's (1973) notion of "wicked problems", water challenges of the 21st century are marked by unprecedented complexity, beginning with global climate change and its hard-to-predict impacts on the environment, natural resources, and human societies. Water challenges cross many scales – temporal, geographic and spatial, ecological and human. Despite impressive scientific and technical advances in humans' understanding of and response to the impacts of their historical relationships to their environment, water crises are characterized by significant uncertainty. Today's water problems are deeply social and political in nature, as well as having scientific and technical dimensions. Global water crises call for global responses, but of what kind? Are appropriate and effective responses only those which involve overarching institutional structures and policies that cut across natural and human made boundaries?

The chapters in this collection point to the importance of water crises in catalyzing governance change. Water problems are experienced and responded to locally in specific contexts, involving discrete sets of stakeholders, and in relation to geographically-located water resources. Water crises are moments in which the assumptions of water users, managers, and policymakers – as well as accepted management practices, are threatened (Ison et al., 2015; Bellamy, Head, & Ross, Chapter 1, this volume). Water crises degrade environments, place untenable burdens on stakeholders, produce or exacerbate conflict, and undermine ecological and social conditions that sustain effective collaboration. Yet water crises also represent opportunities to consider or reconsider governance arrangements that previously may have been unspeakable, if not unthinkable. Water crises may lead, however painfully, to institutional change that transforms governance, as participants respond to specific problems via conflict or collaboration or both, to protect their interests and promote their water resource-related values. Water crises can generate innovative responses or at least responses that are new and appropriate to a particular local context and historical moment. Though local in nature, water crises may yet produce insights useful in other contexts involving different times, places, resources, and people.

Drawing on the analytical framework outlined in the Introduction, this brief epilogue highlights several key implications of cases examined in this collection for the diverse array of stakeholders intimately involved in water governance. It then outlines six insights for scholars, practitioners, policymakers, and others in addressing challenges of water supply, provision, access, and governance. It concludes with a few thoughts on how state policy and legal frameworks might support water governance approaches appropriate for local contexts but that also take into account regional or global aspects of water crises.

Key Implications

Contributions to this volume explore water crises in developed and developing world contexts generated by ecological degradation, rapid state policy and legal changes, material or technical problems of basic water access, and the exercise of asymmetrical power among stakeholders. In these cases, social actors struggled with common governance challenges – to redefine relations between the state and other social actors around water; to manage and coordinate management across scales; to address inequalities in access to the resource and related decision-making because of power differences; and to manage conflict over how to ascribe value to the resource and shape the purpose of governance.

Redefining Relations with the State

Bellamy, Head, & Ross' study of water governance across state borders in Australia's Lake Eyre Basin (Chapter 1) traces multiple shifts over time in the relationship between the Australian state and multiple stakeholder groups. In response to ecological and political–administrative crises, community-based advocacy coalitions including scientists, community members and other stakeholder groups emerged, only to give way later to regional-level national resource policies that increased the power of the state. Eberhard and colleagues' comparative study of water policy governance networks in Australia, the United States, and France (Chapter 4) examines important historical shifts in national policies and legal frameworks; they conclude that, in their case studies, the administrative state rarely ceded significant power to non-state governance stakeholders. In Duncan's study (Chapter 3), however, negotiation and reorganization related to water pollution in New Zealand evolved into new approaches to involving communities in governance. Communities and scientists worked together to develop locally-defined water quality objectives that were arguably more robust than relying solely on often legally vulnerable scientific authority.

Coordinating across Scale

In Huang and Xu's study of multi-level, cross-jurisdictional responses to water pollution in China's Yangtze River Basin (Chapter 2), what they refer to as "scaler configurations of power" among national and local level government officials set the stage for addressing trans-jurisdictional pollution by "jumping scale" to regulate across bureaucratic boundaries. Romano's analysis of cross-scale problems of sustainable water governance in Nicaragua (Chapter 5) explores how local water communities built legitimacy by managing small-scale water delivery with little or no state support. She argues that the resulting "organic empowerment" positioned grassroots groups to act across local scales to help reshape national water legislation.

Addressing Power and Inequality

In Chapter 8, Förster, Downsborough, & Chomba argue that, in South Africa, the implementation of a post-apartheid water governance framework to overcome past racial inequalities in access to water by promoting collaborative water governance, was undermined by the power of local élites. Non-élite farmers and other water users found themselves left out of the new collaborative system. Fonjong and Fokum (Chapter 6) observe that, in peri-urban Cameron, a major shift in state policy to privatize drinking water delivery aimed to resolve efficiency problems of the previous state-run system. Yet because of privatization's conceptualization of water mainly as a commodity, poor coverage, weak bureaucratic institutions, shortages, and inadequate investment continued. They argue that sharing management responsibility in a public–private partnership could build effectively on both the political legitimacy of the state and the potential effectiveness of private institutions in mobilizing capital and expertise.

Struggles to Ascribe Value to Water

Naiga, Penker, & Hogl (Chapter 7) explore the gender-based distribution of the benefits of water governance and of responsibility for operation and maintenance of local water systems in rural Uganda. They argue that there, women bear the brunt of water scarcity yet contribute significant financial and labor resources to water management. Despite national legislation calling for women to participate equally, sociocultural norms and unequal power related to gender block recognition of women's contributions and their potential to improve the effectiveness of water delivery. Norman's study of indigenous peoples' struggle to defend their rights to access and use coastal waterways in northwestern United States (Chapter 9) examines how tribal members organized coalitions to effectively defend their access to the water resource and their traditional ways of life.

Inventions and Reinventions

Taken together, the contributions to this volume provide strong evidence that crises can lead to important and innovative changes in governance by creating conditions conducive to "resetting" existing governance. As stakeholders in these cases struggled to deal with governance issues as described above, in many cases they developed unusual, even innovative responses. These include New Zealand's "community-based catchment limits" (Duncan, Chapter 3); a new, basin-wide identity emerging from value-based water conflicts in Australia (Bellamy et al., Chapter 1); the possibility of "empowerment across scales" (Romano, Chapter 5); and new forms of bureaucratic coordination such as "jumping scale" in China (Huang and Xu, Chapter 2). Stakeholders in multiple contexts also engaged in "reinvention", devising responses that, while perhaps not unique, are new to their contexts. Examples include shifts in Australia's Lake Eyre Basin toward greater state power in regional water policies, while leaving in place enhanced capacity for self-organized collaboration (Bellamy et al., Chapter 1); and collective-organization by tribal groups in the United States' northwest to defend a way of life dependent on access to water resources (Norman, Chapter 9).

Six Insights for Addressing Water Crises

The cases explored in this volume, of course, cannot be representative of all local water crises, nor propose lessons directly applicable to water governance in all other contexts. Nevertheless, as Eberhard and colleagues suggest (Chapter 4), these studies may be viewed as "instrumental cases" with insights whose value "lies not in their ability to speak for other cases, but in what we might learn from them" (quoting Stake and Savolainen 1995). The cases examined in this volume suggest at least six insights that may inform multistakeholder crafting of responses to water crises that are attentive to both local and global dimensions of those crises.

First, while they threatened to upend the status quo of existing water governance, including established institutions and power relations among participants, water crises in these cases also represented *opportunities* for stakeholders, through collaboration, conflict or both, *to redesign and re-implement systems of water supply, provision, and governance*. For example, drawing on experience and legitimacy built over years of *de facto* local responsibility for water provision, Nicaraguan community-based groups organized to demand formal recognition and enhanced state support in new national water legislation (Romano, Chapter 5). In their study of South African water governance reform, Förster et al. (Chapter 8), conversely, found local élites able to derail state efforts to institutionalize collaborative multistakeholder water governance at the local level.

Second, effective water governance in these cases may be best understood as *historically fluid processes* rather than as static institutional structures and practices that once designed, operated consistently over time. Governance involved continual negotiation and renegotiation, cooperation and conflict that resulted in periodic change in the social actors, objectives, and means involved in water governance. This was true in the case of shifting cross-border governance in the Lake Eyre Basin of Australia (Bellamy et al., Chapter 1), and in the six sets of water policy governance networks in Australia, the United States, and France examined by Eberhard et al. (Chapter 4).

Third, despite water stakeholders' significant moves toward inclusivity and collaboration, *governance change* in the cases examined in this volume *has not been singularly directional*. For example, Bellamy et al. (Chapter 1) trace a move over time back to centralized governance power in Australia. And Eberhard et al. (Chapter 4) argue that while the state moved toward increased consultation with other mostly governmental entities, it did not necessarily relinquish significant control over water policy.

Fourth, *uncertainty of science* related to threatened or degraded natural resources and of the political and policy framework of water often has shaped local water crises, but has not necessarily been a barrier to local action. Duncan's New Zealand study (Chapter 3), for example, examined the in-depth action made possible by community-based catchment limits based on scientific modeling and the incorporation of the future as a governance scale. In the South African case studied by Förster and colleagues, local élites reacted to new national-level water governance reform by co-opting the initiative and excluding non-élite water users.

Fifth, *scale matters*. In many of these cases, participants were compelled to think in new ways about the local, global, and in-between, taking into account how water moves across landscapes both physical and social, or how water governance might be organized across institutional boundaries. Huang and Xu (Chapter 2) explore how Chinese policymakers at the river basin and local levels confronted trans-jurisdictional water pollution in face of the uncertainties of water policy that was simultaneously centralized and decentralized. In Bellamy and colleagues' study of cross-border water governance in Australia (Chapter 1), cooperation and conflict revolved around differences across local, regional, and national scales among water-based actors' competing interests and visions of effective water governance.

Lastly, in these cases *power and culture* permeated water crises and related governance change as state and non-state stakeholders struggled to define the nature of those crises and to promote change consonant with their respective understandings of the value of water, and real and perceived interests. Naiga et al. (Chapter 7), for example, describe a move in Uganda in national water law to recognize and formalize women's roles in local water governance, yet conclude that existing socio-cultural gender norms still blocked exercise of women's legal rights to participate actively in water governance. In Norman's study (Chapter 9), United States Federal government efforts to secure national borders following the tragic events of September 11, 2001, were confronted by local indigenous groups defending traditional access to water, the latest in more than a century of struggles to (re-)claim formally-granted tribal treaty rights.

What do the key insights of this collection's instrumental cases – crisis as opportunity; organization as process; non-directional change; action in the face of uncertainty; the importance of scale; and of power and culture – have to offer efforts elsewhere to confront water as global crisis? Above, we invoked Rittel and Webber in referring to global water crisis as a "wicked problem" characterized by unprecedented complexity, cross-scalar causes and impacts, significant scientific uncertainty, and daunting crucial social and political dimensions. These characteristics pose formidable barriers to defining water problems and developing solutions that adequately capture and address those problems scientific and social complexities. Arguably, no single overarching governance as a response to global water crises is possible. Yet, it is difficult to deny that global water crises require global responses.

This collection's exploration of cases of local water crises and responses highlights five governance characteristics that cross-cut these experiences. First, in most cases, as conditions have changed governance arrangements have been significantly open-ended, if far from conflict-free. This relative openness has allowed new stakeholders to appear at the negotiation table and others to be retired. Second, power and influence have shifted among governance actors over time. Third, the objectives of water governance and related means have been frequently renegotiated in response to changing ecological, political, and social contexts. Fourth, governance arrangements and their participants have been compelled to confront rather than avoid ecological, political, and social complexity. Fifth, these experiences have generated significant innovative or rediscovered responses to crisis.

It is important to acknowledge that the outcomes of governance with these five cross-cutting characteristics for threatened environments and the people in them have been highly mixed. None of the cases in this collection represent governance panaceas that adequately satisfied all the important ecological and human needs at stake in these local water crises. On the contrary, in all cases serious environmental and social concerns remain inadequately addressed. What these cases of local water crises and responses suggest, however, is that governance is a live process in which addressing environmental and human needs can result in an institutional dialectic that responds to change and is capable of generating innovation and rediscovery. Even in the face of daunting structural threats, humans are still agents. They can confront crises and learn from them, make changes, and then make changes again.

Conclusion

How might state policy and legal frameworks support governance that is appropriate for local contexts and yet addresses water crises that are also global? The experiences with water crises and responses studied in this collection suggest that appropriate policy and legal frameworks would support a focus on local water problems yet with an analytical and institutional view across scales. Policy and legal frameworks would recognize the need to incorporate diverse stakeholders into governance, yet crucially, ensure that participants also negotiate with relative equity and autonomy vis a vis each other. These frameworks would provide for space, physical or virtual, for ongoing discussion and negotiation. And, they would support an approach to governance that institutionalizes ongoing organizational design, monitoring, implementation, reassessment and redesign, and reimplementation.

In the Introduction, we wrote that water is embedded in all aspects of human existence, natural, and social. Water is, as Pahl-Wostl states, the "source of life" (2015:1). Because of water's centrality in the human experience, water crises give us insight into larger crises of sustainability in humans' relationship to the natural world. This volume's diverse case studies suggest that local governance processes are possible that, in response to crises, are open enough to admit new participants or modify the influence of existing ones, redistribute power among participants, renegotiate objectives and related means, embrace rather than avoid complexity, proceed in the face of uncertainty, and generate innovative or rediscovered strategies.

These governance approaches cannot be assumed to necessarily be "successful" in producing outcomes consistent with any particular stakeholder's needs and goals. Yet they might make progress toward addressing environmental problems that are global in nature but are experienced locally. There is where progress toward sustainability can be stymied or won, where valuable insights may be lost or gained, where innovative tools are crafted or not. A water governance arrangement in which highly complex environmental and social crises are approached as opportunities to rethink existing systems, experiment, implement, and rethink again, might well provide valuable tools for confronting an unprecedented era of uncertainty.

References

Ison, R. L., K. B. Collins, and P. J. Wallis. 2015. "Institutionalising social learning: Towards systemic and adaptive governance," *Environmental Science & Policy* 53: 105–17.

Pahl-Wostl, C. 2015. *Water governance in the face of global change: From understanding to transformation.* New York: Springer.

Rittel, Horst W. J., and M. M. Webber. 1973. "Dilemmas in a General Theory of Planning," *Policy Sciences* 4: 155–169.

Stake, R.E., and R. Savolainen. 1995. *The art of case study research.* Thousand Oaks: Sage.

Index

www.ingramcontent.com/pod-product-compliance
Ingram Content Group UK Ltd.
Pitfield, Milton Keynes, MK11 3LW, UK
UKHW010020280225
455677UK00023B/702